T0301520

Global Talent

APARC
SHORENSTEIN
STANFORD

THE WALTER H. SHORENSTEIN
ASIA-PACIFIC RESEARCH CENTER

Studies of the Walter H. Shorenstein Asia-Pacific Research Center

Andrew G. Walder, General Editor

The Walter H. Shorenstein Asia-Pacific Research Center in the Freeman
Spogli Institute for International Studies at Stanford University sponsors
interdisciplinary research on the politics, economies, and societies of contemporary Asia. This monograph series features academic and policy-oriented
research by Stanford faculty and other scholars associated with the Center.

Global Talent

SKILLED LABOR AS SOCIAL CAPITAL IN KOREA

Gi-Wook Shin and Joon Nak Choi

Stanford University Press

Stanford, California

Stanford University Press
Stanford, California

Printed and bound by CPI Group (UK) Ltd,Croydon, CR0 4YY

Library of Congress Cataloging-in-Publication Data

Shin, Gi-Wook, author.
    Global talent : skilled labor as social capital in Korea / Gi-Wook Shin and Joon
Nak Choi.
        pages cm—(Studies of the Walter H. Shorenstein Asia-Pacific Research Center)
    Includes bibliographical references and index.
    ISBN 978-0-8047-9349-0 (cloth : alk. paper)—
    ISBN 978-0-8047-9433-6 (pbk. : alk. paper)
        1. Foreign workers—Korea (South) 2. Skilled labor—Korea (South) 3. Social capital
(Sociology)—Korea (South) 4. Human capital—Korea (South) 5. Transnationalism—
Economic aspects—Korea (South) 6. Globalization—Economic aspects—Korea
(South) I. Choi, Joon Nak, 1977- author. II. Title. III. Series: Studies of the Walter H.
Shorenstein Asia-Pacific Research Center.
    HD8730.5.S45 2015
    331.6'2095195—dc23

                                                                    2014035015

ISBN 978-0-8047-9438-1 (electronic)

Typeset by Newgen in 11/14 Garamond

Contents

Online appendixes containing the survey instruments used in the research for this book can be accessed at www.sup.org/globaltalent.

Figures, Maps, and Tables

MAP

TABLES

Acknowledgments

We could not have written this book without the support, advice, and encouragement we received from several of our colleagues. We would like to recognize our hard-working research assistants, especially Eun Jung (Jane) Choi, Hilary Izatt, Hyojung (Julia) Jang, Ji-woong Kang, and Joyce Lee, for their extensive efforts collecting and coding data. We would also like to thank Rafiq Dossani, Ho-ki Kim, and Kirak Ryu, who co-authored several policy reports with us and helped us collect some of the data we used here, and Paul Chang and Seung Hoan (Alex) Jeon for introducing us to key interview respondents. We would like to thank Mark Granovetter, Rachel Harvey, Jaeeun Kim, Sookyung Kim, Jung-eun Lee, Rennie J. Moon, Woody Powell, and two anonymous reviewers for providing valuable suggestions, and our editors Andy Walder and Geoffrey Burn for their advice and steadfast support. Last but certainly not least, we gratefully acknowledge the support of the Hana Financial Group and especially former chairman Kim Seunghyu. Of course, any omissions or errors remain our own.

Global Talent

ONE

Toward a New Model of Engaging Skilled Foreigners

The story of Korea's economic miracle is now well known throughout the world. Over the past 50 years, the Republic of Korea (henceforth Korea) has gone from one of the least developed countries to one of the most developed. Today, Korea ranks among the 31 high-income members of the Organisation for Economic Co-operation and Development (OECD) and is classified as an advanced economy by ratings firms, including the FTSE (Financial Times and London Stock Exchange), Standard and Poor's, and Dow Jones. As the only member of this prestigious club that has gone from a recipient to a provider of official development aid (ODA), Korea has become a model for many other developing countries that seek to replicate its success. Korea's economic rise has been accompanied by social development as well; according to the 2010 Human Development Index (HDI), a broad measure of social development, Korea scores virtually identical to Japan and above France, Great Britain, and Italy. Today, Korea has gained a "place in the sun" as an advanced nation with firms like Samsung Electronics and Hyundai Motors, which have become global leaders.

Yet economic development has come with new challenges. As a wealthy, high-income developed country, Korea is increasingly experiencing the same competitive challenges from newly industrializing countries as other advanced nations. In recent years, many countries have followed Korea's formula for development: exporting industrial goods and using the proceeds to invest in more advanced technology, gradually moving up the technology ladder to produce increasingly profitable goods. Through this process, industrializing countries like China have become increasingly sophisticated competitors in the same export industries that Korea has recently dominated, including automobiles, consumer electronics, and shipbuilding. Cutthroat competition in such industries harms Korea more than it does other developed countries that rely less upon manufacturing and more on lucrative service sector industries such as finance and business services. Having reached the limits of export-oriented industrialization, Korea is now attempting to find new engines of economic growth. Toward this end, the previous Lee Myung-bak administration promoted a "knowledge-based economy" while the current Park Geun-hye government is pursuing a "creative economy," emphasizing the development of advanced services and complementing Korea's historical strengths in electronics hardware with software expertise.

Such efforts have been hampered by Korea's shortage of top-tier "global talent." Korea has an extensive system of higher education—indeed, nearly 70 percent of Koreans between 25 and 34 years of age hold the equivalent of a bachelor's degree, the highest in the OECD.[1] Yet, the country faces a shortage of global talent—individuals with key technical or professional skills conferring valuable advantages for firms competing in global markets.[2] For instance, one recent ranking of cities worldwide conducted by the consultancy A.T. Kearney and the Chicago Council on Global Affairs highlighted Seoul's shortage of global talent. This study ranked Seoul as the ninth most important city in the world, with high marks in terms of business activity (7th) and research and development (5th) but much lower marks regarding the quality of its human capital (35th).[3] Similarly, the French business school INSEAD recently ranked Korea 28 out of 103 countries in the 2013 Global Talent Competitiveness Index, a disappointing performance considering its economic strength and vitality. Such evidence suggests that Korea produces an abundant supply of college graduates yet faces shortages of global talent in key sectors, including business services and software engineering.[4]

One potential solution for Korea is to follow countries like the United States and Canada in recruiting talented foreigners who possess the prized skills mentioned above. A large literature on economic growth has long considered skilled foreigners instrumental for enhancing a country's economic competitiveness. As Kirkegaard (2007: 1–2) argues, "The long-term economic growth of an advanced country . . . is with certainty highly correlated with the skill level of its residents. . . . The skill level in turn depends heavily on both the education and immigration policies of the country. The combined outcome of these policies is a ready supply of high-skilled workers, which is critical for globally competing businesses." For this reason, the United States, Canada, and other such countries not only train their own citizens at institutions of higher education but also recruit foreigners possessing desired expertise in fields as diverse as medicine, finance, and software engineering. Foreigners possessing specialized technical expertise or training have played a critical role in endowing such countries with substantial competitive advantages.[5] One needs to look no further than Silicon Valley, which could not have obtained and maintained its status as the center of the global technology industry without an influx of talented Indian and Chinese engineers.

Two global trends are making the recruitment of skilled foreigners all the more important. Economic globalization has facilitated the flow of goods, services, and capital across national boundaries and has increased the demand for top professionals who are qualified to handle such tasks. Demographic changes will further increase the competition for global talent, given a looming shortage of skilled labor in advanced countries.[6] Approximately 20 percent of humanity lives in countries where the number of children being born is lower than that of deaths among the elderly.[7] This transition will affect the workforce sooner than outright population decreases; the number of economically active individuals will begin declining long before the overall population does. Thus, between economic shifts increasing the demand for skilled labor and demographic shifts limiting the supply of such labor, workers with the right skills are becoming increasingly valuable, and the "global war for talent" will only intensify.

In this global war for talent, countries such as Korea that base national identity on shared ethnicity face inherent disadvantages when recruiting skilled foreigners. The countries that have most successfully recruited and leveraged skilled foreigners, such as the United States, Canada, Australia, and New Zealand, have all been "settler societies" characterized by a willingness to accept, assimilate, and naturalize new citizens regardless of their ethnic origins following the legal principle of jus soli (right of soil). Settler societies are attractive to skilled foreigners because their citizens embrace shared narratives of long-term immigration and assimilation, making it possible for new immigrants to become full members of these societies. For instance, the "American Dream" of enjoying a better life as a legitimate member of American society has long drawn skilled individuals of diverse ethnicity to the United States. Such narratives of diversity, tolerance, and accommodation strongly contrast with narratives of national identity prevailing in many other countries. Countries like Korea, Japan, and Germany have all been "nonimmigrant societies" characterized by ethnic identities based upon the belief that its members share a bloodline reaching back several centuries or millennia. For instance, most Koreans hold the idea that all ethnic Koreans are linked through a shared ancestry, and Korean citizenship is awarded based on the principle of jus sanguinis (right of blood). Such an ethnic conception of nationhood and citizenship repels skilled foreigners because outsiders lacking this shared bloodline are not considered fully Korean, regardless how long they stay in the country or how well they assimilate into Korean society and culture (see Shin 2006). Individuals without Korean blood might conceivably obtain Korean citizenship but face discouragingly obstinate barriers. Koreans also remain reluctant to welcome foreigners into their remarkably closed social networks, despite recent efforts by their government to accommodate migrant laborers and foreign brides through multiculturalist policies.[8] For such reasons, a study by the Samsung Economic Research Institute suggests that Korean firms and society would be neither willing nor able to attract top foreign talent.[9]

Across the world, however, such conditions represent the norm rather than the exception. While few countries are nearly as ethnically homogeneous as Korea (see Shin 2006), many if not most countries award citizenship based on jus sanguinis rather than jus soli. As the Center for Immigration Studies notes, only 30 of the world's 194 countries grant automatic birthright citizenship based on jus soli.[10] Data from the World Value Survey further suggest that Korea is representative of a large subset of such nonsettler countries. Koreans distrust foreigners more than people in any other high-income OECD country for which data are available. According to Figure 1.1, Korea differs from three groups of advanced countries. As expected, the settler societies (the United States, Canada, and Australia) are relatively trusting of foreigners. The Scandinavian countries also live up to their reputation for tolerance, as well as two countries (France and Great Britain) that draw large numbers of immigrants from former colonies. However, Korea broadly resembles a fourth group: countries such as Italy and Germany featuring substantial amounts of ethnic nationalism. Other

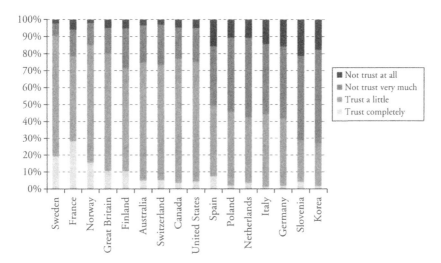

FIGURE 1.1 Trust and distrust of foreigners among selected high-income OECD members
SOURCE: Data from the 2005–2008 World Values Survey.

developed societies in Asia should also fall into this category; in addition to
Korea, Taiwan (not shown) and Japan (no data available) would presumably
fit this pattern.

This fourth group of more ethnically homogeneous countries—including Korea—has even more to gain from skilled foreigners than other developed countries but faces the greatest hurdles in recruiting such individuals.
Most of these countries are projected to face significant population declines
over the next few decades and would benefit the most from an influx of
skilled foreigners. For instance, Korea's recorded birthrate has dropped to
0.89, which has been the lowest in the world for two consecutive years. Indeed, by 2050, Korea is projected as having the highest proportion of people
over 65 of any country in the world. The coming dearth of young workers,
along with a fast-aging population, will make skilled foreigners particularly
valuable to countries such as Korea. Yet, these very countries have the greatest distrust of foreigners—in other words, xenophobia—and thus face special challenges when recruiting skilled foreigners.

In this book, we examine how countries like Korea might recruit and
leverage skilled foreigners to overcome looming economic and demographic
challenges. While most studies on skilled foreign labor have focused on settler societies, we address this issue from the perspective of nonsettler societies using the Korean case, which resembles a large group of Asian and

European countries that have all had difficulty in accommodating immigrants and have consequently been debating the merits and costs of multiculturalism.[11] To the extent that Korea represents those countries, the central arguments and implications developed in this study should apply toward these other countries.

Skilled Foreigners in the Global Economy: Calling for a New Model

In this book we argue that nonimmigrant countries should follow an emerging approach toward leveraging skilled foreigners to improve their economic competitiveness. Skilled foreigners bring *human capital*—specialized skills that are acquired through education, training, and work experience.[12] Skilled foreigners also bring *social capital*—social ties that spread information and innovations and facilitate trust.[13] Existing work on skilled foreigners and current debates on "brain drain" have predominantly focused on the former, overlooking the importance of the latter. For this reason, we call for greater attention to an emerging "new model" of foreigner recruitment. The new model acknowledges the human capital benefits highlighted by the old model but simultaneously focuses on skilled foreigners' ability to bridge their home and host societies. These "transnational bridges" enable the spread of market information, the diffusion of innovations, and greater cultural understanding between these societies. Such benefits not only accrue to the host societies where the foreigners now work and live but also the home societies where the foreigners originated. Thus, the new model highlights bidirectional "brain circulation" rather than a zero-sum brain drain. Saxenian (2006: 5) epitomizes the new model of foreigner recruitment, saying that "the scarce competitive resource is the ability to locate foreign partners quickly and to manage complex relationships and teamwork across cultural and linguistic barriers." Such social capital benefits may even exceed the substantial human capital benefits highlighted by the old model, especially in nonimmigrant societies as shown in this study.

Rationales for Recruiting Skilled Foreigners: The Old Model

The "old model" highlights the human capital benefits of recruiting skilled foreigners. Researchers and policymakers alike have long viewed human capital as an important ingredient for national economic development.

Human capital, defined as "productive wealth embodied in labour, skills, and knowledge" according to the OECD's "Glossary of Statistical Terms" (2012c), enables productive economic activities much like physical capital investments. Gary Becker explains:

> To most people, capital means a bank account, a hundred shares of IBM stock, assembly lines, or steel plants in the Chicago area. These are all forms of capital in the sense that they are assets that yield income and other useful outputs over long periods of time. But such tangible forms of capital are not the only type of capital. Schooling, a computer training course, expenditures on medical care, and lectures on the virtues of punctuality and honesty are also capital. That is because they raise earnings, improve health, or add to a person's good habits over much of his lifetime. Therefore, economists regard expenditures on education, training, medical care, and so on as investments in human capital. They are called human capital because people cannot be separated from their knowledge, skills, health, or values in the way they can be separated from their financial and physical assets.[14]

Although human capital can be increased through investments in formal education, informal training, or simply by workers learning on the job, countries still face a shortage of certain types of skilled labor. A given country's citizens often prefer one skilled occupation over another, even if it creates surpluses in one occupation and shortages in another. For instance, the United States has long had a serious shortage of skilled engineers while training a large surplus of qualified lawyers. Korea has increasingly experienced similar problems, despite historically being known for its deep and talented pool of engineers. According to the OECD's PISA 2006 database, only 8 percent of 15-year-olds in Korea are planning for a career in engineering or computing compared to the OECD average of 11 percent.

TURNING TO SKILLED FOREIGNERS

Recruiting skilled foreigners represents a widespread solution to this problem. Some nation-states (e.g., Canada) have attempted to selectively recruit foreigners who have received tertiary educations, regardless of the specific skills they possess. However, such recruitment has been controversial because an influx of foreigners whose skills duplicate those of native citizens can create greater competition for these citizens. For this reason, most countries have focused specifically on individuals who possess human capital that their own citizens lack, particularly the types of human capital that complement their own citizens' skills. For instance, the United States has selectively recruited skilled individuals who possess engineering skills lacking among its own citizens, who complement its great wealth of marketers, lawyers, and financiers. Policymakers recognize this complementary effect. U.S. Representatives Adam Schiff and Charles Bass introduced the "Invest in America Act of 2012," allowing foreign students who graduate from American universities with science, technology, engineering, or mathematics degrees to start a new business in the United States and earn green cards:

> While it may not be a surprise that a recent study by the National Foundation for American Policy found that nearly half of our country's top 50 venture-funded companies were founded by foreign-born entrepreneurs, it is worth noting that for every foreign-born worker who puts an advanced degree to work in this country, more than two jobs for American-born workers are created. Many other studies all lead to the same conclusion: Entrepreneurial high-skilled immigrants have a strong complementary effect on our economy. . . . Our universities are educating the next generation's Steve Jobs: let's make sure they build the next Apple—and the next iPhone—in the United States.[15]

In general, developed countries have a shortage of skilled engineers while having a surplus of individuals with other skills. Thus, they preferentially recruit skilled engineers and computer scientists, as evidenced by their visa policies for foreign students. Such policies have proven spectacularly successful at nurturing one of the United States' main engines of economic wealth, Silicon Valley. There, collaborations between largely foreign-born engineers and largely domestic-born marketers, managers, and venture capitalists have produced and nurtured hardware companies like Intel and Cisco, software companies like Oracle and Adobe, and Internet companies like Google and Facebook. Had Silicon Valley firms been confined to the United States' limited supply of skilled engineers, they could not have produced the stunning technical innovations underlying their global success.[16]

THE GLOBAL WAR FOR TALENT

As an increasing number of countries recruit skilled foreigners, especially those skilled in engineering and computer science, competition has intensified for such individuals. This global war for talent is expected to escalate in future years given demographic change. Demographers warn of a looming shortage of skilled labor across developed societies throughout Eurasia, which are in the beginning stages of a demographic crisis.[17] Map 1.1

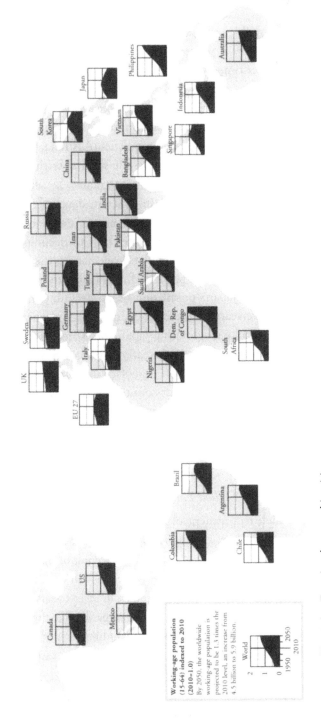

Working-age population (15-64) indexed to 2010 (2010=1.0)

By 2050, the worldwide working-age population is projected to be 1.3 times the 2010 level, an increase from 4.5 billion to 5.9 billion.

MAP 1.1 Upcoming Eurasian demographic crisis

SOURCE: Adele Hayutin, "Population Age Shifts Will Reshape Global Work Force," Stanford Center on Longevity, Stanford University, Stanford, CA, 2010.

illustrates this demographic crisis and its severity across different countries. In the map, each country is represented by a chart showing labor force growth and decline over time, where the X axis presents time from 1950 to 2050 and the Y axis shows the number of working-age adults. The vertical and horizontal lines in each chart indicate the population as of 2010. Less developed societies in Africa and South and Southeast Asia show continued workforce increases. Meanwhile, the settler societies (Australia, Canada, and the United States) show modest increases despite slowing birthrates among native-born citizens, primarily because the immigrants who settle in these societies tend to have higher birthrates. In contrast, developed nonsettler societies in Europe and Asia reveal striking patterns of population decline as they are less receptive to immigration. Note that this decline will affect the workforce sooner than outright population decreases; the number of economically active individuals will begin declining before the overall population does. For instance, Japan's population began declining in 2005, but its workforce peaked five years earlier. Even China will soon experience this demographic crisis, just like neighboring Japan and Korea; its population will begin slowly declining starting in the early 2030s. Such trends presage increasing competition for skilled labor, to replace the loss of native workers. Although developed nonimmigrant countries will continue to import abundant unskilled laborers from less developed, high-birthrate countries like the Philippines beyond 2050, they are likely to find that skilled individuals will become increasingly hard to recruit.

Rationales for Recruiting Skilled Foreigners: The New Model

Under the old model, recruitment of skilled foreigners was considered a zero-sum game where the host society received a net inflow of human capital from the home society, enhancing the competitiveness of the host society at the home society's expense. This model underlies many, if not most, of the policies governing skilled immigration today. In recent years, however, a new model of skilled foreigners has begun to emerge. Unlike the old model described above, the new model centers upon "brain linkages" rather than brain drain and highlights social capital rather than human capital.

SOCIAL CAPITAL AS THE KEY RESOURCE

Social capital refers to the ties linking organizations and/or individuals that can increase the productivity of these actors much like physical capital (e.g., an airport) or human capital (e.g., a law degree).[18] Embodying trust between individuals, social ties provide two clear benefits to the entities they connect. People who trust one another share information, giving one another improved access to market information and innovations. Such people also have less fear of being backstabbed, enabling them to cooperate at a deeper level.[19] These benefits certainly accrue toward individuals acting independently but are amplified for individuals commanding organizations and their resources.[20]

The new model advocated here focuses on a specific type of social capital associated with transnationalism. Putnam (1995) distinguishes between two types of social capital, bonding and bridging. *Bonding social capital* refers to the dense ties linking members of the same group. Social network analysts have long proposed that the social ties linking socially homogeneous individuals facilitate trust and emotional bonding among the group's members, generating solidarity against outside threats.[21] In contrast, *bridging social capital* is created by ties with outsiders. "Bridges" linking otherwise disconnected groups are important as they facilitate trust, spread information, and circulate innovations.[22] Some bridges connect actors in the same geographic area, creating linkages among different groups all located there. Research on Silicon Valley and other "industry clusters" (e.g., Saxenian 1994) has found that such local bridges improve productivity and facilitate innovations.[23] However, recent studies in economic geography and economic sociology have found that bridges are even more useful when they link groups separated by geographic distances.[24] When bridges connect actors in different geographic areas, they link not only social but also geographic distance. Such bridges are relatively rare because most people know predominantly people in the same geographic area and know relatively fewer people elsewhere in their own country, let alone in other countries.[25] Figure 1.2 illustrates the difference between bonding social capital, local bridges, and nonlocal bridges. Note that nonlocal bridges embody transnationalism, a state where actors are simultaneously embedded in different sociogeographic locations across the world (see Schiller, Basch, and Blanc 1995). To highlight this aspect of nonlocal bridges, we henceforth label them "transnational bridges."

Although all forms of social capital provide substantial benefits, transnational bridges are particularly useful. Like local bridges, transnational bridges span gaps in social network structure (i.e., structural holes), linking previously disconnected groups. However, transnational bridges also span geographic and cultural distance. Bridging geographic distance is valuable

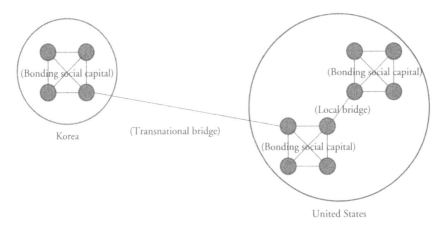

FIGURE 1.2 Types of social capital

because geographically co-located individuals share similar types of knowledge. Even if they are socially disconnected, such individuals are exposed to the same environment and are likely to have similar knowledge and information. Thus, they benefit less from sharing their knowledge relative to individuals in geographically distant locations, who each possess more knowledge novel to one another.[26] However, to fully benefit from sharing novel knowledge, individuals must not only have communication channels but also be able to understand one another. Cultural and institutional differences between two societies can hinder mutual understanding.[27] Transnational bridges mitigate cultural distance because they transmit, in addition to raw information, the background information about local contexts needed to understand such information.[28] For instance, ethnic Korean residents in many foreign countries have been shown to significantly increase the trade between Korea and these foreign countries, indicating that they are playing a bridging role.[29] Although transnational bridges are more difficult to establish, they can provide the valuable opportunity to share information and cooperate across vast distances.

The new model highlights the value of transnational bridges created by the movement of skilled individuals.[30] "Embeddedness" refers to an individual's connections to society through ongoing systems of social relationships.[31] Through their family ties, friendships, and professional relationships, such individuals are anchored into specific communities in specific geographic locations.[32] In other words, individuals are generally embedded into their home societies. An individual who moves to a geographically distant society gains opportunities to build new personal and professional relationships. To the extent that the foreigner has a cultural understanding of both societies and maintains ongoing social ties anchored at both locations, the foreigner can share information and contextual background while brokering cross-national cooperation. This is to say, the foreigner can become a transnational bridge who potentially connects two otherwise disconnected societies.

We note that social ties linking geographically distant individuals are necessary but not sufficient for transnational bridging. Prior studies (e.g., Ong 1999; Saxenian 2006) tended to focus upon individuals who had successfully bridged their societies of origin (i.e., home countries) and those of destination (i.e., host countries), unintentionally overlooking two preconditions for successful bridging. First, transnational bridging presupposes transnationalism, embodying

> immigrants whose daily lives depend on multiple and constant interconnections across international borders and whose public identities are configured in relationship to more than one nation-state. . . . They settle and become incorporated in the economy and political institutions, localities, and patterns of daily life in the country in which they reside. However, at the same time, they are engaged elsewhere in the sense that they maintain connections, build institutions, conduct transactions, and influence local and national events in the countries from which they emigrated. . . . [Thus, transmigrants] construct and reconstitute their simultaneous embeddedness in more than one society.[33]

Scholars have long recognized individual transmigrants as pragmatic actors who try to benefit socially and financially from their status "in between" different societies.[34] When an individual ceases to have ongoing rights, responsibilities, and social ties in either the society of origin (i.e., home country) or society of destination (i.e., host country), the individual no longer channels flows of information, innovation, and opportunity between the countries and ceases to function as a transnational bridge. This means that individuals must notably remain connected to their home societies to function as transnational bridges but also must be accepted as legitimate if partial members of their host societies (Storper 2007).

Second, individuals' ability to function as transnational bridges significantly remains contingent upon organizational culture and structure. An individual socially embedded in both the home and host societies might generate bridging benefits without belonging to an organization. However, organizational conditions represent a multiplier for such benefits. For instance, the information an individual possesses about his or her home society can spread through social networks local to that individual's host society, making host society members more knowledgeable about the transmigrant's home society. However, the same information could have a more direct impact if that individual worked for a corporation. Provided that top managers took his or her knowledge seriously, the individual could help shape the corporation's strategy regarding his or her home society. For this reason, organizational conditions can facilitate or hinder the benefits of bridging. Indeed, recent work (e.g., Wang forthcoming) has found that hierarchical, narrow-minded organizational cultures limit transmigrants' ability to bridge one national context with another. Although bridges provide some benefits to organizations with such characteristics, they should provide far greater benefits to nonhierarchical, open-minded organizations.

BENEFITS OF TRANSNATIONAL BRIDGES

Provided they are properly embedded into both home and host countries, transnational bridges have several important benefits implications. First, skilled foreigners facilitate cooperation across geographic, political, and social boundaries.[35] Skilled foreigners presumably maintain ongoing social relationships with individuals in both home and host societies and are trusted by those on both sides. For this reason, they are in a unique position to broker cross-national deals.[36] Such capabilities can be exceptionally valuable. For instance, countries linked by many bridges have been found to trade specialized, differentiated goods requiring trust and intensive information exchanges, while disconnected countries have been shown to trade only standardized commodities.[37] The ethnic Chinese diaspora in Southeast Asia facilitating the trade of highly specialized goods between that region and China represents a good example.

Second, skilled foreigners spread key innovations across boundaries. Individuals and organizations adopt new innovations largely by learning from their close associates or from monitoring and/or reverse engineering competitors' services and products. Diffusion through both mechanisms occurs easily within a given geographic region, but not between them. As Marshall (1920) once suggested, new innovations spread within the "industrial atmospheres" contained within specific locations, as if "it were in the air." However, they do not spread so readily across geographic space.[38] Such effects play a critical role in differentiating the performance of competitors located in different geographic regions.[39] Transnational bridges represent one of the few mechanisms capable of spreading innovations across national boundaries.[40] For instance, Saxenian (2006) provides ethnographic evidence of the importance of "Argonauts"—highly talented individuals who learned the practices, innovations, and other forms of human capital they accumulated during their sojourns in Silicon Valley, before returning to their home countries to enhance innovation there. Overall, the Argonauts travel back and forth between various technology industry clusters across the world, spreading Silicon Valley information, innovations, and practices to technology clusters overseas.

Third, skilled foreigners can help host society ethnocentric corporations enter home society markets and vice versa. All multinational corporations face a trade-off between local responsiveness and global coordination. On the one hand, they can adopt a decentralized structure, giving substantial autonomy to their foreign subsidiaries and hiring locals as top subsidiary managers. While such corporations are highly responsive to local conditions, they have difficulty coordinating many different subsidiaries around the world in order to play "global chess" against other multinationals. On the other hand, corporations can adopt a centralized structure, using home country executives to run foreign subsidiaries. While such corporations can coordinate various subsidiaries across the world, they have difficulty responding to the specific needs of local markets.[41] Within such ethnocentric corporations, skilled foreigners can bridge the internal gap between home country markets and host country executives.

One noteworthy characteristic of the new model is that it opens up the possibility that home societies can actually benefit by "losing" skilled individuals to their host societies. The old model depicts a zero-sum game in which host societies benefit at home societies' expense. When individuals from less developed home societies emigrate to more developed host societies, they represent a zero-sum brain drain. However, the new model depicts a positive-sum game in which both home and host societies potentially benefit. Prior research has examined what happens when foreigners return to their home societies. For instance, the Argonauts have spread Silicon Valley's culture of innovation to locations like Taiwan and Israel. Such bidirectional movement has been called brain circulation, returning a greater amount of human capital to home societies than what was originally lost. A still more fundamental implication of the new model has to do with social capital. Even if a foreigner never returns home, he or she can bridge the two societies—as someone who spreads information, facilitates cooperation, and generates innovation benefits shared by both societies. Should the benefits generated by this transnational bridge outweigh the host society's initial loss of human capital, even the home society gains more from the emigration of its skilled individuals than it loses.

Synthesizing the Old and New Models

Taking into account both the old and new models, we summarize the main contributions that skilled foreigners can make in Figure 1.3. Unskilled domestic labor contributes little in the way of human capital or transnational bridges. Unskilled foreigners have little potential to contribute human capital but have an inherent potential to contribute transnational bridges to the extent that they maintain ties with their home societies. Yet, such potential often remains unrealized because unskilled foreigners are often segregated within ghettos or ethnic enclaves. Lacking locally bridging social capital, these individuals might possess information and contacts within their home societies that remain unrecognized and underutilized by their host societies. In contrast, locally educated skilled labor provides human capital, especially in societies with excellent tertiary educational systems. It would also provide locally bridging social capital since educated professionals are more likely to build social ties that cut across various social groups.[42] Yet locally educated professionals may not have had the opportunity to build connections with geographically distant counterparts; thus, they generally cannot reliably function as transnational bridges. Consequently, domestic economies with very few foreigners might achieve high levels of productivity but nevertheless remain isolated from the broader global economy and its trends. With little exposure to the broader world, such economies risk becoming insular, developing groupthink and missing important global trends (e.g., shifting consumer preferences away from feature phones toward smartphones).[43] Furthermore, such economies would lack the interpersonal and interorganizational ties that facilitate the most valuable types of international trade and investment.[44] Introducing skilled foreigners could alleviate such risks,

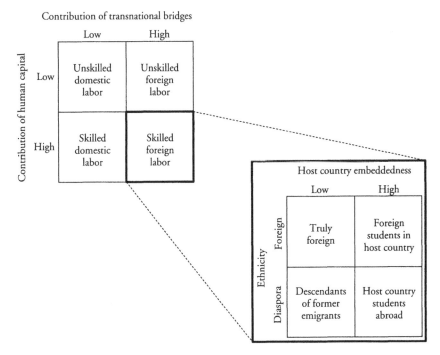

FIGURE 1.3 Types of labor

as even a relatively small number of ties can dramatically increase information flow, exchange, and trust in addition to contributing human capital.[45] For these reasons, in this study we focus on the bottom-right quadrant of Figure 1.3—skilled foreigners—as a source of both human capital and transnational bridges.[46]

The Korean Experiences and Challenges

Focusing on both human and social capital benefits, we examine how recruiting skilled foreigners can benefit Korea, as well as challenges that will inevitably impede such efforts. We first discuss a brief history of foreign labor in Korea before examining the values of skilled foreign workers to the country as both human and social capital.

THE HISTORY OF FOREIGN LABOR IN KOREA

The question of foreign labor is not new to Korea, but until now it has been largely limited to unskilled labor. Beginning in the mid-1980s, Korea experienced a labor shortage due to the exhaustion of its rural labor surplus and the declining participation rate of young adults in the workforce as a result of longer schooling (A. Kim 2009). Furthermore, wealthier and better-educated Koreans started to show a reluctance to engage in so-called 3D (dirty, difficult, and dangerous) jobs. Korea was forced to face the reality that it could no longer be self-sufficient in the labor market, and the sudden influx of migrant workers in the 1990s came in response to this labor shortage. In the late 1980s and early 1990s, the Korean government introduced the Industrial Trainee System (ITS), thereby moving from its long-held "closed-door" policy to one that was at least partially open (W. Kim 2004). The government began systemically coordinating policies that were intended to bring in, and control the inflow of, migrant workers. In 2007, less than two decades after Korea officially opened its doors—first to temporary workers, then to permitted workers—the United Nations declared Korea a receiving country.

The Korean government also opened the door for ethnic Koreans overseas through a new Working Visit program (H-2 visa), allowing ethnic Koreans from China and the former Soviet Union to visit their extended families and find jobs in nonprofessional sectors of the economy. Such returnees usually get jobs in restaurants, as well as in services like cleaning and maintenance, social services, personal care, and housekeeper services. Ethnic Korean returnees, especially from China, have skyrocketed since the adoption of the H-2 visa program: as Figure 1.4 shows, 530,915 foreign workers legally resided in Korea in 2012. However, the 2012 Foreign Labor Survey by Statistics Korea reported 791,000 total foreign workers, suggesting that about 260,000 were illegally residing in Korea largely by overstaying valid visas. However, most such individuals are unskilled workers, and Korea has yet to meet the new challenge of recruiting skilled foreigners that we address in this study.

TOWARD THE RECRUITMENT OF GLOBAL TALENT

Korea is poised to shift its attention away from unskilled foreigners toward skilled foreigners (i.e., global talent) given its enhanced status in regional and global economies. According to research in global and transnational sociology, the role that a specific country plays in the global economy is not necessarily fixed. If a country can develop advanced technology, accumulate financial capital, and educate skilled individuals, it will play a more central

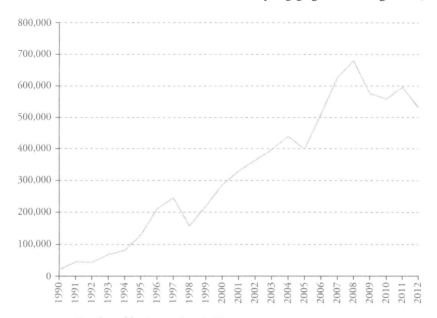

FIGURE I.4 Number of foreign workers in Korea, 1990–2012

SOURCE: Data from the Ministry of Public Administration and Security (1990–2009) and the Korea Immigration Service (number of work visas, 2010–2012).

role in the global economy, becoming a regional or even global hub for higher-value activities.[47] Inflows and outflows of capital, knowledge, and culture will change accordingly. As Korea develops, it is increasingly becoming an economic and cultural hub, especially within Asia. Like Korean manufactured goods, the "Korean wave" (*hallyu*) has been received with particularly great enthusiasm in Asia. One consequence of this economic and cultural outflow has been a reciprocal inflow of many talented students from Asian countries into Korea (see Chapter 2 for details). This phenomenon is consistent with sociological theories suggesting that cultural norms flow from developed "core" countries into the less developed "periphery," while skilled migrants flow in the other direction (Wallerstein 1974; for a review, see Portes 1995a). Another consequence of Korea's more central role in the global economy is that Korean cities such as Seoul can join "world cities" or "global cities" in attracting skilled, geographically mobile individuals from all over the world to work in high value-added activities such as management, finance, and consulting.[48] If so, Korea would become embedded into the core of global flows of human capital, transforming what has largely been a brain drain out of Korea into brain circulation by inducing reciprocal flows of talent into Korea.

Of course, we do not take such brain circulation for granted—we rather aim to explore the factors that enable or constrain it. We focus upon strategic opportunities for Korea to recruit skilled foreigners as transnational bridges, creating win-win-win situations for these individuals, their home societies, and Korea alike. We note that the existence of such connections represent a necessary but insufficient first step, as merely bringing skilled foreigners into a country will not automatically produce social or even human capital benefits to Korea. In addition, the task of properly utilizing such individuals will be challenging for a Korea characterized by strong nationalism and rigid organizational hierarchies—the same barriers to transnational bridging that recent research (e.g., Storper 2007; Wang forthcoming) has highlighted. Therefore, we seek to find strategic opportunities for Korea to utilize skilled foreigners as both human and social capital in the face of many challenges.

CREATIVE SOLUTIONS TO CHALLENGES

One of the most important enabling or constraining factors is Korea's ethnic national identity. Many observers (e.g., Kim 2000) are concerned that Koreans are too nationalistic and intolerant to accept a substantial number of skilled foreigners. Korea is widely regarded as being among the most ethnically and linguistically homogeneous countries in the world. Traditionally, purity of blood and ethnic homogeneity were at the core of dominant notions of national identity and were, moreover, a source of national pride. For this reason, the Korean government has gone so far as to impose various legal measures to restrict immigration into Korea at times. In recent years, the foreign population in Korea has substantially increased, but its enlargement has not been proportional to the Korean public's tolerance of and openness to non-Korean cultures and values. As pointed out elsewhere, contemporary Korean society is becoming diverse but not tolerant of diversity.[49] In the midst of rapidly increasing diversity, notions of ethnic homogeneity and an exclusionary national identity have become serious problems for Korea, as they have driven discrimination and prejudice toward those not considered "pure" Koreans. For these reasons, a recent study by a leading Korean think tank suggested that Korea should focus upon expanding the local pool of skilled workers rather than recruiting foreigners.[50]

However, Koreans may actually be willing to embrace the need to recruit skilled foreigners given a solid economic rationale. A survey conducted by Kim, Yang, and Lee (2009) found that Koreans had a positive impression of foreigners in general (average of 3.23 on a 5-point scale), though such positive impression quickly deteriorated when they were asked about foreigners living in Korea (2.35/5.00) or in their own neighborhoods (2.39/5.00). Yet, this study also found that the overwhelming majority of Koreans believed in the inevitability of Korea becoming a multicultural society: while only 20.8 percent of survey respondents thought that Korea was currently multicultural, an additional 69.1 percent believed that Korea either should become multicultural or will become multicultural. Only 6.8 percent said that Korea either would not or should not become multicultural. Accordingly, there is good reason to believe that Koreans would accept the recruitment of skilled foreigners if it were presented as a strategy of national competitiveness, although we well recognize that a strong sense of ethnic identity held among Koreans will continue to present a key challenge for Korea in recruiting global talent.

It is important for Korea to find creative ways of leveraging skilled foreigners that diverge from traditional thinking. While a strong sense of ethnic identity might make Korea less attractive to ethnic non-Koreans, it might simultaneously induce overseas Koreans back "home" provided that they have maintained close ties to their homeland. Additionally, Korea's cultural heritage represents the foundation of the Korean wave of popular culture, which has spread across Asia and has induced foreigners to better appreciate Korean culture and society. As shown in the next chapter, it has also attracted Asian students to Korean colleges. Given these factors, it may actually be possible for Korean society and firms to benefit from skilled individuals, whether or not they live and work in Korea, converting brain drain into brain circulation.

Overall, Korea differs from the settler societies that have been the focus of the vast majority of studies on the skilled foreigners phenomenon. Rather, Korea represents a group of East Asian and European countries basing their national identities upon shared ethnicities. Unlike the settler societies, which have long used their natural advantages to recruit some of the most talented individuals in the world, these countries—including Korea—must seek creative ways to recruit skilled foreigners.[51] Thus, Korea's experience as presented in this study can shed light upon the way these "nonimmigrant" countries can utilize skilled foreigners, which is especially important as these same countries are the ones facing the most severe demographic crises.

Four Segments of Skilled Foreigners

Given the diversity of potential targets of skilled foreigners, we focus on four groups in this study. Skilled foreigners represent individuals who each have valuable skills and live overseas but may have little else in common. Recognizing this, we differentiate four segments divided along two dimensions, ethnic identity and embeddedness in the host society, among the skilled foreigners in Figure 1.5. The first segment consists of true foreigners without any host country embeddedness. The second segment consists of foreigners with substantial host country embeddedness, notably foreign students who have studied in the host society. The third segment consists of members of the diaspora with shared ethnic identity but little embeddedness in their ancestral homes, descendants of emigrants who left generations ago. The fourth segment consists of host society nationals who left to study overseas, but who retain family and friends from their primary and secondary educations.[52] While the first segment has received the most attention from policymakers and business leaders as well as in academic research,[53]

Embeddedness in Korea

	Low	High
Not Korean	Foreigners without Korean ties (Chapter 5)	Foreign students studying in Korea (Chapter 2)
Korean	Descendants of Korean emigrants (Chapter 4)	Korean students studying abroad (Chapter 3)

Ethnic origin

FIGURE 1.5 Typology of skilled foreigners in Korea

each of the other segments is equally important as human and social capital and similarly receptive to recruitment. Accordingly, in this study we divide foreigners without an ethnic connection to Korea into true foreigners and foreign students educated in Korea, and ethnic Koreans overseas into Korean citizens educated overseas and members of the overseas diaspora, who may be generations removed from their Korean ancestors.

TRUE FOREIGNERS

When most people think of skilled foreigners, they envision foreigners with few ties to the host society. Such "true" foreigners are recruited primarily for their human capital—their technical skills or professional experience and prior research has rightly focused on this aspect. However, being educated individuals possessing professional ties in their home countries, they could also become strong bridges between home and host societies. Therefore, a key opportunity as well as challenge in this regard is to transform their value from human into social capital.

In our study we focus on engineers of Indian descent as a case to illustrate the value of "true foreigners" as human and social capital. Korea faces a shortage of engineers, especially software engineers, and India offers the deepest and largest pool of untapped engineering talent that would be useful to Korea. While many of them would prefer a place like Silicon Valley, there is ample evidence to suggest that they would be interested in working in Korea, though only for a few years. We seek to examine how engineers of Indian descent can contribute to the Korean economy first as human and ultimately as social capital as well.

FOREIGN STUDENTS EDUCATED IN KOREA

Foreign students, whether or not they remain in host societies after graduating, are much better embedded into their host societies than true foreigners who come to work without much knowledge or prior experience of a country. While most of these students may return home after graduation, some remain in the host countries, contributing to their domestic economies. Foreign students are better embedded into their host societies by virtue of their educational experiences, their familiarity with the culture and language, and their ties with their classmates. Most of them also maintain close ties to their home countries—after all, many students are supported by their extended families back home. Accordingly, foreign students have great potential to contribute to the host countries as human and social capital, and some nations (e.g., the United States) have been particularly adept at retaining many talented foreign students after graduation.

In this study, we examine foreign students studying in top Korean universities. Although the best Korean universities rank below the most prestigious U.S. universities, they are competitive within Asia: eight Korean universities are ranked among the top 100 in Asia according to the Academic World Ranking of World Universities, and 9 Korean universities are ranked among the top 100 in Asia by the Webometrics Ranking of World Universities. As a result, Korean universities attract students from foreign countries, especially from China and Southeast Asia. In addition, some foreign students are attracted to Korea by the recent popularity of Korean culture and recognition of the Korean developmental model. The Korean government has also been actively recruiting foreign students to Korean colleges by offering various scholarships. According to the Korean Ministry of Education, Science, and Technology, a total of 86,878 foreign students were studying in Korea as of 2012. They should be expected to be more embedded there than true foreigners, and this study examines how Korea can utilize these foreign students as human and social capital for its society and economy.

CITIZENS EDUCATED OVERSEAS

Most countries not only receive foreign students but also send their own citizens abroad to study. According to the OECD's 2011 *Education at a Glance* report, there were almost 3.7 million tertiary students enrolled outside their country of citizenship in 2009. The report also revealed that just over 77 percent of them studied in OECD countries, and Asians accounted for 52 percent of all students studying abroad worldwide. Korea has a long history of sending its brightest students to foreign countries for study, and as of 2013, there were 227,126 Korean students studying abroad, at the tertiary level, mostly in Asia and North America (see Chapter 3). Koreans are the third largest international students behind Chinese and Indians, but Korea is sending the largest proportion of its population to study abroad, since its population is less than one-twentieth of that of China and India.

Students studying abroad often return home after receiving first-rate educations and contribute to their economy and society. As Kirkegaard

(2007) notes, Korean students who receive a PhD in the United States return home at far higher rates than their Indian or Chinese peers; almost two-thirds return home. In fact, Korean scientists and economists educated in the United States returned home to make tremendous contributions to the economic development of the country in the 1970s and 1980s. However, some students may never return home or may return long after working in the host country, contributing toward a brain drain for Korea. Yet, following the new model specified above, we need to explore how Korea might still benefit from the ties that these students maintain with the homeland they have left behind.

OVERSEAS DIASPORA

The last group that we examine in this study is the diaspora community. According to the OECD's *Global Profile of Diasporas* report (2012a), there were approximately 214 million migrants worldwide in 2010—a 177 percent increase from five decades ago. People migrate to other countries for various reasons, and later-generation immigrants overseas may or may not retain their ancestral ethnic identities. More likely than not, these migrants would have gained citizenship in their country of residence, and they would face higher barriers than first-generation immigrants if they were to return to their homelands. Still some may maintain ties with their homeland while being closely embedded in their country of residence.

When seeking skilled foreigners, Korea can target over 7 million ethnic Koreans living overseas who left the country for a wide variety of reasons: China (2.7 million), the United States (2.0 million), and Japan (0.9 million) host the largest numbers.[54] In particular, descendants of Korean immigrants in advanced countries like the United States can be an excellent pool of global talent as they are among the most educated and skilled group even in that society. Despite being economically and socially integrated into their host societies, many of them are also attached to their ancestral homeland. In this study we focus on the children and grandchildren of first-generation emigrants, from the so-called 1.5 generation onward living in North America, who could contribute to Korea as both human and social capital. The challenge here would be to create an environment that either encourages later-generation ethnic Koreans to become professionals in Korea and/or encourages them to bridge their ancestral and adopted homelands. Yet little research has been done to assess this group's potential as a source of skilled labor in both ways, and we examine it with ethnic Koreans from North America in this study.

For each of the four groups under consideration—true foreigners, foreign students educated in Korea, Korean students studying abroad, and members of the Korean diaspora—we examine how these groups can contribute both human and social capital to Korea.

Data and Methods

We investigate each of the four target segments identified above with both quantitative and qualitative data and methods as summarized in Table 1.1. The specifics of the data vary across chapters, reflecting differences between our focal groups and the data associated with these groups. Although we conducted online surveys of three of our focal groups, we chose not to do so with foreign students in Korea (Chapter 2) because we interviewed nearly all such students we were able to contact. Our quantitative analyses for this chapter resemble those that we used in other chapters, but use data coded from our interviews. Conversely, we surveyed Indian engineers (Chapter 5) but had difficulty scheduling one-on-one interviews with them. In response, we conducted focus groups in Silicon Valley and India instead. Overall, our data for different focal groups varies somewhat, but we follow similar patterns of analysis across the chapters as much as possible, that is, quantitative analysis followed by in-depth qualitative analysis.

TABLE 1.1

Data sources and research methods for empirical chapters

Chapter	Focal group	Quantitative data source	Qualitative data source	Quantitative methods
2	Foreign students in Korea	No quantitative data used	Interviews at elite Korean universities	Correspondence analysis of coded qualitative data
3	Korean students abroad	Online survey of Korean students in North America	Interviews at elite U.S. universities	Correspondence analysis of quantitative survey data
4	Ethnic Koreans in North America	Online survey of Korean American students	Interviews at elite U.S. universities	Correspondence analysis of quantitative survey data
5	Engineers of Indian origin	Online survey of engineers in Silicon Valley and India	Focus groups in Silicon Valley and India	Correspondence analysis of quantitative survey data

For each group, we first categorized individuals into distinct subgroups using correspondence analysis, a statistical technique that divides individuals according to their empirical characteristics.[55] This was necessary because each of the four groups was internally diverse, and it was important for us to capture their heterogeneity. In correspondence analysis, individuals with similar characteristics are placed closer together in two-dimensional space, while those with dissimilar characteristics are placed further apart. Simultaneously, it places variables closest to the individuals they best describe. Thus, correspondence analysis produces a two-dimensional map of individuals based on the similarities or dissimilarities of their characteristics, where the dimensions represent bundles of characteristics that vary together (for an overview of correspondence analysis, see Barnett 1993).

Second, we calculated subgroup averages for key variables, enabling meaningful comparisons between different subgroups of the same subject. Some subgroups uniformly scored high on the key variables of interest (i.e., willingness to work in Korea, willingness to bridge Korean society and businesses to geographically distant locations), while others did not. By identifying subgroups and their key characteristics, we were able to determine which subgroups could potentially contribute the greatest amount of human and social capital as skilled foreigners.

Third, we used qualitative evidence from interviews to check the validity of the quantitative findings and to provide further insight into the mechanisms underlying these findings. We sought to interview as many survey respondents as possible using ethnographic techniques (Spradley 1979), a proportion that differed across our four target segments. We interviewed most of the foreign students in Korea (Chapter 2) that we contacted, dispensing with a survey altogether. In contrast, we could not interview all of the Korean students and Korean Americans and Korean Canadians (Chapters 3 and 4) who responded to our online survey, partly because so many responded and partly because they were geographically spread out across North America. As interviewing all respondents would have been impractical, we chose those respondents clustered in two geographic locations where we had particularly large concentrations of respondents—New England and Northern California. We had to take a more opportunistic approach toward Indian engineers (Chapter 5), who were working full time in India, the United States, or various locations in Asia. Considering the difficulties involved in interviewing such individuals on an individual basis, we conducted focus groups in California, India, and Asia where we adapted the ethnographic approach toward a group setting. Regardless how we chose our interviewees, we followed the ethnographic interview approach as closely as possible, asking individuals to describe the phenomena they considered relevant in their own words. We found evidence that members of the same subgroups shared the same characteristics (i.e., biographical peculiarities, motivations, etc.) that would cause them to either work in Korea or bridge Korean society and businesses with another geographic location. We detail this evidence in the empirical chapters.

Overall, our mixed methods used quantitative data to provide a broad snapshot of our key findings, before using qualitative research to interpret and add depth to these findings. Such qualitative data proved critical for explaining several counterintuitive quantitative findings.

What Is Ahead?

This book seeks to examine the utility of skilled foreigners beyond their human capital value by focusing on their social capital potential, especially as transnational bridges between host and home countries. We build on an emerging stream of research that conceptualizes global labor mobility as a positive-sum game in which countries and businesses benefit from building ties across geographic space, rather than the zero-sum game implied by the global war for talent metaphor. This new orientation in research focus is necessary and timely as the competition for skilled foreigners will only increase with economic globalization and demographic transition in many parts of the world. We empirically demonstrate our arguments with the Korean case, which has embraced economic globalization while facing a demographic crisis. As our research and its key findings are relevant to other advanced societies that seek to utilize skilled foreigners for economic development, central arguments made in this book are expected to offer generalizable insights that extend beyond Korean experiences.

We begin our empirical chapter with an analysis of foreign students in Korea. While the influx of such students in Korea is a relatively recent phenomenon, there is an urgent need to turn to them as an important resource of skilled labor. Yet little research has been done on this subject, as much existing work focuses on unskilled foreigners in Korea. We then turn to Korean students abroad in Chapter 3, engaging in the current debate on brain drain as many of them leave the country to study abroad at an early age and some may not return home after education. In particular, we address the question of how to convert potential brain drain into brain circulation. In Chapter 4, we examine the Korean diaspora with a focus on Korean American students who study at top North American universities. Many of them are well embedded in the host country but also maintain a sense of ethnic identity as Korean descendants and thus could well bridge between Korea and their country of residence. Chapter 5 deals with Indian engineers as true foreigners, with a focus on how they can help the Korean software industry as human resources and also how their value could be transformed into social capital. Chapter 6 summarizes how these empirical chapters demonstrate the utility of skilled foreigners as both human and social capital to Korea and beyond in a rapidly globalizing world.

TWO

Foreign Students in Korea

Ganbaatar is a foreign student from Mongolia studying at a top university in Korea.[1] As an undergraduate studying management, he possesses skills similar to those of legions of young unemployed or underemployed Koreans. Furthermore, Ganbaatar has shown little evidence of being exceptionally talented, unlike some other foreign students who won prestigious academic competitions before arriving in Korea. At first glance, he does not appear to be the kind of "global talent" to be desired by Korean companies.

Nevertheless, Ganbaatar can potentially provide immense benefits to Korean society and ethnocentric companies alike. Having been an avid consumer of Korean cultural products, he has a strong, positive impression of Korean culture and society:

> I first learned about Korea by watching Korean dramas, which have been popular in Mongolia since about 2000. . . . Having watched *Dae Jang Geum* and other Korean dramas as well as listening to hallyu music, I developed a favorable impression of Korea.

Ganbaatar also came to Korea because he admires the Korean developmental experience. He sees Korea as a role model for his home country, as an Asian nation populated by people who look like he does but have nevertheless achieved economic, social, and political parity with the most advanced Western societies:

> I also chose Korea for another reason. Korea looks very small on the map, when I look at the world map while studying. Even though it is so small, Korea developed tremendously over the past 30 years. Also, Korea is Asian—in Korea, people

have the same face as I do, and have a hard time recognizing me as a foreigner. They think that I am a Korean until I speak, when they ask me where I come from.

With these motivations, Ganbaatar has a strong desire to bridge Korea with his homeland economically, connecting Korean capital and know-how with Mongolia's abundant natural resources:

> I want to stay in Korea for two, three, or four years. . . . I want to work at a large Korean company . . . especially one that does business with Mongolia. Korea has capital and expertise while we [Mongolians] have natural resources and talented individuals. So, I want to connect Korea and Mongolia economically, using the things I learned in college . . . I want Korea to benefit and Mongolia to benefit. Already, there are some Korean companies in Mongolia, and in the future, there will be much more Korean investment in Mongolia. I want to find opportunities as someone educated in Korea.

He is an exemplary case of a foreign student who has the potential to play the role of transnational bridge between Korea and his home country.

In this chapter, we examine how individuals like Ganbaatar can provide benefits to Korean society and companies. Besides apparent human capital contribution, such individuals can bridge the geographic, cultural, and social gaps separating Korea from potential partners and/or consumers in developing Asian countries and reinforce Korea's emerging centrality within the Asia-Pacific region. We find that a substantial number of foreign students come to Korea swayed by the music and dramas constituting hallyu or strong desire to learn Korea's developmental success. Such students want to build economic and cultural partnerships between Korea and their home countries. By bringing Korean products, services, capital, and know-how back home, they hope to help their countries develop into an advanced and recognizably Asian society like Korea. In short, we find that foreign students can mitigate Korea's shortage of certain types of skilled workers (e.g., engineers with advanced degrees)—but that the potential for building stronger connections with key countries in developing Asia represents the real payoff for Korean society and companies alike.

Foreign Students in Korean Universities

Foreign students studying in Korea is not a new phenomenon, but their number has skyrocketed in recent years. As Figure 2.1 shows, the number of foreign students at Korean universities has increased fivefold within the past decade. Not surprisingly, most foreign students in Korea originate from Asia, as Tables 2.1 and 2.2 illustrate. As of April 1, 2011, Chinese students top the list with 59,317 (66 percent), followed by Japanese (4,520), Mongolians (3,699), and Vietnamese (2,325). There are also 1,618 ethnic Koreans from China studying in Korea. About one-fifth of these foreign students study the Korean language, and about half of them pursue undergraduate degrees in Korean universities: 21 percent are in graduate school, with 5 percent pursuing PhDs. About half of the foreign students study humanities and social sciences, and about 16 percent study engineering/natural sciences.

Several factors have contributed to the growing presence of foreign students at Korean universities. First, Korean universities have significantly improved their reputations overseas. Although they rank below the best U.S. and European universities, they are nevertheless competitive within Asia. Among the top 100 universities in Asia, 8 Korean universities qualify according to the Academic World Ranking of World Universities while 9 Korean universities qualify according to the Webometrics Ranking of World Universities. Korea is particularly known to offer an excellent education in engineering and the sciences with a highly organized system of research, experiment-based training, and an established research network.[2] Thus, many Korean universities are now prestigious enough to attract students from foreign countries, especially from less developed parts of Asia.

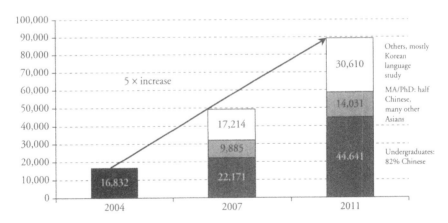

FIGURE 2.1 Increase in the number of foreigners studying in Korea, 2002–2011
SOURCE: Data from the Ministry of Education, Science, and Technology.

TABLE 2.1
Number of foreigners studying in Korea by educational level

Educational level	Language study	Humanities and social sciences	Engineering	Natural sciences	Arts and physical education	Medical and medicine	Other	Total
Language study	18,424	—	—	—	—	—	—	18,424
Other training	—	—	—	—	—	—	7,460	7,460
Bachelor's degree	—	32,329	6,018	2,678	3,443	173	—	44,641
Master's degree	—	10,257	2,257	1,027	756	219	—	14,516
PhD	—	1,433	1,617	1,077	129	240	—	4,496
Total	18,424	44,019	9,892	4,782	4,328	632	7,460	89,537

SOURCE: Data from "Foreign Students Statistics in 2011," Ministry of Education, Science, and Technology.

TABLE 2.2
Number of foreigners studying in Korea by region of origin

Region of origin	Language study	Field of study						
		Humanities and social sciences	Engineering	Natural sciences	Arts and physical education	Medical and medicine	Other	Total
Asia	16,366	41,167	9,297	4,483	4,130	480	4,843	80,766
Africa	195	531	219	71	5	12	30	1,063
Europe	794	577	123	36	48	5	1,358	2,941
North America	790	1,357	145	160	116	126	1,075	3,769
South America	206	251	91	14	21	3	74	660
Oceania	73	136	17	18	8	6	80	338
Total	18,424	44,019	9,892	4,782	4,328	632	7,460	89,537

SOURCE: Data from "Foreign Students Statistics in 2011," Ministry of Education, Science, and Technology.

Second, the Korean government has devoted substantial resources to recruiting foreign students to Korean universities. In 2001, the Ministry of Education, Science, and Technology initiated a program called "Study Korea" designed to attract foreign students, aimed at bridging developed and developing countries, globalizing domestic higher education to improve its competitiveness, and marketing a foreigner-friendly image of Korea.[3] The subsequent influx of foreign students has diversified the student population at many Korean universities and increased the demand for English-language courses. By all accounts, this initiative has bolstered Korean universities' attempts at globalization and helped to improve their rankings in the world.

Third, the presence of foreign students in Korea is inextricably linked to Korea's socioeconomic development. During 2004–2011, Korea became a wealthy economy, increasing its per capita gross domestic product (GDP) at purchasing power parity from $19,200 to $32,100.[4] Korea simultaneously improved its rating under the Human Development Index from 0.888 in 2002 (27th in the world) to 0.897 in 2011 (15th in the world). Korea is not only a member of OECD but the only member of the prestigious club that has become a provider from a recipient of official development aid (ODA). In addition, Korea's continued development has had a disproportionately large impact upon its standing within Asia. In 2010, 52 percent of Korean exports went to Asian countries—31 percent to China, including Hong Kong; 12 percent to Association of Southeast Asian Nations (ASEAN) members; 6 percent to Japan; and 3 percent to India.[5]

Fourth, Korea has modified its immigration policies to help foreign students seek employment opportunities in Korea after graduation. For instance, the Ministry of Justice has started to issue Gold Cards for skilled professionals.[6] Holders of these cards are guaranteed three years of unlimited entry and departure, as well as permission to hire household assistants. Foreign students in science majors have been added to this program.

Nowhere has Korea's influence on developing Asia been more visible than in the cultural sphere. Korea's cultural industries (e.g., music, TV programs, movies) experienced a renaissance after Korea's 1987 democratization, exploring topics previously prohibited or frowned upon under authoritarian rule. As these cultural industries developed through the late 1990s, they began to attract overseas audiences. For instance, "K-Pop" or Korean popular music exploded in popularity from 2000 through 2010, when Korean music exports rose from just over 3 percent of world music exports to around 4.5 percent, and Korea's ranking in musical exports rose from 11 to 6.[7] Such exports of cultural products have had a profound impact on the increasing popularity of everything Korean, especially in Asia.[8] Beyond financial benefits,[9] the lasting impact of hallyu appears in the increased interest in Korean culture and society in developing Asia, reflected by a growth in the number of foreign students coming to study in Korea attracted by it. The link between hallyu and the increase in foreign students has yet to be demonstrated by rigorous research, but as Ganbaatar's case illustrates, there seems to be an important correlation.

Foreign Students as Human and Social Capital

Whether pursuing a quality education, scholarship assistance, or a uniquely Korean experience, foreign students can potentially provide Korean society and companies with valuable resources.[10] Korea's opportunity is hardly unique; as we discuss in the next chapter, foreign students (including Koreans) in the United States power many of its most lucrative economic engines, including Wall Street and Silicon Valley. Below, we explore specific opportunities for Korea to leverage foreign students' human and social capital.

HUMAN CAPITAL

Many Koreans may argue that there is no place in their country for the foreign students that its universities educate. The Korean economy, they may believe, cannot provide enough jobs even for its own college graduates, who face years of unemployment or underemployment as contract workers. At first glance, the data appear to support such claims. For instance, Korea has no immediate need for foreign engineers outside of a few sectors such as software engineering (see Chapter 5).

Nevertheless, we argue that Korea could benefit by employing foreign students for their technical skills. Some foreign students possess crucial skills not commonly found among Korean university graduates. For instance, Korea has an immediate and unfulfilled need for PhDs in engineering. As discussed in Chapter 5, the Korean economy requires about 10,000 more PhDs in engineering than it trains. Foreign students studying for a PhD in engineering would fill an immediate need in the Korean economy. Moreover, as noted in the previous chapter, Korea is experiencing an unprecedented demographic transition where population growth will shift to population decline more rapidly than ever before recorded. This transition will be felt most strongly in fields such as engineering, which are becoming increasingly unpopular among young Koreans. Indeed, only 8 percent of 15-year-old Koreans plan to have a career in engineering or computing, below the OECD average of 11 percent (OECD 2006). For these reasons, Korea may face a shortage of engineers sooner than it might expect, suggesting that Korea should at least begin planning to recruit foreign students more systematically.

SOCIAL CAPITAL

Korean society and companies, however, also have another reason to recruit the foreigners that its universities educate. Foreign students in Korea have great potential to bridge Korea with their home countries. As the Ministry of Education, Science, and Technology recognized as early as 2001,

Korea would benefit by "foster[ing] human resources that bridge developed and developing countries."[11] Foreign students in Korea can play this role particularly well, being familiar with Korean society as well as their home societies. On the one hand, foreign students are often transmigrants who maintain rights and responsibilities back home; many are financially supported by large networks of extended family and send back remittances from future earnings to reciprocate such support (see Schiller, Basch, and Blanc 1995; Tilly 2007). On the other hand, foreign students would build at least a few connections with their classmates, and with local networks in place, they are quite likely to find an appropriate job in Korea.[12] Overall, foreign students are embedded within both their homelands and host societies and are particularly well suited to function as transnational bridges.

This is particularly salient given Korea's pattern of globalization. As Katzenstein (2005) notes, globalization often refers to integration within world regions (e.g., Asia) rather than integration across world regions. Korea has been no exception. From the beginning of their modernization, Koreans have confronted, embraced, or otherwise dealt with a pan-Asian identity (Shin 2006). In recent years, hallyu has found an enthusiastic reception in East and Southeast Asia but only a limited market in North America and Europe. Through this Korean wave, millions of people in Asia have become familiar with Korean culture, and connections with countries like Vietnam and Mongolia would strengthen the country's place within Asia.[13]

FOREIGN STUDENTS AS TRANSNATIONAL BRIDGES
IN THE MULTINATIONAL ENTERPRISE

Social capital has particular relevance to Korean companies with a multinational scope. Academic research suggests that all multinational corporations face competing pressures to centralize or localize.[14] At one extreme, multinational corporations can adopt a highly centralized structure. Such structures often feature so-called ethnocentric management, where home country executives lead local subsidiaries. Having spent most of their careers at corporate headquarters and being familiar with their home countries' business cultures, such executives can easily understand and execute the directives issued by headquarters. Indeed, such executives often consider a stint overseas a step toward receiving a promotion back home. For these reasons, subsidiary managers in an ethnocentric company tend to follow headquarters' directives without raising many objections, giving such companies the ability to easily coordinate the activities of their disparate subsidiaries. Such global coordination comes at a cost, however. Managers sent outward from the home country have neither social ties with local customers and partners nor a cultural understanding of the local environment. Thus, ethnocentric companies have difficulty adapting to local conditions and producing goods suitable for local markets. At the other extreme, multinational corporations can adopt a highly decentralized structure constituted of overseas subsidiaries led by managers hired locally. Being acculturated to the local environment and having ties with local customers and partners, such managers are in a better position to produce and market goods and services for the local environment. In contrast with ethnocentric management, however, highly decentralized companies have limited ability to coordinate their subsidiaries' global activities. Locally hired managers may share little trust with headquarters executives, whom they often view as outsiders seeking to impose their rule upon subsidiary managers. For these reasons, locally hired managers may be less receptive to central coordination, being attuned to their local markets rather than the global interests of the company as a whole.

Korean companies with a multinational scope—the *chaebŏl*—invariably use ethnocentric management. Without exception, the chaebŏl are headed by Korean chairmen and managed by Korean presidents; they are almost always operated by Korean vice presidents and directors. With rare exceptions, the chaebŏl assign Korean managers who have spent most of their careers working at headquarters to head their overseas subsidiaries. Largely for these reasons, the chaebŏl have excelled in manufacturing-oriented industries where central control and global coordination provide competitive advantages. Such industries feature opportunities to achieve economies of scale by aggregating the design and production of manufactured goods. Well-known examples include automobiles, memory chips, and mobile phones. In contrast, the chaebŏl have failed at nearly all attempts to expand overseas in localization-intensive industries featuring goods and services that must be tailored to local tastes. Such industries include business services (e.g., consulting), consumer services (e.g., online social networks), and retail. Notable examples include CyWorld and Helio (see Chapter 5 for a detailed discussion). This does not mean, however, that the problems of ethnocentrism are limited to localization-intensive industries. Our conversations with the human resources teams at several leading companies indicate that many of the Korean managers of their overseas subsidiaries have had substantial problems managing local staff, working with local partners, and selling to local markets.

Prior research recommends that ethnocentric companies resolve such problems by moving away from ethnocentricism. Decades ago Perlmutter (1969) recommended that companies take a "geocentric" approach, staffing positions with the most appropriate individuals regardless of national origin, a recommendation echoed by more recent researchers (notably Bartlett and Ghoshal 1989). Indeed, Perlmutter viewed the turn of ethnocentric companies toward the geocentric model as both desirable and inevitable. Four decades later, however, ethnocentricism still persists among multinational corporations hailing from nearly all nonimmigrant countries, including industrial powerhouses like Germany, Japan, and Korea. Indeed, it is difficult to imagine such companies easily abandoning strong orientations to their home countries and people. To preserve ethnocentric orientations while localizing to overseas markets, these companies have long attempted to hire local managers. This solution is not optimal, however, because local hires have neither professional ties with headquarters-based executives nor an understanding of the culture and motivations driving such executives. These twin gaps hinder local hires and home country executives from trusting one another and working together.

Assuming that ethnocentric companies will not easily abandon alignments toward their home countries, we propose an alternative to geocentricism that leverages foreign students studying in Korea. Such students have largely acculturated to Korean society and its peculiarities. When hired by Korean ethnocentric firms, such individuals have a better chance to adapt to these firms' strong corporate cultures, which typically magnify the peculiarities of Korean culture in general. After serving a stint at corporate headquarters and developing relationships with headquarters-based colleagues, these individuals could become trusted insiders. When assigned overseas to their home countries, such individuals can bridge their companies with their home countries, bringing three specific benefits. First, foreign students can help Korean firms develop highly localized products suitable for specific export markets, to the extent that they understand both their home markets and Korean corporate culture. Second, foreign students can bridge the gap separating Korean executives and local hires; being trusted by both sides, such individuals can reduce cultural misunderstandings and keep interactions cooperative. Third, foreign students can bridge Korean companies with potential local partners using their preexisting social connections as well as their cultural fluency in the local environment. For these reasons, foreign students who have studied at Korean universities represent good candidates to eventually manage Korean companies' local subsidiaries.

Leveraging foreign students in Korea improves upon and complements existing solutions to the problem. Forward-thinking Korean corporations have begun taking advantage of this opportunity, by initiating programs designed to recruit foreign students fluent in Korean to eventually lead home country subsidiaries. For instance, LG Electronics recently initiated a program to hire foreign students from top Korean universities, focusing upon the production engineering, marketing specialist, and general management roles. Trainees in this program spent a year at LG Electronics' Seoul headquarters not only building their domain expertise but also forging key relationships with managers and learning LG's corporate culture. Afterward, such trainees are assigned to LG's subsidiaries in their respective home countries, where they would bridge the Korean senior manager in charge of the subsidiary with LG's local partners and employees.[15] Several other chaebŏl (e.g., Lotte) have also initiated analogous programs, although the trend is far from universal—for instance, LG Electronics' arch-rival, Samsung Electronics, has no specialized program for recruiting foreign students in Korea.

We interviewed representatives from several different chaebŏls operating such programs and found that these programs were generally considered highly promising. They described these programs as a way to bridge the gap between the companies and far-flung local markets. Considering how new these programs were, the companies we interviewed had yet few means to assess the long-term success of these programs. However, anecdotal evidence suggests that graduates of such training programs were working as expected. For instance, one company representative observed that graduates of that company's training program had been particularly effective in clearing up misunderstandings between Korean managers and their local staff. The same representative also emphasized that Korean managers running overseas subsidiaries were literally "clamoring" for additional graduates of its training program. Most representatives emphasized their respective companies' willingness to promote successful hires into high-level positions in the local subsidiaries, not only because they were more effective and cost effective than Korean expatriates sent overseas but also because Koreans were becoming increasingly unwilling to relocate to some important but less developed markets.[16]

Realizing Potential Benefits

Given these potential benefits, we investigate how Korean society and companies can realize the benefits described above. To leverage the *human capital* capacity that foreign students possess, Korea and its ethnocentric companies would need to incentivize them to stay in Korea long term and build a career there. To leverage the *social capital* capacity that foreign students possess, however, Korean companies would need to recruit them into highly specified roles bridging their home countries with Korea before repatriating them as economic ambassadors. Although these solutions appear simple, they build upon characteristics of foreign students that are deeply rooted in their biographies and experiences.

To understand these characteristics and their effects upon foreign students' willingness to remain in Korea and/or bridge Korea with their home countries, we build an end-to-end theoretical model of foreign students, including not only economic considerations but also social and cultural motivations for why they might come to Korea to study, and how these motivations morph into deployable career interests and objectives. As Figure 2.2 suggests, we theorize that the reasons why foreign students choose to study in Korea are directly related with their potential to provide Korean companies with human and/or social capital in a mutually beneficial arrangement. We now explain the key elements of this model.

INSTRUMENTAL MOTIVATIONS TO STUDY IN KOREA

Foreign students undoubtedly choose to study at Korean universities for instrumental reasons—to get a quality education, build a good career, and/or earn a decent living. Such instrumental motivations come in two varieties. On the one hand, foreign students seek to increase their attractiveness to potential employers by attending universities that have strong reputations and provide excellent skill sets. On the other hand, foreign students seek to limit the financial and intangible costs of their educations. Scholarships offer an important incentive to study in Korea. Of the 89,537 foreign students in Korea as of 2011, 2,513 (2.8 percent of total students) were sponsored

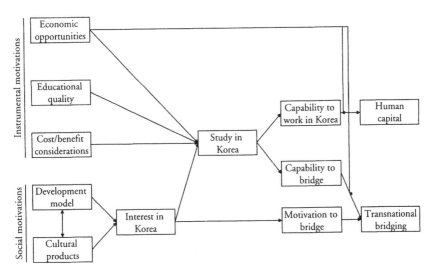

FIGURE 2.2 Theoretical model for Chapter 2

by the Korean government and a further 8,504 (9.5 percent) were invited by their respective universities, receiving substantial financial aid from these sources. An additional 3,195 (3.6 percent) received assistance from other sources, including their home country governments (Korean Educational Development Institute 2012). Even for those who were self-funded, Korean universities can be attractive as they, unlike many universities in other OECD member nations (OECD 2012b), generally charge the same tuition for international students as for Korean nationals. Geographic proximity also matters for Asian students because they can visit home more often, lowering the social costs they bear. Furthermore, these students face lower psychological barriers adapting to environments that are culturally similar to their own.

Economic opportunity also motivates students to choose countries offering attractive career options. Universities located in developed but growing countries offering many desirable, high-paying jobs should be more attractive than others located in poor countries. In the Korean case too, as Hye Jin Kim (2008) finds, foreign students (mostly from developing Asian countries) choose the country largely because they like to remain there, to find jobs with good salaries and benefits. Foreign students also hope to work for Korean multinational corporations, which have made foreign direct investments in their homelands. This is consistent with previous findings in management research (e.g., Tharenau and Caulfield 2010) that highlights the importance of economic opportunities among voluntary expatriates and repatriates.

SOCIAL MOTIVATIONS TO STUDY IN KOREA

Foreign students may also come to study in Korea for reasons relating to their social identities. As noted above, cultural flows outward from more developed toward less developed countries should acculturate individuals living there. Such individuals would develop familiarity and fondness for the source country of these cultural products and be motivated to study abroad there. Simultaneously, Korean cultural products should resonate well with people living in developing Asia because Korea represents a role model for their own countries—a recognizably Asian country that has overcome colonization, war, poverty, and authoritarianism to join the ranks of advanced industrialized democracies. Such admiration for the Korean historical experience would instill a desire to learn more about it—and to bring relevant elements of this development model back home.

Motivations related to social identity differ from instrumental motivations in one crucial way. From an instrumental perspective, Korea is just one of several destinations that offer comparable benefits. Many individuals may even consider Korea an excellent low-cost steppingstone to more desirable environments in the settler countries such as the United States or Canada. In contrast, from a social identity point of view, Korea can be a special place. For a hallyu fan, for instance, other countries cannot provide the unique experience that Korea does. The same applies in the case of those interested in replicating Korea's development model in their own countries. That of the United States or even Japan would be more difficult to emulate, whereas the Korean model may offer a more practical option for them.

CENTRAL ARGUMENTS

According to the framework we illustrate in Figure 2.2, both instrumental and social factors would motivate foreign students to come to Korea. While studying in Korea, these students should gain substantial language and cultural fluency as well as technical and professional skills. Provided that Korean firms offer the right economic opportunities, such students would be willing to remain in Korea for many years, contributing the human capital they possess. Individuals motivated mainly by economic opportunity and other instrumental reasons should view Korea as a good place to build skills and earn money. However, they may also consider Korea just a steppingstone to more desirable destinations. In contrast, foreign students motivated to study abroad in Korea for reasons related to their social identities should view Korea as a special place offering unique experiences and opportunities. To the extent that they also possess strong home country identities, they should be particularly well positioned to bridge Korea with their home countries. While instrumentally motivated foreign students may also recognize the special opportunities created by a bridging role, those motivated by their social identities may be particularly passionate about becoming Korean companies' economic and cultural ambassadors back to their home countries. We examine the validity of these arguments by investigating motivations and interests of foreign students in Korea—and their potential to make human and social capital contribution to Korean society and companies.

Understanding Foreign Students in Korea

This study is based on in-depth interviews of 52 foreign students in Korea who were studying at top Korean universities—Seoul National University, Yonsei University, Korea University, KAIST, Pohang University of Science and Technology, and Hanyang University—during spring 2012. We focused on students studying either technical subjects (primarily engineering) or business-related studies (economics, management, finance). Our respondents are split nearly evenly among women (40 percent) and men (60 percent), business or economics majors (50 percent) and technical majors (56 percent) with a few interviewees pursuing both, undergraduates (46 percent) and graduate students (54 percent), and individuals who proactively learn Korean (46 percent) and those who do not (54 percent). Nearly half of our respondents come from China (42 percent), followed by Central Asia and Russia (19 percent), Malaysia/Indonesia (12 percent), Vietnam (10 percent), and South Asia (10 percent).

Our interviews, consisting of one 90-minute session each, used an approach designed to facilitate interviewees' explanations of their own experiences in their own words (Spradley 1979). In particular, we sought to capture characteristics describing interviewees' biography and geographic origin, as well as whether or not interviewees mentioned one of several different motivations for why they chose to study in Korea, characteristics of their social lives while in Korea, and views of their future plans. To be clear, we make no claims about the representativeness of our sample, considering that we focused exclusively on attendees of elite universities studying either engineering or business-related fields.[17] Still, we sought to capture diversity in our sample by engaging with students from a wide variety of countries other than China, the main source of foreign students in Korea. In most other respects, our sample is quite comparable to the population of foreign students in Korea, except the lack of Japanese students. Our findings illustrate how foreign students might make important contributions to Korea's economy and society as human and social capital, a central theme of this study.

Motivations for Studying in Korea

Our interviewees reveal several common reasons why they came to study in Korea. A substantial number of students pointed to one of several instrumental reasons, such as recruitment by government, corporate, and/or school-sponsored scholarships (40 percent) or otherwise receiving some level of scholarship support (an additional 46 percent), the superiority of Korean education compared to alternatives (31 percent), Korea's low geographic or social distance from their home countries (23 percent), advertising and exchange programs set up by Korean universities (21 percent), and Korea's status as an affordable alternative to North America or Europe (19 percent). Also of particular interest and relevance to our study is the finding that many students mentioned three factors associated with their social identities—their interest in Korea as an exemplary development model for their own countries (29 percent), interest in Korean cultural products (19 percent), and interest in learning the Korean language (17 percent). In short, as expected, motivations for coming to study in Korea are diverse. While some are instrumental, others relate to students' social identities.

Characteristics of Social Lives

Our interviewees also show several common characteristics of their social lives in Korea. Nearly half of all respondents say they have close Korean friends (46 percent) or many Korean friends (48 percent). These characteristics are negatively correlated with each other (–0.17), perhaps reflecting personality differences between introverts with a few close friends and extroverts with many activity partners. Either way, these findings suggest that the majority of our interviewees are embedded within Korean society in a meaningful way.

About equal proportions consider Koreans friendly to foreigners (40 percent) and unfriendly to foreigners (40 percent). These perceptions are independent of each other (correlation coefficient of –0.04); indeed, many interviewees simultaneously consider Koreans both friendly and unfriendly to foreigners. Even the best-adjusted interviewees believe that Koreans treat Caucasians or fluent English speakers exceedingly well, but treat others less hospitably, showing "hierarchical racism" in Korea (Shin 2012). Our interview with Mingzhu exemplifies this trend. Mingzhu, a female Chinese student, majored economics at a top Korean university and now works for a leading Korean mercantile firm. As an undergraduate, she was engaged in many student activities and has made many Korean friends. Indeed, she has a Korean boyfriend, whom she intends to marry. Despite being so well-adjusted to Korean society, however, Mingzhu noted that

> I feel certain things because I am Chinese. I feel that here, they treat fluent English speakers really well, but not Chinese, Vietnamese, or even the Japanese. Indonesians, Indians, Africans—people who live in countries below Korea—people are not friendly towards. . . . It's really bad when I go to the department store while speaking Chinese with my friends. . . . For instance, when I'm walking around with my friends without speaking, the salespeople approach me so courteously. At first, they ask how they might help. But, when I don't talk to them and talk to my friend in Chinese, they just leave. They sometimes say something like "these girls are just looking." Also, it's different when I go with Chinese friends from when I go with my Caucasian friends.

Mingzhu, however, noted that things have improved markedly since she first arrived in 2007.

Other interviewees suggested that certain groups of Koreans treated them very well, while others discriminated against them. Several, for instance, mentioned that middle-aged men discriminated against them, while middle-aged women and younger Koreans tended to be quite friendly. At the same time, many other interviewees mentioned that they had experienced no discrimination. Yuting, an undergraduate studying management, mentioned that she had read about discrimination in the news but never experienced such things personally and wondered if discrimination actually existed. These findings indicate that foreign students have heterogeneous experiences of discrimination, making it difficult to generalize about their views.

Many interviewees (25 percent) also reported discomfort with Korea's drinking culture. Muslim interviewees were particularly uncomfortable with one common social bonding activity among Koreans—drinking while eating grilled pork—both banned under Islamic law. Abdullah, a Bangladeshi male pursuing a graduate degree in international business at a top Korean university, specifically referred to "alcohol and pork" as the "uncomfortable part" about being in Korea. As he said in an interview with us:

> Among foods, these two things are inconvenient. While being part of a group or doing *hwoisik* [informal bonding dinners among co-workers], there's often barbecued pork and alcohol. When I'm having dinner with one, two, or three people, these friends know about me and understand. I ask to eat fish or chicken. However, I can't attend monthly meetings of our international business majors, because they eat pork. So I say sorry and don't go. Since they're eating pork and drinking alcohol, if I am the only one eating something else, it's awkward. It's uncomfortable.

Such responses highlight social awkwardness more than coercion. However, other interviewees (27 percent) also expressed discomfort with Korea's rigidly hierarchical social structure. For instance, Bojing, a Chinese male studying information systems at Hanyang University, stated,

> I am uncomfortable with Koreans' emphasis on the *sŏnbae-hubae* [senior-junior] relationship. Back home, we have no need for such relationships. If someone is older by two or three years, they're simply friends. Here, when I started as a first year, I wasn't able to greet my *sŏnbae* in my department the right way. The other people in the department thought I was very weird. Later, they asked me why I couldn't greet my seniors. I simply had no idea of this concept. . . . My *sŏnbaes* said that I had bad manners.

While several foreign students were dismayed by Korea's drinking and hierarchical culture, others found neither to be a major problem. For instance, Yebzhan is a Kazakh male pursuing an MBA from a top Korean university and has substantial prior experience working for Korean companies. As a nondrinker, he was often told by Koreans that he would have a tough time building interpersonal ties if he did not begin drinking. Yet, Yebzhan actually "found that this wasn't important. Not drinking had no effect on my interpersonal relationships or social life." Once again, responses such as Yebzhan's highlight the heterogeneity of foreign students in Korea.

Future Plans

Our interviewees repeatedly mentioned seven distinct plans for the future. Nearly half (42 percent) wants to work in Korea for a Korean firm, but only in the short term to build their careers. A smaller proportion (25 percent) desires to work in Korea long term. A third (33 percent) would like to work back home but not for a Korean company. In contrast, a slightly larger proportion (38 percent) wants to work for a Korean firm back in their home countries specifically aiming to play a bridging role. A smaller proportion (12 percent) prefers to work at some other location altogether, most often a settler society like the United States or Australia. Among undergraduates and MA/MS students, a substantial number wants to pursue further studies. When asked about their preferred location of further studies, a far larger proportion of interviewees (31 percent) wants to go elsewhere, compared to the proportion that mentions Korea (15 percent). For instance, Jing, a female from China majoring in computer science, described her postgraduation plans as follows: "I can either work or go to graduate school. If I work, I would like to do it in Korea, and if I go to graduate school, I would like to go somewhere else." When asked about her preferred country for graduate study, she referred to "English-speaking countries such as the United Kingdom, the United States, or Canada."

Such responses portray Korea as a good place to work and pursue undergraduate studies but not necessarily the best place for graduate studies. Nevertheless, many current PhD students in Korea expressed satisfaction with their educational and research experiences there.

DIVERSITY OF FOREIGN STUDENTS

Our data contain rich insights about the way foreign students perceive their experiences and opportunities in Korea. However, as shown above, we recognize substantial variations, making it difficult to generalize about foreign students in Korea as a whole. Thus, we cluster groups of students who share much in common, before assessing their perceptions and experiences through interview data. For this purpose, we conducted a correspondence analysis of our 52 interviewees, using dichotomously coded variables capturing whether or not an interviewee mentioned one of the common themes. Table 2.3 lists these themes, along with typical biographical characteristics for interviewees classified into a given group.

TABLE 2.3
Themes and characteristics recurring across interviewees

Category	Recurring theme or characteristic	All	I	II	III	IV
Biography	Age	25.45	23.73	26.78	27.43	23.85
	Gender (female)	0.40	0.43	0.40	0.36	0.43
	Major—business/economics	0.50	0.86	0.60	0.07	0.50
	Major—technical	0.56	0.14	0.50	0.93	0.64
	Undergraduate study	0.46	0.64	0.20	0.00	0.93
	Graduate study	0.54	0.36	0.80	1.00	0.07
	Proactively learned Korean	0.46	0.64	0.40	0.21	0.57
Region	Central Asia / Russia	0.19	0.57	0.10	0.00	0.07
	China	0.42	0.14	0.10	0.43	0.93
	Malaysia/Indonesia	0.12	0.21	0.30	0.00	0.00
	South Asia	0.10	0.00	0.40	0.07	0.00
	Vietnam	0.10	0.07	0.00	0.29	0.00
	Other	0.08	0.00	0.10	0.21	0.00
Why Korea?	Interest in Korean cultural products	0.19	0.29	0.20	0.00	0.29
	Interest in Korea as developed country	0.29	0.57	0.20	0.29	0.07
	Interest in learning Korean language	0.17	0.21	0.00	0.07	0.36
	Superiority of Korean education	0.31	0.07	0.50	0.71	0.00
	Advertising/exchange	0.21	0.07	0.10	0.29	0.36
	Recruited as scholarship student	0.40	0.43	0.60	0.50	0.14
	Receiving some scholarship support	0.46	0.36	0.40	0.50	0.57
	Low physical/cultural distance	0.23	0.14	0.00	0.14	0.57
	Family or friends linked to Korea	0.21	0.21	0.00	0.14	0.43
	Affordable alternative	0.19	0.29	0.50	0.00	0.07
Social	Considers Koreans friendly to foreigners	0.40	0.36	0.70	0.50	0.14
	Considers Koreans unfriendly to foreigners	0.40	0.43	0.50	0.36	0.36
	Participated in tongari	0.29	0.43	0.00	0.07	0.57
	Participated in international studies activity	0.15	0.29	0.20	0.07	0.07
	Has close Korean friends	0.46	0.50	0.40	0.50	0.43
	Has many Korean friends	0.48	0.50	0.50	0.36	0.57
	Has had Korean boyfriend or girlfriend	0.10	0.14	0.10	0.00	0.14
	Discomfort with drinking culture	0.25	0.36	0.30	0.07	0.29
	Discomfort with hierarchy	0.27	0.29	0.20	0.07	0.50
	Happy living in Korea	0.15	0.21	0.20	0.00	0.21
Future	Work in Korea, Korean firm (for experience, short term)	0.42	0.14	0.60	0.64	0.36
	Work in Korea, Korean firm (long-term plans)	0.25	0.07	0.20	0.29	0.43
	Work back home, not for Korean firm	0.33	0.21	0.30	0.50	0.29
	Bridge home/host (Korean firm)	0.38	0.64	0.70	0.14	0.14
	Work elsewhere	0.12	0.07	0.10	0.21	0.07
	Further study in Korea	0.15	0.00	0.00	0.14	0.43
	Further study elsewhere	0.31	0.07	0.30	0.21	0.64
Number of interviewees		52	14	10	14	14

As Figure 2.3 shows, this analysis finds two main dimensions, dividing our sample of foreign students into four groups corresponding to the quadrants. The first dimension, shown on the X axis, corresponds with an interviewee's resemblance to a "typical" undergraduate or graduate student. Interviewees located to the right in Figure 2.3 resemble the typical graduate student while those located to the left are more like the typical undergraduate student. The second dimension, shown on the Y axis, is far more interesting—it corresponds with an interviewee's view of Korea. Interviewees located near the bottom view Korea primarily instrumentally, as one of several alternative geographic locations offering attractive resources. The implication is that such individuals would be likely to abandon their attachment to Korea should they find a more attractive opportunity elsewhere. Conversely, interviewees located near the top see Korea as something unique or special, largely because of its association with familiar hallyu cultural products or as a uniquely Asian development model. On both dimensions, the zero point indicates the sample mean.

The quadrants define four different groups of students, whom we label youthful instrumentalists (quadrant IV), focused instrumentalists (quadrant III), youthful Koreaphiles (quadrant I), and focused Koreaphiles (quadrant II). We now describe each category and relay experiences and attitudes that shape the key factors we investigate—their willingness to work in Korea long term or to bridge Korea with their home countries. We start with students who have the least potential to provide either human or social capital (youthful instrumentalists), before examining others who have greater potential to provide human capital than social capital (focused instrumentalists). Then, we examine the inverse of this situation (youthful Koreaphiles) before finishing with students who may provide both human and social capital (focused Koreaphiles).

YOUTHFUL INSTRUMENTALISTS

We start with a group of foreign students, corresponding to quadrant IV in Figure 2.3, who have only limited potential to contribute either human or social capital to Korean society and businesses. On the one hand, youthful instrumentalists are open to new experiences and actively explore social opportunities. Mostly lacking a graduate education, however, such individuals have less potential to contribute the specialized human capital that Korea currently needs than others pursuing a more advanced degree. On

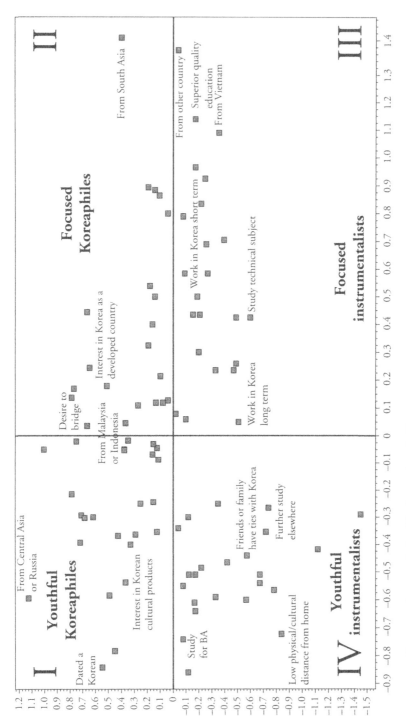

FIGURE 2.3 Correspondence analysis of foreign students in Korea

the other hand, youthful instrumentalists do not consider Korea special, so only 14 percent of this group expresses interest in bridging Korea with their home countries. Thus, such individuals are less likely to contribute social capital to Korea by becoming transnational bridges. Nearly all of this group's interviewees (93 percent) come from China, which is not surprising considering that Chinese students constitute the majority of foreign undergraduates in Korea. Overall, youthful instrumentalists have less potential to provide either human or social capital than the other groups we examine here, although some may develop skills useful to Korean firms—or maintain their ties with Korea after they leave.

The Steppingstone Approach

Youthful instrumentalists have primarily instrumental motivations for studying in Korea. Cultural, social, and geographic proximity appears to play a key role among this mainly Chinese group. Shi, a male undergraduate studying computer science, wanted to go to a "far English-speaking country." His high school teacher even recommended him for an opportunity to study there. However, his mother objected to the suggestion because she worried about the geographic distance, despite the fact that his father thought that studying in the United States, the United Kingdom, or Australia would be a good idea. She finally allowed him to study in Korea because Shi has a relative there. However, many of these undergraduates plan to attend graduate school in a different country—most likely in the United States or Europe—after Korea. For them, Korea represents a convenient steppingstone to more desirable destinations. For instance, Mingzhu—whose attitudes on Koreans' selective discrimination against certain groups of foreigners we described earlier—initially considered Korea a steppingstone to a more attractive destination. As she stated, "In the first four years I spent in Korea, I thought of Korea as a springboard, a jumping board. Back then, I figured I would study here before going to Europe or the U.S. to receive a PhD."

Even for these instrumentally minded students, however, Korea seems to present an attractive opportunity for building career experience through a short-term sojourn working at well-known Korean firms. One male Chinese student said that he would stay in Korea only because "if you get a good job here, you get an adequate salary, and if you join a big company, you join a Global 500 company. You get good experience at a large company." His goal is clearly career related: "If I move jobs or return home, I would make my résumé look better by having such experience." Students like him are more interested in working in Korea (either long term at 43 percent or for short-term experience at 36 percent) than bridging Korea with their home countries (14 percent).

Although the steppingstone approach characterizes many youthful instrumentalists' views of Korea, some may change their opinions or plans over time. For instance, Mingzhu changed her plans midway through her sojourn in Korea, after spending a year studying in the United States and then finding a Korean boyfriend:

> . . . after I spent a year in the U.S. studying it was really hard, so I did not go back. [Laughs.] I started thinking that "Korea is comparatively better." Soon after I returned . . . I met someone I liked in a *tongari*.[18] [Laughs.] So, for that reason, for him, I decided that I wanted to live here. So, to live with this person, I started planning to remain here.

Chinese Students and Instrumental Motivations

Why do youthful instrumentalists express predominantly instrumental motivations and eventually desire to go elsewhere, rather than seeing Korea as their destination or a place to bridge with their home country? They resemble other undergraduates (youthful Koreaphiles, as we describe below) in many respects, showing an affinity for Korean language (57 percent) and cultural products (29 percent). Nevertheless, only 7 percent of them show interest in Korea as a developmental model, suggesting that they are simply not that impressed with Korea and its economic development even if they find its culture entertaining. Such a view seems plausible considering that the vast majority of youthful instrumentalists are from China—a gargantuan country itself experiencing rapid development.

Another possible explanation is that Chinese undergraduates might feel disappointed by their reception in Korean society, more so than other foreign students. Considering the geographic and cultural proximity of the two countries, as well as China's rising global status, Chinese students may have expected to feel welcome in Korean society. However, even exceptionally well-adjusted individuals like Mingzhu often felt left out. As she relates, "Koreans like to say 'Let's get dinner' and such friendly words. They say this a lot but don't actually have dinner with you. . . . Not only about getting dinner but also whenever we'd meet, they'd say, 'We're friends now so let's spend a lot of time together. Let's drink.' They say stuff like this . . . but I never hear back from them." Many other interviewees echoed her sentiments. For instance, another well-adjusted Chinese undergraduate laments that "there's a cultural difference. No matter how much I think about it. I went to this and that tongari and made a lot of friends. At first they were so friendly. Until . . . the kinds of things they talk about is so different, like their high school experiences and stories like being in the [Korean] Army. . . . I cannot get in. They do everything in groups. I want to talk with them but can't. As things get more and more like this, I don't want to stay in this kind of environment."

Some Chinese students even refer to Korean racism, especially its hierarchical nature that regards Caucasians more positively than other Asians, including Chinese. As Xi, a Chinese student studying computer science, says, "Ah, what I can think of regarding that point is that Koreans are very positive towards Americans but not some other people. This is strange, but I understand." Such Chinese students leave Korea with ambivalence. Xi recounts his experiences in Korea as follows: "Before I came to Korea, I enjoyed Japan's language and manga, video games. So I had a very good image of Japan. However, the Japanese had a bad impression of us Chinese, and I did not appreciate how they acted primarily to earn money from China. Korea is similar to Japan in this manner. Of course I feel good about Korean dramas or culture, but there's a difference in the way we think. . . . As time goes by, I want to go back to China." His view appears to summarize youthful instrumentalists,' differentiating this group from other Chinese undergraduates classified as youthful Koreaphiles. The words of Jing, the same student who expressed a desire to pursue a graduate education elsewhere, capture this ambivalence. Talking about her friend, she said that "he graduated from Korea before going to study to another country. When he was in Korea, he used to talk about how Korea wasn't all that great. However, after he left, he says he often thinks about Korea." Although such individuals feel uncomfortable living in Korea, they nevertheless leave the country with many memories and social ties. In this regard, one should not rule out the possibility that they could someday become a source of social capital for Korea, but this potential is limited given their overall ambivalence toward the country.

FOCUSED INSTRUMENTALISTS

Like youthful instrumentalists, focused instrumentalists (corresponding with quadrant III in Figure 2.3) value the opportunities Korea provides for them without viewing Korea as something unique or special. Unlike youthful instrumentalists, however, focused instrumentalists are more interested in achieving their specific objectives than exploring their social domains. Indeed, nearly all in this group are graduate students pursuing technical studies, as shown in Table 2.3. As such, members of this group have strong potential to contribute the kind of human capital that Korea needs—the skills obtained through advanced degrees in science and technology—even if they do not necessarily contribute greatly to its social capital.

Dominance of Instrumental Motivations

Like youthful instrumentalists, focused instrumentalists are predominantly motivated by specific interests. Yet, in contrast to the former whose main motivations have much to do with cultural, social, and geographic proximity, large proportions of this group cite aspects of their education, including the superiority of a Korea-based education (71 percent) and their recruitment as scholarship students (50 percent), as main reasons that they came to Korea.

Being oriented toward technical research, many focused instrumentalists care most about the high-quality research conducted in the Korean lab environment. For instance, Bilal, a South Asian studying for a PhD in engineering from KAIST, emphasizes that he came to study at the school because "KAIST has quite a reputation among foreign academics. It produces a lot of good research, and it has a very good reputation among researchers." In particular, he refers to the quality of his research lab as his main reason for having chosen KAIST. Many other respondents echo the sentiment that Korean universities offer an excellent education, particularly top Korean technical universities such as KAIST and the Pohang University for Science and Technology. One student said that "PosTech [the Pohang University for Science and Technology] was better than the American universities where I was accepted."

Of particular interest are the views Chinese students have about Korean universities, because they account for 43 percent of focused instrumentalists in our study. Many Chinese interviewees expressed concerns about higher education back home as a motivation for studying abroad. One such student, who had previously worked as a computer programmer in Beijing, derided the quality of education at Chinese universities, saying "I did not feel like pursuing further education in China. . . . I did not trust Chinese universities very much. I spent four years working on my undergraduate degree in China, and after four years, I kind of got a feel for the system. Even if I attended graduate school, there wasn't very much there."

Beyond the high quality of Korean universities, focused instrumentalists often mention the availability of scholarships as another key factor for studying in Korea, as well as its cultural proximity to their homelands. For instance, Xi—a computer science PhD candidate from China studying at a technical university—mentioned that he came to Korea largely because of the financial assistance: "I liked the U.S. and Japan [as potential destinations] as well. However, the financial assistance [my university] provided was quite attractive. So, I chose Korea without hesitation." Such interviewees also emphasize the lower time and effort needed to adjust to Korea versus other countries. For instance, one industrial engineering student from China noted, "Many students desire to study in the U.S. However, for many Asian students, Korea and Japan are good alternatives to the U.S. because Korea and Japan are more similar culturally and physically closer." Yet some focused instrumentalists are critical of Korean work culture. The South Asian doctoral student who praised KAIST above also said that "at labs, Koreans work too hard. They are workaholics. Rather than working smart, they just work hard."

Focused instrumentalists, like youthful instrumentalists, also mentioned convenience and practicality as primary reasons to choose Korea. While many students wanted to study in Korea, others had no choice—they simply could not go to their preferred countries and chose Korea as a backup option. One such individual, a chemical engineering student from Vietnam, frankly shared with us his main reasons for coming to study in Korea:

I studied a little bit in Germany but faced difficulties funding my education. I could have also studied in the U.S., but my GRE scores [Graduate Record Examinations, demanded by many U.S. universities] were a bit low. Also, my English language vocabulary was somewhat lacking. So, I thought of Japan, but my father, who is a professor in Vietnam, thought that Korean students were somewhat better than Japanese students. . . . So, he recommended Korea over Japan.

Others were even more explicit about their lack of qualifications to study elsewhere. For instance, the Chinese computer programmer we discussed earlier said, "I tried to apply to English-speaking countries, but my TOEFL [Test of English as a Foreign Language, an English proficiency test] scores were only like 67 or 69 out of 120 points. So the only country I could go to with these kinds of scores was Korea. I was scared to select an English-speaking university."

Following Future Opportunities

Like youthful instrumentalists, focused instrumentalists see nothing special about Korea. Instead, they seek opportunities anywhere in the world, as reflected in the interviews above. Such individuals generally plan to work in Korea short term to build work experience (64 percent) or return home without working for a Korean firm (50 percent), given that some individuals mentioned several alternative plans. For instance, when Bilal—the afore-mentioned engineering student at KAIST—was asked about his future plans, he replied, "I will return home. But before I return, I want about three years' experience working here first. After that, I will return home." Such replies reveal that focused instrumentalists see value in gaining experience in Korea, suggesting that they would be willing to stay in Korea to utilize their specialized technical skills—but only given compelling economic opportunities.

However, unlike both youthful and focused Koreaphiles, focused instrumentalists have no particular attachment to Korea or compelling reason to prefer Korea over other countries. In fact and not surprisingly, many focused instrumentalists express a preference for the culturally more diverse settler societies—the United States, Canada, Australia, and New Zealand—over nonimmigrant ones like Korea. Even when they are content with the high quality of Korean education, they are concerned with the overall living and working environment for foreigners in Korea. The South Asian PhD student in engineering at KAIST mentioned above said, "When I leave KAIST, I have difficulty because I cannot speak Korean. I sometimes have to receive help from Korean friends." One student from the Middle East explains how cultural barriers would bar him from staying in Korea beyond short-term economic opportunities:

> Canada offers an easy path to residency, and the U.S. is similar. I don't know about Korea. . . . There is a problem communicating [because of the need to

speak Korean], and the culture is completely different from my home culture. So, I want to go somewhere like Canada where there are a lot of immigrants, where I can adjust more easily because there's a vast diversity of ethnicities living there. I do not want to stay in Korea—I want to go to the U.S. or Canada. The possible option is to stay here while I learn English. Korea offers a high salary so I can work in Korea for about a year.

Overall, focused instrumentalists value and follow practical interests, suggesting that Korean companies could retain such individuals by offering attractive opportunities. Many of them possess technical skills useful to Korean firms, more so than youthful instrumentalist, though both groups are opportunistic. That said, focused instrumentalists, like youthful instrumentalists, have no compelling reason to stay in Korea, implying that their sojourns in the country will be short in length. For them, Korea may not be attractive compared with settler societies that better appreciate and promote ethnic and cultural diversity. Nevertheless, such individuals represent a pool of high-end technical talent that Korean society and firms can potentially draw upon if they provide the right incentives.

YOUTHFUL KOREAPHILES

A third group of students, corresponding to quadrant I in Figure 2.3, is diametrically opposite from focused instrumentalists in two dimensions. First, youthful Koreaphiles are still exploring new experiences and opportunities, rather than being focused on their education. According to Table 2.3, interviewees placed in this category tend to be undergraduates (64 percent) majoring in business or economics (86 percent). Large proportions participated in tongari or general student activities (43 percent) or specific activities for international students (29 percent). Second, youthful Koreaphiles believe that there is something special about Korean culture and society. Ganbaatar is broadly representative of this category—higher-than-average proportions of youthful Koreaphiles came to Korea because their interest was sparked by the Korean development experience (57 percent), hallyu (29 percent), or a desire to learn the Korean language (21 percent). For instance, Nigora, a female student from Uzbekistan studying management, initially had a strong interest in the English language and going to English-speaking countries, before unexpectedly developing an interest in Korean drama. She became interested in Korea, began to learn Korean, and ended up studying in Korea. Overall, such individuals have less technical training and skills to offer than focused instrumentalists but have stronger host country embeddedness and show a willingness to actively bridge Korea with their home countries. So, these individuals may not provide valuable human capital (beyond what Korean students already provide) but have great social capital potential.

Why do youthful Koreaphiles consider Korea so unique or special? Ganbaatar's keen interest in and appreciation of the Korean development model was shared by many other members of this group. For instance, Wing, a female Malaysian, cites Korea's phenomenal economic success compared to her own country as a primary reason to study in Korea:

> South Korea and North Korea only stopped being at war around 1953. Meanwhile, Malaysia gained independence around 1957. While Malaysia and Korea are separated by only four years, Korea developed so much faster when compared with Malaysia. Now, Malaysia is about 20 years behind. So, I was curious how Korea did so well.

Many such students are interested in taking the Korean experience back to their home countries, as a template for future development.

Motivation and Ability to Bridge

Such viewpoints are strongly associated with an interest in bridging Korea with their home countries. Ganbaatar is hardly alone in his desire to bridge—indeed, according to Table 2.3, nearly two-thirds of youthful Koreaphile interviewees (64 percent) indicate their desire for future transnational bridging. The following responses are broadly representative of the comments made by many youthful Koreaphiles. Such responses do not always provide the same level of detail as Ganbaatar's response but reflect the same broad motivations and ideas.

The availability and lucrativeness of opportunities to bridge are often cited in conjunction with the desire to bridge. For instance, Wing is aware that large Korean companies are "looking for Asians, from places like India and Malaysia, because they are looking to expand into South Asia." For this reason, she "wants to work for two years in Korea before returning home to Malaysia" so that she could "gain experiences before being sent out to Malaysian subsidiaries."

To improve their chances at such opportunities, youthful Koreaphiles are willing to acculturate even further into Korean society than they already have. At a basic level, this willingness is reflected in their widespread desire to learn to speak Korean. Additionally, many—but not all—students are willing to fit into Korean work culture, even if it means that they would violate taboos and prohibitions prevalent in their home countries. For instance, Nigora, who practices Islam, mentioned that she "changed a great deal while in Korea." She began drinking to better enjoy life in Korea and began eating pork even though she "really shouldn't have." Overall, she has changed because she "wanted to get friendlier with people and to understand Korean culture more."

Several interviewees indicate that they would prefer to work in their home countries while performing a bridging role rather than living in Korea because of the pull exerted by friends and family who have remained back home. For instance, Suleyman, a Turkmen male who majors in electrical engineering, wants to "work for a company like Samsung or LG that focuses on electronic components." However, he would like to return home after one to two years, partially because "LG and Samsung do a lot of business with [his] home country" and partly because he has lived apart from his family for eight years already and feels as if he should return home. Nevertheless, Suleyman emphasizes his desire to bridge:

> And—to help my country develop, and to make Korea and my country have good relations, I want to go back and forth between Korea and my home country. I want to do something that will help link the two countries often.

We take this view with caution, however, as some evidence suggests that such individuals' attitudes may change once a student has begun to work in Korea. To supplement our interviews of foreign students in Korea, we also talked to senior human resources personnel at several major Korean companies. During one such interview, we were told that many foreign students who initially expressed a desire to return home ended up preferring Korea's environment over their home countries' less desirable living conditions.

Our study shows that some students are willing to bridge Korea with their homelands because of a sense of gratitude for the opportunities they received from Korean universities and firms. One such interviewee, Honghui, majored in international trade before working for a large Korean securities firm. As soon as he was hired, his company's human resources department told him that he would probably have to go back home to China as the company's business there expanded. Honghui felt strong loyalty to his company given such opportunities:

> I think that my company is giving me a great opportunity. I told my company that I would first work two to three years as a financial analyst and later become a fund manager. As a fund manager, I believe that I should return the favor my company provided me.

Evaluations of such positive sentiments, however, must be tempered by Korean companies' previous experience with foreign students, especially those from China. One human resource executive from a major Korean company made the rather harsh remark that foreign students from some countries tended to "suck out the sweet juice" from job opportunities by building their résumés before "looking for opportunities elsewhere." Although such concerns remain unanswered, youthful Koreaphiles represent a segment of the foreign student population with both the motivation and the ability to bridge their home countries with Korea.

FOCUSED KOREAPHILES

Our final group, corresponding to quadrant II in Figure 2.3, includes foreign students also viewing Korea as special, but focusing upon their studies rather than generally exploring their social environments. Thus, it is not surprising that just like focused instrumentalists, focused Koreaphiles tend to be graduate students (80 percent; see Table 2.3). At the same time, members of this group, like youthful Koreaphiles but in contrast to focused instrumentalists, consider Korea unique—and correspondingly have an interest in bridging Korea with their home countries. Thus, members of this group have the potential to not only contribute specialized technical expertise (i.e., human capital) but also bridge Korea to their home countries (i.e., social capital).

Like focused instrumentalists, many focused Koreaphiles cite the quality of a Korea-based education (50 percent) as well as its affordability (50 percent) as main reasons to come to study in Korea. However, like youthful Koreaphiles, they also refer to an interest in hallyu (20 percent) and the Korean development model (20 percent). For instance, Abdullah—the Bangladeshi student who expressed discomfort with alcohol and pork—emphasizes the critical role played by both instrumental and social identity-related reasons:

I came as a scholarship student invited by the Korean government, but I had an interest in Korea from when I was young. And I knew a lot about Korea. When I was attending middle school, there were many Bangladeshis working in Korea. From them, I heard a lot about Korea. And Korea is among the countries in the world with very fast economic development. I was curious how Korea developed so quickly. Because of this curiosity, I came to Korea.

When asked why he chose Korea over other countries like the United States, however, Abdullah admitted that he had had "inadequate means" to study elsewhere. Yet he exemplifies many students motivated by both instrumental and social identity factors.

Compared to youthful Koreaphiles, focused Koreaphiles have different experiences. Rather than socializing and participating in tongari, this group focuses on research. One graduate student in life sciences, studying at a leading engineering and sciences institution, describes his experience in Korea as spending time in research labs:

I have no free time. Honestly speaking, among various fields ours is the hardest, and among these, my lab is the toughest. Basically, I arrive at my lab around 9:00 in the morning and leave around 2:00 late at night. I follow this schedule even during the weekends. Sometimes I get to spend time with my girlfriend during weekends, during the occasional Sundays off. When I rest like this, I go to various places and eat Italian or other types of food. Because I spend so much time at school, I don't do other social activities very well. There's just no time for it.

Interestingly enough, many other students claim their fields to be the hardest—and their labs as the most rigorous—suggesting that this characterization is representative of the experience of PhD and research-oriented MS foreign students in Korea. Consider Bahar—a graduate student in engineering—who notes that he is very happy with the education he is receiving in Korea but has had difficulty keeping up with the workload. He attributes this primarily to cultural differences, given that Koreans are trained to work hard from secondary school onward.

Motivations and Ability to Bridge

Like youthful Koreaphiles, focused Koreaphiles express a strong desire to bridge Korea with their home countries (70 percent), but they also show interest in working in Korea short term to build their work experience

(60 percent) that could also be useful to their future bridging role. One Indian interviewee from PosTech even applied to a Korean firm anticipating that opportunities to bridge the two countries would materialize in the future. Interestingly, he wants to remain in Korea until that time—and mentions the possibility that he might stay there instead of returning home.

Like their youthful Koreaphile counterparts, focused Koreaphile interviewees often expressed gratitude for the opportunities they had received in Korea. Yebzhan, the same Kazakh MBA student who had previously worked in a Korean firm and found that not drinking was not a problem, said, "By working with Korea, my family situation became much better so that my family feels gratitude towards Korean people." Simultaneously, focused Koreaphile interviewees are older and more mature than their youthful Koreaphile counterparts and have a more nuanced and perhaps more realistic perspective on a bridging role. A good example is Meng, a Malaysian student more focused upon his studies than most other undergraduates. According to him, Korean firms employ many Malaysians and generally have a good image of Malaysians. However, Meng cites language as a barrier: "In Malaysia, we use mainly English. If you work for a Korean company, you have to use Korean. Malaysian people do not speak Korean well and don't understand the words, so there are some difficult situations that arise, according to what I've heard." Also, he adds that Malaysians working in a Korean firm would have to endure longer hours than they would at a local firm. He appreciates the idea that Malaysians who have studied in Korea have something special to offer to Korean firms in Malaysia but prefers to work overseas first: "If I return to Malaysia right away, the salary is not very high. The monthly salary is about 120 man-won (KRW 1,200,000 or approximately USD 1,100), but if you work overseas, you can earn a lot more money. If you work overseas for about five years, you can buy a house in Malaysia." Our interviews with Korean companies' human resources executives corroborate such accounts. Indeed, these executives mentioned that foreign students expected to be compensated the same as Koreans sent abroad. What is notable about this account, though, is that at least some focused Koreaphile interviewees have an informed view of the realities of bridging a Korean firm with their home countries and nevertheless embrace such a role.

Overall, members of this group with advanced degrees in science and engineering not only possess the technical expertise to contribute the kind of human capital needed by Korean firms but also the willingness to provide the social capital that could help Korean firms and society play a more central role within the Asia-Pacific region.

Foreign Students as Human and Social Capital

Our investigation of foreign students in Korea reveals substantial heterogeneity that affects in various ways their potential to contribute the kinds of human capital and/or social capital that could benefit Korean society and firms. Youthful instrumentalists have neither the skills of the kind immediately needed by Korean firms (i.e., those provided by advanced technical degrees or technical work experience) nor the inclination to build transnational bridges linking Korea to their home countries. Focused instrumentalists, however, are obtaining advanced degrees in technical subjects, providing them with skills badly needed by Korean firms. They can be tapped into as an important pool of human capital for Korea. In contrast, youthful Koreaphiles do not necessarily possess useful human capital capability, but nevertheless they have a strong interest in building social ties between Korea and their homelands. They can be a good source of social capital, if not of human capital, for Korea. Finally, focused Koreaphiles can potentially provide both human and social capital valuable to Korean society and economy.

These findings both support and challenge a widespread perception among Korean policymakers and academics that only foreign students studying engineering or the natural sciences have much to contribute to the Korean economy, while others studying business, the social sciences, and the humanities have little to offer. This perception seems to be built upon two assumptions. First, foreign students studying technical subjects are thought to be more skilled, talented, and intelligent than those studying other subjects. While technically oriented foreign students are viewed as internationally competitive global talent, others are viewed as individuals who chose to study in Korea given financial pressures or rejection from prestigious schools in North America or Europe. Second, the Korean educational system is assumed to produce an insufficient number of technical professionals but an excessive number of other graduates. Regardless of the quality of nontechnical foreign students, they are welcomed less than their technically oriented peers, as they are believed to compete with—and sometimes displace—deserving Korean university graduates. Evidence appears to support both assumptions. Korean universities have globally competitive programs in engineering and other such technical subjects but are relative laggards in business education, the social sciences, and the humanities. It follows that Korean universities can attract better technically oriented foreign students than nontechnical foreign students. The Korean economy indeed faces a labor shortfall in some technically oriented fields—but a surplus in other fields.

Yet the findings we present in this chapter illustrate that foreign students studying either technical or nontechnical subjects have much to contribute to the Korean economy. To be sure, the specific skills (i.e., human capital) possessed by foreign students matter, but their willingness and ability to bridge Korea with their home countries may matter just as much. Indeed, we reiterate that a larger proportion of students willing to provide the most important benefit—bridging Korea with their home countries—come from business-related fields rather than technical fields. This finding challenges current thinking among researchers and policymakers in Korea, which primarily focuses on the human capital contribution, overlooking the greater potential of these students as social capital.

Overall, Korean universities, companies, and society at large all need to carefully rethink foreign students' role in Korea. We wish to reiterate that the transnational bridges created by foreign students can benefit everyone involved. Korean companies receive a chance to expand overseas to new markets and increase the efficiency of offshore operations. Foreign students' home countries profit by absorbing the expertise and know-how brought by Korean companies, carried back by the students they sent to Korea. Finally, foreign students have the opportunity to gain attractive employment where they can express their desire to bring two countries they have feelings about—Korea and their respective home countries—closer together. As these positive-sum benefits become realized, foreign students can play a valuable role in consolidating Korea's newfound centrality within Asia. As Korean companies have entered markets in East and Southeast Asia, and as Korean artists have popularized Korean culture through the Korean wave, Korea has become increasingly central to these regions. In comparison, Korea's social ties with its Asian neighbors have not kept pace with its economic and cultural reach. As foreigners embedded in Korean society, Korean-educated students can forge such ties that are valuable for both Korea and their homelands.

THREE

Korean Students Overseas

Korea not only receives foreign students but also is a leading nation in sending its own young people for education abroad. Moreover, the number of Korean students studying at foreign colleges and universities has been on the rise with globalization. Korean students are the largest group of international students in China and the third largest in the United States. While North America remains to be the preferred destination to obtain advanced degrees, about two-thirds of students studying languages go to the Asia-Pacific region, presumably to China.

Despite becoming rich, Korea is still losing many bright students to other advanced countries. Some of the best students in Korea have long studied overseas, and many of these students never returned. The Brain Drain Index developed by the International Institute of Management Development (IMD) suggests that Korea has experienced "brain drain" more severely than other advanced economies. From 2005 to 2013, Korea has fluctuated between 3.40 and 5.91 on an index where 0 indicates severe brain drain and 10 indicates no brain drain at all. Korea did worse than Japan, which ranged between 4.87 and 6.75, but better than China, which scored between 2.93 and 3.66. In comparison, the United States ranged between 6.64 and 7.88 during the same time period. Overall, Korea experiences less brain drain than developing countries like China but more so than other advanced countries like Japan and the United States.[1]

The recent *chogi yuhak* trend has further exacerbated this situation. Chogi yuhak refers to Koreans sending their young children overseas to avoid a secondary educational system in Korea that is known to be very stressful not only for the students but also for the parents. The chogi yu-hak practice originated among middle- and upper-class families who sent their children abroad to elite private institutions in the United States and Europe, even though they could have attended top universities in Korea. In recent years, however, the practice spread among a wider range of socio-economic backgrounds, and chogi yuhak students have spread out across a broader range of institutions and countries. As Figure 3.1 shows, the number of chogi yuhak students remains a small proportion of all Koreans studying abroad but reached over 20,000 in 2008 (declining after the global recession), reigniting the brain drain question.

To be sure, many such students return to Korea after receiving first-rate educations overseas; almost two-thirds of Korean students who receive PhDs in U.S. universities return home.[2] Such individuals have made key contributions to the rise of Korea in the second half of the twentieth century. For instance, Kim Jae-Ik—a Stanford-trained economist—returned home and became a key architect of Korea's economic development. Such individuals

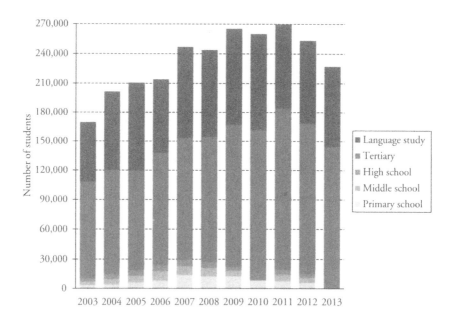

FIGURE 3.1 Number of Koreans studying overseas
SOURCE: Data from Statistics Korea.
NOTE: Data on primary, middle, and/or high school students not available for 2010 and 2013.

have long provided the country with crucial human capital, helping fill Korea's need for "global talent."

Some Korean students may not return home for some time after their education, if ever, and the conventional view considers this a loss of human capital for Korea. However, as we argued in Chapter 1, Korea nevertheless benefits from the transnational bridges that these Koreans generate. Saxenian (2006) examines the life journeys of Taiwanese, Indians, and Israelis who attended U.S. graduate schools and chose to remain in the United States to work in Silicon Valley after receiving degrees. Her study finds that such individuals had played a critical role in establishing high-technology industry clusters in Hsinchu, Bangalore, and Haifa, among other locales. Not only did these Argonauts bridge Silicon Valley with these industry clusters, but they also actively proselytized Silicon Valley's culture of innovation and entrepreneurship in their homelands. While Saxenian does not cite the Korean case, her story can apply to Koreans as well, especially given Korea's recent focus on building Silicon Valley–like ecosystems for creative entrepreneurship.

By transforming brain drain into brain circulation, Korea would continue to gain not only high-value human capital but also connections to the world's most advanced economies, increasing Korea's centrality in the global economy. Yet, we know little about key factors that transform the brain drain into brain circulation—the long-term objectives of Koreans who leave Korea to study abroad and factors affecting their decisions to eventually return home. We also consider the possibility that some students may never return home and ask how Korea as a country may nevertheless benefit from the ties that these students will maintain with a homeland they left behind. Thus we need to address two interrelated questions. Will the multitudes of talented young Koreans educated in foreign countries eventually return to Korea? Even if they do not, could they benefit Korea by constituting a global network bridging Korea with their host societies, channeling information, innovations, and opportunities back and forth for mutual benefit?

In this chapter we investigate these questions through an analysis of Korean students studying at top colleges in North America, at both the undergraduate and graduate levels. As of 2010, a full 4.1 percent of Korean tertiary students studied abroad, 52.4 percent of these students in the United States and a further 6.2 percent in Canada. Furthermore, Koreans constituted 10.4 percent of all foreign students in the United States and

4.5 percent of such students in Canada (OECD 2012b). Our goal in this chapter is to understand the motivations and concerns of Korean students overseas and their likelihood of returning to Korea or remaining overseas but working closely with Korean individuals and firms.

Study Abroad for Koreans

Study abroad, brain drain, and brain circulation have great relevance to Korea today. Yet, they are far from new to the country. Indeed, Koreans have been studying abroad for most of the past two millennia. Many of the brightest minds of the Silla, Koryŏ, and Chosŏn dynasties studied Buddhist and Confucian classics in China. Korea supposedly experienced brain drain when some of these students chose to remain in China. One such individual was the Buddhist monk Wŏnch'ŭk. Born in Silla, he became one of the two star pupils of Xuanzang—the inspiration for the famed novel *Journey to the West*. Wŏnch'ŭk himself gained wide renown in the Tang dynasty and never returned home. Simultaneously, dynastic Korea benefited from notable examples of transmigration and brain circulation. Perhaps the most famous example is Jang Bogo. Born in Silla, Jang traveled from there to Tang China and eventually became a junior general in the Wuning district (today's Jiangsu Province) where he built ties with ethnic Silla communities in China. After returning to Silla, these transnational ties enabled Jang to dominate trade between Silla, Heian Japan, and Tang China for decades.

As Korea entered the modern world, young Koreans looked away from China and toward Japan for modern education. Many of the leaders of the Kapsin coup in 1894 were students of Fukuzawa Yukichi at his newly established Keio Institute (later Keio University). This pattern continued and intensified throughout the colonial era, as many Korean families sent their sons to study at elite Japanese schools. One notable example was Shin Kyŏkho, who left Korea to study at a high school affiliated with Waseda University. In 1948, Shin founded the Lotte Group, and later became a transmigrant when he reestablished a presence in Korea after Japan and Korea normalized relations. Today, he splits his time between Korea and Japan, and Lotte is one of the few large bi-national corporations in the world along with Royal Dutch Shell.

Since Korea's liberation after World War II, the United States has emerged as Koreans' preferred destination of study abroad, and the number of Korean students going there has steadily increased over the years. Of the 123,370 Korean students overseas for an undergraduate degree as of 2011, 36,234 (29.4 percent of the total) were studying in the United States. Of these students, 19.2 percent majored in the sciences and engineering. An additional 18,223 (14.8 percent) and 12,629 (10.2 percent) were, respectively, studying in Australia and Canada. The United States remains a more attractive destination for Korean graduate students, educating 23,386 (57.3 percent) of 40,799 total worldwide. Of these students, 30.4 percent pursued degrees in the sciences or engineering.[3] As Figure 3.2 shows, the number of Korean students in the United States increased rapidly through 2008, before leveling off during recessionary conditions.

The main reason Koreans prefer to study in the United States is essentially the same as why their forefathers previously went to China and Japan—they expect to receive a better education there, despite the rapid improvement of Korean universities. A recent survey (Hong and Cho 2012) found that 87.9 percent of surveyed Korean students in the United States

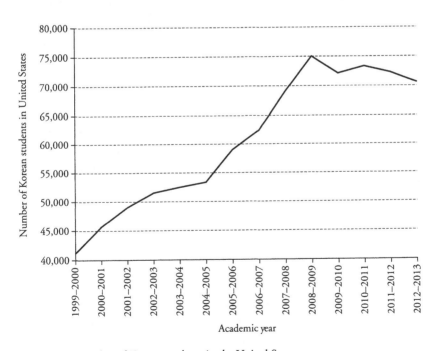

FIGURE 3.2 Number of Korean students in the United States
SOURCE: Data from "Open Doors Data, International Students: Leading Place of Origin," International Institute of Education.

believed that they were receiving a better education there. Indeed, 57.4 percent of them listed the superiority of an American education as the primary motive for studying abroad. Largely for this reason, the number of Korean students in the United States nearly doubled in the decade following 1999–2000.

We recognize that Koreans study in many countries all over the world but focus on Korean students in North America for two reasons. First, Korean students more likely enroll in full-time, degree-seeking programs in developed countries like the United States and Canada. On the other hand, Koreans who study at English-language programs in less developed countries like the Philippines are not likely to enroll in longer-term degree-seeking programs. Such short-term students are much less likely to become meaningfully embedded in their host societies, reducing their bridging potential. Second, North America still attracts the most talented and ambitious students. Other developed countries (e.g., Japan, Australia, New Zealand, Great Britain) certainly draw top Korean students too, but the United States in particular attracts a disproportionately large group of such students. We focus on such students because they have the greater potential to develop into the kind of global talent that the Korean economy increasingly needs.

Overseas Students as Human and Social Capital

The large number of talented young people leaving the country for study abroad presents concerns and challenges for Korean society and economy. First, they represent a deep pool of quality human capital that could be lost to other nations, raising the question of brain drain. In fact, the number of Koreans returning home after receiving a PhD overseas has decreased gradually since 2007 and exponentially since 2011. Almost 70 percent of science and engineering Korean PhD holders in the United States in the period of 2006–2009 reported that they would prefer to stay and work in the United States. Furthermore, the growing trend of chogi yuhak makes it only more difficult for Korea to count on the return of individuals studying abroad, as chogi yuhak students who are exposed and accustomed to their host countries' advanced levels of education and technology early on are less likely to want to return home after their studies. The challenges that Korea faces in bringing its students back home have little to do with identifying the right individuals; as Korean citizens, they have a right to return should they choose to do so. Re-embedding such students into Korean society is likely to be much easier than acculturating true foreigners to Korea's hierarchical structures and ethnic nationalism. Even with some difficulties reintegrating into Korean society—a phenomenon called "re-entry shock"—Korean students who have studied abroad should eventually readjust to the local environment better than just about any other group of foreigners.[4] Still, Korea would be competing with other countries, including the countries hosting Korean students, for their talent, and thus one important question is how to offer attractive incentives to bring them back home to enlarge Korea's pool of human capital.

A perhaps more serious challenge is to transform brain drain into transnationality. Regardless of how successful the government and businesses become at recruiting Korean students to return home, some will choose to remain overseas for various reasons. By staying overseas, such students will not be contributing human capital to Korea—the phenomenon regarded by the old model as brain drain—and concerns about this drainage has remained intense over the years. However, the current discourse has mainly focused on human capital, in large part overlooking the social capital potential of brain circulation, and as such there has been a lack of strategic policies that would generate, support, and promote brain circulation. In contrast, the new model of expatriate recruitment that we advocate in this study highlights the building of transnational bridges connecting Korea to important foreign societies rather than accumulating human capital inside a nation's geographic boundaries. As discussed in the previous chapter, foreign students in Korea can add their human capital to the host society (i.e., Korea) but at the same time can contribute social capital to both home and host societies. Likewise, Korean students settling abroad may contribute human capital to their respective host societies, but also can make social capital contribution to both host societies and Korea. Given this, the goal would be to encourage these students to maintain personal and professional ties with Korea and to increase their interest in working with Koreans or working for Korean firms while residing overseas.

Recruiting Korean students back home or encouraging them to work with Koreans while remaining abroad requires a careful understanding of such students' motivations and concerns. To explain what factors might entice students to return home, or failing that, remain abroad but work with Koreans, we build on a model developed by Tharenou and Caulfield (2010) that seeks to explain how expatriates voluntarily living abroad decide whether to remain in their host countries or return home. This model has two stages. First, the motivation to return home must be strong enough to overcome motivations to remain abroad. On the one hand, an individual's host country embeddedness, in both professional and social spheres, moves an individual to remain in the host country. On the other hand, an individual's home country embeddedness works to pull him or her back home, as does his or her sense of national identity. These opposing forces condition an expatriate's level of satisfaction with the host country, which, in turn, condition an expatriate's intention to return home. Second, the motivation to return home must be supported by the ability to return home. Even if an individual desires to return, the individual will find it difficult or even impossible to return if he or she cannot find appropriate opportunities there. In other words, the effect of a motivation to return home upon an actual decision to do so is mediated by the ability to return home.

Taking this general model, we apply its central arguments to Korean students studying abroad. Like voluntary expatriates, students decide whether or not to return home after their education. This decision is conditioned by the relative availability of career opportunities in the home and host societies, as well as the individual's national identity and level of embeddedness in both societies. The key difference is that students do not have a current job to anchor them to the host societies; also, the work visas available to students often differ from those available to skilled, working expatriates. Here, we focus upon factors affecting students' motivation to return, given that our data do not allow us to track which students ended up returning home.

Understanding the Motivations of Korean Students Abroad

To understand their motivations and concerns, we conducted an online survey of Korean students overseas as well as Korean American students (and Korean Canadian; for simplicity's sake, "Korean American" will henceforth refer to both Korean Americans and Korean Canadians as they constituted the majority of the sample) in April 2011.[5] We primarily asked questions relating to the respondents' biographies, social networks, educational attainment, job aspirations, and social and national identities. We received 253 total responses, of which 215 (85.0 percent) were complete. Of the completed responses, 126 came from respondents who held U.S. or Canadian citizenship or permanent residency. We consider these respondents to be Korean Americans regardless of whether they also identified themselves as Korean; we investigate them in the next chapter.[6] The remaining 89 responses came from individuals without permanent residency, whom we regard as Korean students studying abroad, even if they consider themselves American or Canadian rather than Korean. These individuals are our focus in this chapter. We use this criterion for a very practical reason. Individuals who have citizenship or permanent residency in the United States or Canada have the legal right to stay where they are. In contrast, those who lack such rights must return to Korea after graduation unless they receive a work visa. Although we acknowledge that Koreans and Korean Americans can also be differentiated based on self-described identity rather than legal right of abode, we believe the practical considerations of citizenship or permanent residency to be more important here.

In Table 3.1, we describe our surveyed respondents without U.S. or Canadian citizenship or permanent residency—our sample of Korean students abroad. Respondents tend to be very well educated, highlighting the human capital potential that they possess. About a third of respondents have undergraduate degrees from the top 30 U.S. universities, with most of the others having received undergraduate degrees from top Korean universities. Furthermore, graduate students without undergraduate degrees from the top 30 universities currently attend well-known universities in North America. Indeed, we received the highest number of responses from current undergraduate and graduate students at Stanford, Cornell, and the University of Chicago and also got many responses from Brown, Yale, Emory, the University of California, Los Angeles, and the University of Toronto. About 40 percent of respondents major in engineering as undergraduates; about 20 percent of respondents have either obtained or are pursuing Masters or PhD degrees.

In addition to the online survey, we conducted in-depth interviews with 24 Korean students selected from our sample of 89 respondents during spring 2012 (with a few follow-up interviews during summer 2013) at one of several different locations, including a top public university in California, an elite private university also in California, and an elite private university in New England. Our interviews consisted of one 90-minute session each, during which respondents were asked questions by a bilingual researcher

TABLE 3.1

Comparison of four quadrants: Averages of biographical characteristics

Variable	Mean	I	II	III	IV
Respondent biographical factors					
Age	25.24	25.06	28.40	27.66	21.99
Years spent in the United States / Canada after age 7	4.90	9.00	2.87	2.58*	5.67
Years spent in Korea after age 7	11.42	7.88	16.93	16.12	6.94
English language fluency	4.22	4.06	3.87	3.96	4.67
Korean language fluency	4.68	4.56	4.80	4.96	4.45
Female	0.41	0.81	0.13	0.19	0.52
Married/engaged	0.23	0.19	0.47	0.38	0.03
Educational characteristics					
BA from a top-30 university	0.34	0.38	0.07	0.15	0.61
BA in physical sciences	0.09	0.00	0.20	0.15	0.03
BA in biological sciences	0.14	0.31	0.20	0.04	0.12
BA in engineering	0.37	0.25	0.60	0.50	0.21
BA in business	0.10	0.13	0.07	0.04	0.15
BA in economics	0.18	0.13	0.07	0.15	0.27
BA in other social sciences	0.23	0.44	0.00	0.00	0.42
BA in arts and humanities	0.18	0.19	0.07	0.23	0.18
MA in any field	0.27	0.31	0.47	0.42	0.03
MA in engineering or sciences	0.14	0.13	0.40	0.19	0.00
PhD in any field	0.22	0.19	0.33	0.42	0.03
PhD in engineering or sciences	0.13	0.06	0.27	0.27	0.00
Plans after graduation					
Work in business-related field	0.29	0.13	0.07	0.19	0.55
Work as an engineer	0.23	0.19	0.47	0.31	0.09
Work in academia	0.28	0.19	0.53	0.42	0.09
Work in medicine	0.10	0.38	0.00	0.00	0.09
Pursue a nonprofessional MA or PhD	0.20	0.13	0.20	0.15	0.27
Respondent opinions					
Korean economy	3.67	3.81	3.53	3.58	3.73
Korean security	3.52	3.44	3.60	3.81	3.30
Korean politics	2.27	2.44	2.27	2.12	2.30
Korean culture	4.00	4.00	4.00	3.81	4.15
Korea overall	3.88	3.88	3.73	3.77	4.03
Family network characteristics					
Number of parents in the United States / Canada	0.21	1.00	0.00	0.04	0.06
Number of parents in Korea	1.61	0.94	2.00	1.88	1.55
Number of siblings in the United States / Canada	0.36	0.63	0.20	0.31	0.33
Number of siblings in Korea	0.67	0.38	0.93	0.81	0.58
Close extended family in the United States / Canada	0.60	0.88	0.40	0.62	0.55
Identity and culture					
Self-described as Korean	0.92	0.81	1.00	1.00	0.88
Self-described as Korean American	0.19	0.63	0.00	0.00	0.21
Frequency of attending Korean church	3.18	8.59	7.43	0.52	0.73

TABLE 3.1 (*continued*)

Variable	Mean	I	II	III	IV
Respondent interest in:					
Returning to Korea long term	3.31	2.75	3.13	3.88	3.21
Working with Koreans	3.43	3.38	3.40	3.46	3.45
Working for Korean firms	3.01	3.00	3.07	2.85	3.12
Marrying a Korean	4.54	4.56	4.80	4.54	4.42
Marrying a Korean American	3.70	4.31	3.40	3.15	3.97
Marrying a non-Korean Asian	2.27	2.19	1.93	1.92	2.73
Marrying a Caucasian	2.02	2.06	1.73	1.69	2.39

NOTE: "Korean American" refers to both Korean Americans and Korean Canadians.

fluent in both Korean and English, coming from a similar background. Respondents were interviewed in the language they preferred, either English or Korean. They were asked to explain their experiences in their own words, prompted by active listening cues designed to engage the respondent and elicit responses with clarity and depth.

In what follows, using both survey and interview data we relate the sociodemographic characteristics of our respondents to their interest in returning to Korea long term, interest in working with Koreans, and interest in working for Korean firms, to identify what factors would motivate students to return home, or failing that, remain abroad but work with Koreans. Although our sample of Korean students is not necessarily representative of the total population, our findings should nevertheless illuminate such students' value as human and social capital.

INTEREST IN RETURNING HOME

Our respondents viewed a possible return to Korea moderately favorably, averaging 3.31 on a 5-point Likert scale. This is consistent with prior research. Examining U.S. government data, Kirkegaard (2007) found that a sizable proportion of Korean students in the United States return home, although others choose to remain in the United States. Surveying Korean students in the United States, Hong and Cho (2012) found that 56.7 percent of these students intended to return to Korea for their first jobs and that an additional 12.7 percent intended to return at some point after their first jobs. Our analysis goes one step further to determine the reasons why these students would be interested in returning home. We find that a combination of several factors—time spent in Korea, embeddedness in Korean society, and a Korean social identity account for these students' moderately high interest in returning to Korea. We examine each of the factors contributing to this general trend before further investigating two important deviations from it.

Biography and Time Spent in Korea

Following Tharenou and Caulfield (2010), biographical factors related to the length of an individual's stay in North America should be expected to affect his or her interest in returning to Korea in ways that are quite intuitive. Students who have spent more time in Korea would return home at higher rates, while students who left at an earlier age will have experienced less acculturation into Korean society and greater acculturation into U.S. or Canadian societies, and will be less likely to return. Language skills should show a related pattern, as language is one of the most essential skills needed to function in a society. Thus, English-language proficiency should be expected to increase an individual's interest in remaining in the United States or Canada and, conversely, decrease an individual's interest in returning to Korea. Simultaneously, Korean-language proficiency should increase interest in returning home.

Given these predictions, our respondents' moderately high interest in returning to Korea is not surprising. As Table 3.1 shows, the average respondent was 25 years old, having spent an average of 4.9 of his or her years past age 7 in the United States or Canada versus an average of 11.4 years in Korea, meaning that the typical respondent was far more familiar with Korea than North America. Language skills do not seem to be a severe limitation, considering that respondents rated their English-language ability at an average of 4.22 on a 5-point scale (i.e., 4.22/5.00) and their Korean-language ability at 4.68/5.00. This suggests that the sample includes many bilinguals—individuals fluent in both English and Korean and able to function adequately in both their home and host societies.

Our interviews with Korean students confirm that familiarity strongly contributes to their interest in returning home. Students who had spent a great deal of time in Korea, regardless of the age that they had left, invariably expressed regret about being outside their familiar Korean environment. For instance, Kyusik, a graduate student in linguistics who had received his undergraduate degree in Korea, stated, "I want to go back to my own country. . . . I am familiar with Korean culture, and want to live in that culture. I care less about the external environment than people of a specific culture. That's what is really important." Another student who had recently arrived at an elite private university in the United States after spending most of his life in Korea reported, "I used to have a home base in Korea, which is good. . . . I like Korea because I'm familiar with it. . . . I grew up there and received that culture so I feel comfortable." Such sentiments were so strong that even those aspects of Korean culture that outsiders generally consider negatively were portrayed as familiar and even desirable. For instance, Sarah—a premed undergraduate who finished high school in Korea before enrolling in an elite private university in the United States—said that

> Korea's work environment is not as dry as America's—people take each other out drinking all the time—people are good friends there. So, they let each other get away with breaking rules and if they don't like one another, they put each other down severely. The work and personal spheres are not distinct . . . and display a rigid hierarchy. . . . High-status people talk down to lower-status people. If you're an employee, you need to act like an employee. . . . Things might look authoritarian but they nevertheless do very, very well. If you go to restaurants where people get together after work, the Samsungs hang out with other Samsungs and the LGs hang out with other LGs. Collectivism is strong there to that extreme degree. Isn't this the nature of Korea? Korean nature is very good in that way—there's very much an indescribable aura of feelings and emotions that go back and forth. This must be good, because it apparently raises productivity. (translated from Korean)

This account is remarkable as it portrays aspects of Korean work culture generally regarded as negative in positive terms. Interestingly enough, Sarah had adjusted to the U.S. environment very well, using an American name and speaking fluent English. Nevertheless, she emphasized a strong familiarity with Korea, especially with the Korean neighborhood where her parents still lived in the apartment in which she had grown up. In these regards, she is quite typical of many Korean students abroad, who strongly desire a return to their home despite their ability to function effectively in North America.

Networks and Embeddedness in Korean Society

A very closely related factor is home country embeddedness, best measured by the presence of family and friends in Korea, which should also increase interest in returning home. As Tilly (1990: 84) notes, the "effective units of migration were (and are) neither individuals nor households, but sets of people linked by acquaintance, kinship, and work experience." When anchored to specific geographic locations, such networks pull embedded individuals toward host societies or, conversely, back home.[8] Thus, Korean students who have family in the United States or Canada would be more likely to stay; by contrast, if they have family and friends in Korea, they would be more likely to return. The location of parents should have an even greater effect than the locations of siblings or friends.

As might be expected, Korean students had predominantly Korea-based family networks, with an average of 1.61 parents living in Korea, according to Table 3.1. Respondents also had more siblings residing in Korea (an average of 0.67) than in the United States or Canada (0.36). Similarly, they had few extended family members they felt close to in the United States or Canada (0.60). Given this, it is not surprising that Korean students abroad might want to return home. Indeed, nearly all of our interviewees indicated a desire to be closer to their parents back in Korea.

Identity

Even after accounting for familiarity and embeddedness, sociocultural identity should also play an important role in students' interest in returning home. That is, students who continue to identify as Korean should want to return home. Indeed, a survey of Koreans studying for PhD degrees abroad reveals that the predominant reason that such individuals return home is that they do consider Korea "home" (Korean Research Institute for Vocational Education and Training [KRIVET] 2008). In contrast, students who begin to self-identify as Korean Americans despite their Korean nationality have a greater desire to stay in the United States or Canada. Among many different markers of identity, marriage preferences are among the strongest, as a long-term indicator of the life course an individual desires.

Our findings show that a Korean identity is one of the key factors driving respondents' interest in returning home. As Table 3.1 presents, 9 out of 10 (92 percent) respondents described themselves as Korean, while only 2 out of 10 (19 percent) regarded themselves as Korean American; respondents were allowed to select multiple identities. Also, a Korean identity manifested itself in respondents' marriage preferences. Koreans have long considered "international marriage" (i.e., marrying a nonethnic Korean) negatively since they have regarded doing so as if contaminating the "purity" of the Korean nation. In this sense, it is not surprising to find that respondents have great interest in marrying a Korean (4.54/5.00) and are progressively less interested in marrying a Korean American (3.70/5.00), a non-Korean Asian (2.27/5.00), or a Caucasian (2.02/5.00).

Our interviews with several students confirm that their Korean identities contribute to their desire to return to Korea. For instance, Kyusik—the same graduate student in linguistics who expressed his desire to return home—mentioned that "there is nothing wrong with wanting to return to *my own country*" (emphasis added). Similarly, Changsik, a graduate student in computer science, noted that he had difficulty fitting in American society despite speaking fluent English and having spent the previous 10 years there:

> The language is not much of a problem . . . [but] in the East or South, you don't see a lot of Asians around. I don't know if it's me being self-conscious. Sometimes when I go to conferences, it's a pretty white town. In the restaurant they all kind of look at you for a while. That's when I still feel like I'm an *outsider*. When I meet a new person and they say, "Wow, your English is so good," it's kind of a compliment but not really because in the mind of every American they think Koreans don't speak English too well. *I don't feel part of the society.* (emphasis added)

For Korean students like him, identity matters more than anything else: they would just like to return home where they feel like a part of the society.

Job Opportunities

Korean students tend to be far more familiar with Korea than the United States or Canada, have parents who typically remained behind in Korea, and have preserved their identities as Koreans. Thus, they would naturally be expected to express a very strong interest in returning home. Nevertheless, our respondents averaged only 3.31 on a 5-point scale, where 5 indicated an extremely strong interest in returning home, posing a puzzle. Why do Korean students express somewhat less interest in returning home than might be expected? Our analysis shows that perceptions of economic opportunities in Korea versus North America can offer a clue to answering this question.

Regardless of how much an individual might want to return home, a lack of proper opportunities, especially jobs, will often deter them from returning. Students remaining overseas to pursue career-related opportunities represent a clear case of career migration as defined by Tilly (1990). However, such career migration might function in reverse as well; economic opportunities back home would make a return more attractive. Tharenou and Caulfield (2010) go so far as to describe economic opportunities back home as the mediating factor between an intention to return home and actual repatriation. Indeed, our interviewees agreed that economic opportunities enabled or constrained their intentions to return home. For instance, Joonseok—a graduate student studying operations research and an aspiring management consultant—said that, "in the end, many people who were debating whether or not to return home decide to go when they receive a good job offer" (translated from Korean). Such a view was not limited to individuals focused on business careers. Woojin—a graduate student in earth sciences and a recent arrival from Korea—made it clear that economic opportunity would trump his desires to return home, saying, "Right now, I am in a situation where I have to say 'Thank you very much' to whichever side [Korea or the United States] offers more money. Everything depends on the job . . . I have to get a job once I graduate. I am not in a situation where I can argue against this reality."

Given this, Korean students' perceptions of job and career prospects in Korea must have a strong impact on individuals' interest in returning home. At first glance, Korean students would seem to have a favorable opinion of career prospects in Korea. Our survey respondents had a moderately favorable view of the Korean economy, averaging 3.67/5.00 during a period when the United States in particular was still suffering the effects of the global recession starting in 2008. Yet interviewees repeatedly stressed two broad concerns about economic opportunities in Korea that may discourage their return. First, they gestured to the lower salaries paid in Korea relative to the United States. For instance, Joonseok—the aspiring management consultant—mentioned that

> even within the consulting industry, compensation is indexed to the wage level of that country—Korean wages cannot compare to high American wages. No matter how well paying consulting [in Korea] can be, there's a very big difference between being well paid in Korea and being well paid in the U.S. So, if I had a choice between these two regions, I would prefer to find a job in the U.S. (translated from Korean)

Second, Korean students were concerned about career development opportunities and geographic mobility. Many interviewees were critical of the hierarchical nature of corporate and even academic culture in Korea, which might limit their career development. Similarly, many of our interviewees considered it easy to return to Korea at any time—but difficult to go back overseas. James—a graduate student in neuroscience—emphasized both points:

> I think it boils down to the prospect of self-development. If [a] job is dead and that's all you're going to do and you're not going to learn anything, then there's less chance the person will take that job. If it's in terms of [self-development], it's great they would go. I think the other thing is it's hard to go from Korea back to the States. . . . It's hard to leave Korea and find job in the States again although it's easy the other way around. . . . There are many cases where Koreans working here are recruited back to Korea, but there is no opposite flow. (a few words were translated from Korean)

Korean students gave two very different responses to these problems. On the one hand, some expressed a desire to return home but to work overseas first to increase their value on the Korean job market. For instance, Gahyeon—a psychology undergraduate who had only recently arrived from Korea—said that she would "continue looking for jobs internationally since I'm already overseas" (translated from Korean). Kiseok—an engineering and information systems graduate student who had previously studied in Korea—expressed similar but still more strategic views:

> For instance, if I worked here for two years [before returning to Korea], I would get credit for two years' worth of work experience [on the Korean job market]. But if I worked here longer and raised my salary more, I not only get credit for more work experience, but I would also get additional bargaining points. . . . There are also things that I can only do here, that will help me get a better position back in Korea. (translated from Korean)

On the other hand, others had a more emotional response, being afraid of being called a "loser" for returning home. Citing the conventional view that the United States in particular offered better opportunities than Korea, such individuals felt that they would be looked down upon as people who had to return home because they had failed to succeed overseas.[9] Wonjoon—a graduate student in physics who had received his undergraduate degree in the United States—used sports analogies to illustrate this point:

Ah, they will say that this person is coming home because he fell behind his competition in the U.S. . . . Korea is always the second option. Nobody knows who is number one in Korean soccer or baseball, but everyone knows Park Ji Sung [player for Manchester United in the English Premier League] and Park Chan Ho [player for the Los Angeles Dodgers in Major League Baseball]. Also, when Park Chan Ho came back to Korea to look for a baseball team, nobody thought of this as success. "He played in the U.S. and Japan but now he's only in Korea," they said.

Although such sentiments were by no means universal among our interviewees, they seemed prevalent enough to attenuate Korean students' interest in returning home. Our findings are consistent with a survey of graduate students in the United States (Hong and Cho 2012) reporting that among students not intending to return immediately to Korea, 66.7 percent referred to U.S. jobs as superior opportunities for career development and 28.6 percent cited the ability to command a higher salary in Korea after working overseas first. Had Korea been perceived as providing superior opportunities, their interest in returning home may have been stronger than the moderately high levels that our survey shows.

INTEREST IN WORKING WITH KOREANS OR FOR KOREAN FIRMS

Respondents have a moderately high interest in working with Koreans (3.43/5.00) and a slightly lower but nevertheless solid level of interest in working for Korean firms (3.01/5.00). These figures, however, should be interpreted in conjunction with their moderately high interest in returning to Korea (3.31/5.00). Individuals returning to Korea would reasonably expect to work with Koreans, even if they do not necessarily work for Korean firms. For our purpose here—to examine students who could bridge Korea with key overseas markets, and to understand their motivations—we must first identify those students who intend to remain overseas who nevertheless have an interest in working with Koreans or for Korean firms.

DIFFERENTIATING KOREAN STUDENTS STUDYING ABROAD

To properly identify Korean students who wish to remain in the United States but would like to maintain their ties with Korea and Koreans, we conducted a correspondence analysis of the 89 Korean students, including all relevant characteristics of these respondents (i.e., variables). Although casual observers may consider Koreans studying abroad to be fairly homogeneous, our analysis reveals that they differ from one another in two important dimensions specified below. Furthermore, these differences appear to have great bearing upon our other focal area of interest—why some Korean students want to return home more than others.

As Figure 3.3 shows, our correspondence analysis produces results that closely match two intuitive ways to explain the variation among Korean students. The most important dimension differentiating Korean students from one another, shown on the X axis, corresponds to chogi yuhak versus traditional yuhak. On the one hand, individuals located to the right of Figure 3.3 are older, married, or engaged, spent greater time in Korea, and have either obtained or are currently pursuing MAs or PhDs. Such individuals fit the profile of traditional yuhak students who received an undergraduate education in Korea before seeking advanced degrees in the United States. This group predominantly consists of males studying science or engineering. On the other hand, individuals located to the left are younger, single, have spent less time in Korea, and tend to be female. Furthermore, such individuals are more likely to attend universities in the United States or Canada for undergraduate programs and have a parent living in North America, and may even have acquired an identity as Korean American in addition to their strong affinity with Korea. Such individuals fit the profile of chogi yuhak, students who head overseas before graduating from college or even high school, sometimes accompanied by one or more parents. In short, the traditional yuhak versus chogi yuhak student status is one important dimension to separate Korean students overseas from one another.

Another and perhaps less obvious but more interesting dimension, shown on the Y axis, corresponds to a respondent's church attendance. Korea has the largest Christian population by percentage of all the countries in Asia at 29 percent, and many Korean students coming to study in North American are from Christian families. Observers have long noted that they avidly attend Korean churches, especially Protestants that combine religious worship with activities to promote Korean culture and identity, while studying in North America. Members of Korean churches often assert that "attending a Korean church is a declaration not only of one's religious affiliation, but of one's ethnicity and commitment to that particular ethnic community as well."[10] Individuals located near the top of Figure 3.3 tend to attend a Korean church more often than individuals located near the bottom. The likelihood of Korean church attendance is strongly associated with the

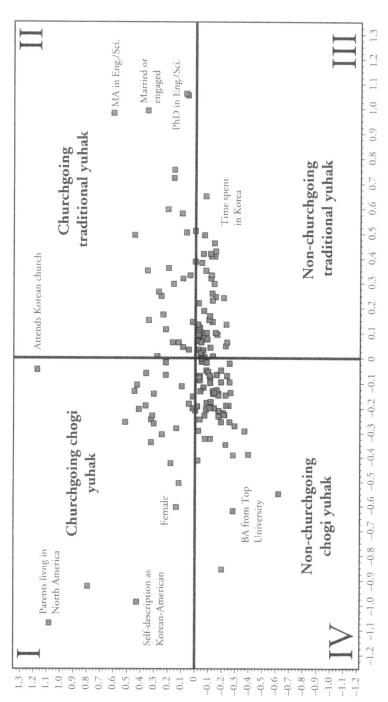

FIGURE 3.3 Correspondence analysis of Korean students in North America

presence of parents living in North America, but no other variable is correlated with it. In other words, the frequency of Korean church attendance differentiates Korean students from one another, unrelated to any other variable except that frequent churchgoers tend to have more family members living in North America.

These two dimensions divide sampled Korean students into four groups corresponding to the quadrants shown in Figure 3.3. Group I represents chogi yuhak churchgoers, Group II represents traditional yuhak churchgoers, Group III represents traditional yuhak non-churchgoers, and group IV represents chogi yuhak non-churchgoers. To be sure, as Table 3.1 shows, these groups share many important features with one another, including Korean-language fluency, opinions of Korea, self-described Korean identity, and marital preferences. Most importantly, they present little variation in average interest in working with Koreans (ranging from 3.38 to 3.46 on a 5-point scale) or working for Korean firms (ranging from 2.85 to 3.12). However, the groups reveal differing levels of interest in returning to Korea—traditional yuhak non-churchgoers (group III) show the strongest interest (3.88/5.00), followed by traditional yuhak churchgoers and chogi yuhak non-churchgoers (groups II and IV, respectively, 3.13/5.00 and 3.21/5.00) and finally chogi yuhak churchgoers (group I, 2.75/5.00), which shows at best a lukewarm interest in returning home.

This pattern suggests that chogi yuhak status and Korean church attendance have independent and additive effects diminishing students' likelihood of returning home. We elaborate on this observation with details below.

The Effects of Chogi Yuhak on Returning to Korea

Not surprisingly, chogi yuhak students have less interest in returning home. As Table 3.1 indicates, the two groups of chogi yuhak students (groups I and IV) are mainly undergraduates having spent an average of 7.88 and 6.94 years, respectively, in Korea after age 7, while the two groups of traditional yuhak students (groups II and III) are mostly older graduate students who, respectively, spent an average of 16.93 and 16.12 years there. We count the years following age 7 because socialization outside the family environment intensifies after a child enrolls in primary school. On the other hand, the chogi yuhak groups have spent far more time in North America (9.00 and 5.67 years, respectively, for groups I and IV) than the traditional yuhak groups (both averaging less than 3 years). Largely for this reason, some chogi yuhak students have developed Korean American identities (63 and 21 percent of groups I and IV, respectively) in addition to their native one (81 and 88 percent, respectively), while no respondent in groups II and III reported such an additional identity. Group I (chogi yuhak churchgoers) is also unique in having an average of one parent living in North America, while other groups typically have both parents staying in Korea. Considering that groups I and IV are less familiar with Korean culture and society, have a greater familiarity with North America, have acquired emerging Korean American identities, and often have parents living in North America (for group I), it is not surprising that such students have less interest in returning to Korea.

Our chogi yuhak interviewees support this general observation. Gahyeon—the psychology undergraduate who mentioned that she might as well look for jobs overseas considering that she was already in the United States—noted that she had grown unfamiliar with Korean culture and even her Korean friends during her stay overseas. Saying that she is "worried that I can't adjust over there," she emphasizes her lack of socialization in college:

> I saw that my friends learned different things [than I did] as they passed through college in Korea. They drank a lot and treated seniors and juniors differently than they do in the U.S. . . . People change a great deal during college life. My friends are like that. Someone who attended college in the U.S. will need much time to adjust to this culture. I am worried about this. (translated from Korean)

Similarly, Seonyoung—a graduate student in engineering who had originally arrived as a chogi yuhak student—mentioned that

> when I go to Korea, I often hear that "You've become like an American." I am neither this nor that. Still, for me to live alone, it's more convenient here [in the United States]. I've traveled all over the place here since high school, so it's more convenient for me here. For instance, I made my first checking account in Korea. But this was the first time I've tried anything like that . . . here [in the United States]. I can easily go to the bank and register for a credit card and pay. In Korea, I had no idea what to do. (translated from Korean)

Seonyoung also resisted Koreans' attempts at resocializing her into the local environment during a summer internship in Korea. She described her time interning in Korea as "not a pleasant experience. . . . [as she] experienced quite a bit of culture shock." Although she "wanted to add value," she "felt that the hierarchy was quite severe." Indeed, she ended up being a "gofer" for more senior colleagues, fetching coffee and making photocopies. She later felt more comfortable interning at an Indian firm, the employees of which were "very professional" and "gave me real responsibility and training." After that experience, she "kind of lost the motivation to work in Korea." Such accounts illustrate how *chogi yuhak* students might be aware of the re-entry shock they potentially face if they return to Korea and how this would reduce their interest in returning home.

The Effects of Korean Church Attendance on Returning to Korea

Frequent attendees of Korean churches also have less interest in returning home. Among *chogi yuhak* students, churchgoers (group I) expressed much less interest in returning home (2.75/5.00) than non-churchgoers (group IV) (3.21/5.00). Likewise, among traditional *yuhak* students, churchgoers (group II) revealed a weaker interest in returning home (3.13/5.00) than non-churchgoers (3.88/5.00). The negative relationship between Korean church attendance and interest in returning to Korea is surprising given that Korean churches are believed to function as a stronghold of Korean community, culture, and identity. According to the conventional wisdom, frequent churchgoers would be expected to retain more of a Korean identity and be more interested in returning home.

What explains this counterintuitive finding? Prior research on ethnic enclaves (Portes 1995b; Portes and Rumbaut 2001) provides some clues. Several geographic locations in North America (e.g., Koreatown in Los Angeles, Flushing in New York City, and Bloor Street in Toronto) host high concentrations of Korean immigrants. Like other ethnic enclaves— or localized concentrations of immigrants from a given foreign country— Koreatown and other Korean enclaves provide the comforts of home in a distant land. For instance, Koreatown in Los Angeles, the largest Korean enclave in North America, is dotted with Korean-language signs advertising coffee shops, stores, *noraebang* (karaoke bars), and other services more typical of Seoul than a typical North American city. Spoken Korean language is so pervasive that it is commonly said that a Korean immigrant can live there quite comfortably without ever having to learn English. Providing key services in a familiar environment, Korean enclaves should not only reinforce Korean students' native identities but simultaneously root them to their host countries.

Korean churches seem to play much the same role. Besides their religious functions, as a meeting place for ethnic Koreans, often in a predominantly non-Korean neighborhood, Korean churches are sites for intense social interaction that reinforce Korean language, identity, and social cohesion.[11] It follows that Korean churches provide their members with a strong sense of belongingness and social support, functioning much like ethnic enclaves, but distributed all over North America. In 2013, there were 4,233 Korean churches in the United States alone, one church for every 403 Koreans living in the States.

Our interviews with students who are frequent Korean churchgoers highlight the importance of churches as key places to meet and socialize with other Koreans. Some students attend Korean churches to expand their social circles. For instance, Chris—a graduate student at an elite private university—shared his reason for attending an on-campus Korean church: "to meet [Korean] friends and they have some outside activities that I participate in." Jungeun—a former chogi yuhak student—also emphasized that, besides "spiritual reasons," social motivations provided a strong secondary rationale for finding a specifically Korean church. She related the lengthy process that she undertook to find the church that offered the most comfortable social environment. She moved to the United States in her early teenage years with her parents and a sibling, partly because her father found work in the United States but more to avoid the stressful Korean educational system:

> We started looking for a church immediately following our move to the U.S. . . .
> We attended several different churches in our neighborhood before we settled
> for one; I think my parents chose the church we ended up attending because
> they felt the most welcomed. I think they also took into account the fact that
> my sibling and I told them we felt most welcomed in this particular church over
> others. It didn't occur to us to try attending a church with those with different
> ethnic backgrounds.

Note that Jungeun differs from the Korean Americans (and Korean Canadians) we investigate in the next chapter, as she has yet to apply for permanent residency in the United States—reflecting her family's initial intention of returning to Korea. Regardless of their initial intentions, however, such individuals and families could very well end up remaining in North America.

There are other individuals who had no choice but to seek out Korean churches. For instance, Kangmun, who arrived in the United States at the age of 24, emphasized that he could not speak and understand English fluently, and that he did not consider going to non-Korean churches. He also illustrated the role that social networks played in connecting new arrivals to specific Korean churches. Upon arriving in the United States, he stayed with his uncle for the first few months, who was an elder at a local Korean church. He naturally gravitated toward that particular church.

CHURCHGOING CHOGI YUHAK STUDENTS AS TRANSNATIONAL BRIDGES

Our discussions above clearly suggest that among Korean students in North America, chogi yuhak students who regularly attend Korean churches (Group I) are the least likely to return home but at the same time may have the highest potential to function as transnational bridges, becoming Korean transnationals embedded within American and Canadian societies. Korean churches may represent sites for "selective acculturation," which occurs when immigrants maintain their home cultures while becoming full members of the host society. Selective acculturation, however, requires that immigrants connect with the host society at their own time and choosing, protected by a safe enclave or other agglomeration of co-ethnics. Korean churches can provide such safe havens, enabling Korean students to retain their native identities and maintain their connections to Korea and Koreans while gradually embedding themselves in American or Canadian society.

Our survey data support this proposition. On average, group I respondents have a lower interest in returning home than other groups (2.75/5.00) but a moderately high interest in working with Koreans (3.38/5.00) and some interest in working for Korean firms (3.00/5.00), just like other groups. While most (81 percent) continue to identify as Korean, many (63 percent) also identify as Korean American. The proportion identifying as Korean American is far higher for this group than otherwise comparable chogi yuhak students who do not regularly attend church (21 percent). This suggests that the selective acculturation occurring in Korean churches actually accelerates the emergence of a Korean American identity. Group I members attend Korean churches an average of 8.59 sessions per month—about twice a week (see Table 3.1).

During interviews, chogi yuhak students said that belonging to a Korean church helped them selectively acculturate to the United States by allowing them to retain a sense of being Korean and remaining tied to Korea, while simultaneously building connections to a larger society outside this protected enclave. As Jungeun related her own experience:

> I think attending a Korean church was very helpful during my teenage years. Just being able to relate by code switching or talking about Korean pop culture was a huge relief in those years. I believe I sought out people with similar external appearances, language, and culture in order to understand and identify myself as a Korean American. . . . Being part of a Korean church gave me many opportunities to be involved with the Korean culture and language. I think those exposures have definitely played a big role in forming my identity right now as a Korean American. Now, along with many other Korean Americans at my Korean church, I identify myself as the 1.5 generation, which, in a way, is another subgroup within the Korean American communities. Being connected to the language, culture, food, and people has altered my views on the American culture. Since I was very much part of the Korean culture as well as the American culture, I feel that I have the ability to view both cultures from an outsider's perspective.

Chogi yuhak students such as Jungeun have a strong potential to bridge the United States and Canada with Korea because they have retained Korean identities and ties to Korea while building connections with their surrounding environments. Such individuals benefit from selective acculturation. In contrast, traditional yuhak students attending Korean churches do not experience such benefits. Indeed, Korean church attendance appears to retard their ability to acculturate to North America and build social ties outside the Korean community. Kangmun—who had arrived in the United States as a 24-year-old graduate student—emphasized that by attending Korean church, he gained many benefits but was also deterred from gaining new experiences: "I didn't have a chance to learn English and different ethnic cultures. Therefore, I have only few non-Korean friends for twelve years in the U.S." Such individuals have limited potential to bridge Korea with North America, largely because they are not embedded within their host societies.

Chogi Yuhak Parents as Anchors

As mentioned above, churchgoing chogi yuhak students more likely have parents who accompanied them to North America—and chose to stay after their children entered college. In Table 3.1, group I members average one parent living in North America, unlike other groups whose parents nearly always stay in Korea. One common pattern is that of a mother accompanying young chogi yuhak children to North America while the father remains in Korea to earn an income and support the family. They are different from immigrants whose families usually move together to a new country, and in Korea such "separated" families are called *kirŏgi kajok*, or geese families. As discussed above, the presence of parent(s) in the United States or Canada significantly diminishes students' interest in returning home to Korea.

Our interviews with chogi yuhak students show that Korean churches play a particularly important role in helping their parents to settle in the United States or Canada, so that they remain there even after their children enter college. Jungeun related such a story:

> My parents are in the States, and they do attend a Korean church. I know that church membership has played a great role in shaping their new lives in the States. There wasn't any tangible help that they received, but I know that my mother received much information about school districts, tutors, *hakwŏns* [cram schools], and other such topics through the [church elders] she had befriended at church.

Other students also talked about how church elders assisted their parents by informing them of economic and other opportunities that helped them to remain in North America.

Church membership also helps anchor parents to locations in North America, in turn assisting their chogi yuhak children to be embedded in local communities there. Jungeun emphasizes that her parents' church membership:

> . . . has played a big role in them entertaining a move to a different state or a region. I think my mother sometimes even says that she likes those Korean friends she has met in church here in the States more than her friends in Korea. She has been away for a long time, and she feels that she associates more with the Korean community here in the States rather than Korea itself. I also know that if my mother had not found a church she could be actively engaged in, she would have liked to return to Korea because there was little available for her to do with her time. Actually, I do believe that my mother is more content with her life here in the States thanks to her church membership, and that has led to my father switching jobs so that he will also stay in the States. [Moving to the United States] was for my sibling's and my education, but I know that having a Korean church provided comfort and security for my parents in terms of social interaction.

Another student, Hyejin, still lives together with her parents and attends the same church. She emphasized that her parents' "involvement with the Korean church definitely gives them comfort and a sense of security." She also related how her parents deliberately avoided moving to a different part of the United States because they felt part of the "Korean community through the Korean church." Overall, such narratives demonstrate how Korean churches shelter parents accompanying their chogi yuhak children, anchoring the family in North America.

Overall, churchgoing chogi yuhak students and their parents have been given the opportunity to acculturate to the United States on their own terms, maintaining close ties with Korea and their Korean identities while becoming embedded in their new environment and even coming to identify with their host society. In particular, students who have one parent living with them in North America while the other still lives in Korea have an extra motivation to bridge their two "homes." Simultaneously, such students have the same level of interest in working for Korean firms or otherwise working with Koreans as other groups of Korean students studying abroad. Consequently, churchgoing chogi yuhak students have a particularly good chance at functioning as transnational bridges between Korea and North America.

Conclusion: From Brain Drain to Brain Circulation

With globalization, increasing numbers of young people are leaving their countries for advanced studies overseas. Upon their return with advanced degrees, they can provide an important pool of human capital to their home countries. However, some students may choose to stay in the host countries after graduation, or undertake "voluntary migration," thus raising brain drain as a possibility. Countries seeking to induce their students overseas to return home face the difficult task of transforming brain drain into brain circulation. According to Tilly (1990), voluntary migration takes three basic forms. *Career emigrants* migrate to take advantage of professional opportunities overseas. *Chain migration* occurs when past emigrants facilitate further emigration by informing friends and family about overseas opportunities and perhaps even sponsoring them. *Circular* or *transmigration* occurs when emigrants maintain rights, responsibilities, and relationships with their home countries by sending home remittances and regularly returning there.[12]

Tilly's framework of migration helps identify both opportunities and challenges for countries that send many talented students overseas. From the "old model" perspective, these returning students can be an important source of human capital to their own society and economy. The challenge is to reduce career migration, especially by increasing the number and quality of opportunities back home. Reducing career migration has a further benefit: it diminishes future chain migration. However, from the "new model" perspective, which attends to the value of social capital and transnational bridges, countries can also benefit by leaving their students overseas. By facilitating transmigration, countries can become better connected with the rest of the world, gaining transnational bridges, but this is not an easy task.[13] Reducing career migration and encouraging transmigration are particularly important for a country like Korea, which has long educated many of its brightest individuals overseas.

Our study reveals that Korean students' interest in returning home, working with Koreans, or working for Korean firms is conditioned largely by two factors— chogi yuhak versus traditional yuhak and active participation in a Korean church. Sojourn length and age differentiate older graduate students who attended college in Korea from younger chogi yuhak students. Older graduate students unsurprisingly express more willingness to repatriate than their younger chogi yuhak counterparts. Chogi yuhak students often acquire a Korean American identity, which diminishes their interest in returning. One fascinating and unexpected finding is that frequent attendees of Korean churches also have less interest in returning home, surprising given that Korean churches have been viewed as a stronghold of Korean community, culture, and identity. We interpret this counterintuitive finding as indicating that Korean churches function much like ethnic enclaves that provide key services in a familiar environment, not only reinforcing students' Korean identities but also rooting Korean students in their host countries. As a result, they would feel quite comfortable in staying at the host countries after education.

Existing studies focus primarily on students who return home, while overlooking how those remaining in the host country after graduation might function as social capital. In the old model, such remaining students have little to contribute to the home society and can be considered a case of brain drain and the current debate on Korea's brain power also focuses on this aspect. However, in the new model that we advocate here, they can potentially bridge Korea and their host countries. Accordingly, we pay special attention to Korean students who may not return home but who are nevertheless willing to work with Koreans and perhaps work for Korean firms. Indeed, we identify churchgoing chogi yuhak students as individuals who are simultaneously embedded within their host society (the United States or Canada) and their home society (Korea). These individuals have the most potential to bridge the United States or Canada with Korea, providing new model social capital benefits to Korea if not providing old model human capital benefits. Such a pool can be also found in the Korean diaspora, to which we turn now.

FOUR

The Korean Diaspora

Like first-generation Koreans studying abroad, the Korean diaspora, especially the one in advanced countries, represents a potent source of human and social capital. Many of these individuals are well educated and embedded in their own societies but still maintain some affinity with Korea and interact with other ethnic Koreans in their adopted homelands.[1] Such individuals might have a more difficult time embedding themselves into Korean society compared to first-generation students returning home but would nevertheless experience less difficulty than true foreigners with no connection to Korea whatsoever. Overall, Korean immigrants could provide human capital if they returned to their ancestral homeland and, even if they did not return long term, could provide transnational bridges if they built or rebuilt their ties to Korea.

Overseas diaspora communities have frequently had significant economic impacts upon their ancestral homelands. For instance, the Jewish diaspora has had a profound influence upon the Israeli economy, largely by linking Israel with advanced economies in Europe and North America. For instance, ethnically and religiously Jewish individuals helped seed the thriving Israeli technology industry by spreading the culture of technology entrepreneurship from its Silicon Valley roots (see Saxenian 2006). Recognizing such crucial benefits, the Israeli government collaborated with large private donors to create Birthright Israel in 1999, a program designed to reach out to the Jewish diaspora. By bringing 51,000 young adults into Israel every year for short sojourns, Birthright Israel not only reawakens Jewish

identities among members of its diaspora but also forges connections between them and resident Israelis. This program is unique because it focuses
upon building a Jewish identity and social connections among its diaspora
instead of recruiting individuals back "home." Given a strong sense of ethnic identity held among members of the diaspora community, countries
such as Korea could likewise benefit by shifting their focus away from the
old model of expatriate recruitment toward the new model of building lasting connections between diaspora and homeland.

In this chapter, we explore how Korean society and economy could benefit not only from recruiting its diaspora back home but also by strengthening its ties to diaspora members for the purpose of building transnational
bridges. Until now, most ethnic Koreans who returned to Korea for work
came from China as unskilled labor, and prior research has focused on this
group. However, such individuals mostly cannot provide Korea with the
"global talent" that we examine here (see Chapter 1). We turn our attention instead to highly educated members of the Korean diaspora in North
America who could offer Korea both human and social capital.

We utilize data from the same survey used in Chapter 3, focusing on
Korean Americans and Korean Canadians—the 126 respondents who had
citizenship or permanent residency in the United States or Canada. Such
individuals differ from those on student visas, as citizenship or permanent
residency expresses the legal rights and intention to remain in North America long term. We also use interview data with 16 of these respondents to
gain deep insights into their motives and interest in returning to Korea or
working with Koreans or Korean firms while remaining in North America. As noted in the previous chapter, they are graduate and undergraduate
students currently attending a top public university in California, an elite
private university also in California, and an elite private university in New
England.

Korean Immigration in Historical Context

Starting in the late nineteenth century, Koreans began emigrating in substantial numbers. This outward movement accelerated during Japanese
colonial rule. Some left Korea in search of work or simply to avoid Japanese
repression, but many others were forced to work in the factories and min-
ing operations in the Japanese empire. Although some returned home after

1945 when Korea was liberated from Japanese rule, many of these Koreans remained overseas, especially in Japan and China. By 2010, over 7 million ethnic Koreans, or about 10 percent of ethnic Koreans worldwide, lived outside the Korean Peninsula. Over half live in Asia, with 2.7 million in China and 904,806 in Japan, most being descendants of ethnic Koreans who left the Peninsula before 1945. North America hosts an additional 2.5 million, mostly in the United States, with 1,094,290 possessing U.S. citizenship, 603,402 having permanent residency, and the rest having been granted educational and other short-term visas (see Table 4.1 for details). Most of these are relatively recent immigrants who left Korea for better work or educational opportunities. Here, we focus on Korean Americans and Korean Canadians who are among the best-educated and most economically

TABLE 4.1
Overseas Koreans by status of sojourn as of 2010

Region	Country	Citizens	Residents	Sojourners General	Sojourners Students	Total
Asia	Japan[a]	326,671	461,627	96,146	20,362	904,806
	China[b]	2,335,968	4,161	307,142	57,723	2,704,994
	Other	38,883	54,464	276,845	83,228	453,420
	Subtotal	2,701,522	520,252	680,133	161,313	4,063,220
North and South America	United States	1,094,290	464,154	512,938	105,616	2,176,998
	Canada	102,666	85,951	22,094	20,791	231,492
	Central and South America	34,018	53,297	24,898	767	112,980
	Subtotal	1,230,974	603,402	559,930	127,174	2,521,470
Europe	Former USSR (CIS)	523,542	433	9,380	2,470	535,825
	Continental Europe	15,927	22,404	43,178	37,017	117,892
	Subtotal	539,923	23,644	53,920	39,220	656,707
Mideast		139	20	15,509	634	16,302
Africa		189	1,573	8,072	1,238	11,072
Total		4,472,747	1,148,891	1,317,554	329,579	7,268,771

SOURCE: Data from "Overseas Koreans," Ministry of Foreign Affairs and Trade, available at Korean.net.

[a]Japanese citizens include Korean Japanese who naturalized into Japan during 1952–2005, including those with North Korean nationality. Statistics are drawn from the Ministry of Justice.

[b]1,923,800 Korean Chinese with Chinese nationality were reported to be living in China according to its 2000 census.

successful individuals in the Korean diaspora community, offering a key potential source of global talent for Korea.

Koreans came to the United States in three waves. The first wave migrated to Hawaii to work on sugar and pineapple plantations after Emperor Kojong approved emigration in 1902. These Koreans were well assimilated into American society, and by 1970 Koreans in Hawaii had the highest per capita income and the lowest unemployment of any ethnic group on the islands. A second wave entered the United States following the Korean War and consisted mainly of students and wives of U.S. servicemen. A third wave and its descendants constitute most Korean Americans today. This wave, arriving after changes to U.S. law in 1965 that liberalized immigration from non-Western countries, differed from the prior waves in two ways. These new immigrants were often college educated with professional work experience and brought their families with them. Although limited proficiency in English impaired their initial socioeconomic progress in the United States, their commitment to education and attainment powerfully affected the next generations, who became some of the best educated people in the world; nearly half of Korean Americans have college degrees, compared to the U.S. national average of 26.8 percent.

Today, a disproportionately high number of Korean Americans enter professional careers such as law, medicine, and management. Korean Americans have significantly outperformed other ethnic immigrants and Caucasian Americans in educational attainment.[2] The "Korean effect" has persisted through the generations: second- and third-generation Korean Americans have remained better educated than comparable Caucasian Americans, even after they have assimilated in many other respects, such as language spoken at home.[3] Considering that skilled professionals (e.g., financiers, businessmen) bring crucial human and social capital to a society, such well-educated individuals represent a largely untapped source of global talent for the Korean economy. At the same time, second- and third-generation returnees will face far more serious re-entry shock than that faced by Korean students returning from their studies abroad.

Korea's economic prosperity has created new opportunities for such highly educated individuals in the diaspora community. Especially during the recent economic recession, which Korea weathered much better than the United States, many Korean Americans sought job opportunities in Korea given the paucity of comparable ones in the United States. Although

Korean Americans and Korean Canadians are not awarded Korean citizenship, the possibility has received substantial attention in recent years as the Korean government extends dual citizenship to some overseas Koreans not subject to military service. However, the debate has been spurred by Korean domestic politics more than the needs of overseas Koreans beyond the first generation, whom the new policies are intended to serve. The primary reason is that immigration policies already meet the needs of second- and third-generation ethnic Koreans. Most Korean Americans and Korean Canadians are eligible for permanent residency through the F-4 visa, which gives former Korean citizens and their children unrestricted access to jobs and services in Korea without the military service requirements demanded of male Korean citizens. As of 2008, 37,740 overseas Koreans lived in Seoul under the F-4 visa program.[4]

Against this backdrop, we attempt to understand how the Korean diaspora in North American can be a valuable pool of global talent for their homeland by examining why Korean Americans and Korean Canadians past the first generation (henceforth labeled Korean Americans for convenience) may desire to return to Korea, work with Koreans, and/or find employment at Korean firms.

Identifying and Understanding Potential Returnees

We begin our analysis with key descriptive statistics as presented in Table 4.2 for all 126 respondents in the sample. Compared to the Korean students on temporary visas we examined in the previous chapter, our Korean American respondents were substantially less willing to repatriate to Korea long term (2.37 on a 5-point Likert scale, versus 3.31/5.00 for Korean students). This is not surprising, given that the Korean Americans had spent the vast majority of their lives after age 7 in the United States or Canada (an average of 11.4 years) versus Korea (an average of 3.4 years). Similarly, their level of Korean language fluency (3.79/5.00) was lower than that of Korean students (4.68/5.00). Nevertheless, Korean Americans were nearly as willing to work with Koreans as Korean students (3.23/5.00 versus 3.40/5.00) and had similarly positive opinions of Korea (3.90/5.00). Also, 41 percent had not formally renounced Korean citizenship, even after obtaining U.S. or Canadian citizenship. This practice is technically illegal under Korean law but has nevertheless been widespread. An additional 5 percent had given up

TABLE 4.2
Comparison of four quadrants: Averages of biographical characteristics

Variable	All	I	II	III	IV
Respondent interest in:					
Living in Korea short term	3.77	3.87	3.81	3.64	3.71
Living in Korea long term	2.37	2.05	2.69	2.88	2.11
Working with Koreans	3.23	3.05	3.27	3.08	3.51
Working for Korean firms	2.56	2.25	2.92	2.68	2.57
Respondent opinions					
Korean economy	3.75	3.80	3.35	4.00	3.80
Korean security	3.29	3.18	3.27	3.48	3.29
Korean politics	2.51	2.65	1.96	2.40	2.83
Korean culture	3.93	3.80	4.04	4.20	3.80
Korea overall	3.90	3.75	3.81	4.04	4.03
Respondent biographical factors					
Age	22.58	22.42	24.87	22.52	21.09
Years spent in the United States / Canada after age 7	11.40	14.37	8.15	7.32	13.3
Years spent in Korea after age 7	3.94	1.00	9.38	7.68	0.60
Summers in Korea while overseas	0.79	0.75	0.92	0.76	0.77
Language study in Korea	0.14	0.15	0.15	0.08	0.17
Korean language fluency	3.79	3.60	4.27	4.40	3.20
Female	0.52	0.75	0.65	0.20	0.37
Married/engaged	0.09	0.05	0.12	0.12	0.09
Visa status in Korea					
Korean citizen	0.41	0.15	0.65	0.64	0.37
Permanent resident (F-4)	0.05	0.08	0.00	0.12	0.00
Characteristics of BA degree					
From a top-30 university	0.51	0.63	0.38	0.44	0.51
In physical sciences	0.11	0.00	0.15	0.20	0.14
In biological sciences	0.35	0.35	0.50	0.32	0.26
In engineering	0.16	0.18	0.23	0.12	0.11
In business	0.12	0.05	0.04	0.28	0.14
In economics	0.17	0.05	0.15	0.32	0.23
In other social sciences	0.24	0.43	0.12	0.12	0.20
In arts and humanities	0.17	0.28	0.12	0.00	0.20
Characteristics of MA degree					
Has MA degree	0.18	0.25	0.27	0.16	0.06
Characteristics of PhD degree					
Has PhD degree	0.14	0.20	0.23	0.12	0.03

Korean citizenship but had acquired permanent residency in Korea through the F-4 visa.

In addition to respondents' biographical ones, we also examine their social characteristics. As Table 4.3 shows, the Korean Americans considered here were much more likely to have family members living in the United States or Canada than the Korean students examined in Chapter 3. Seven out of 10 described themselves as Korean American (or Korean Canadian), while only 3 of 10 described themselves as Korean. Korean Americans watched nearly as much Korean television and movies and listened to nearly as much Korean music as Korean students in our sample. However, Korean Americans were interested in a much greater range of future careers than Korean students. In general, the statistics describing Korean Americans' social characteristics were more dispersed than Korean students', as measured by standard deviation. This indicates the greater heterogeneity of Korean American students and should be considered in examining their interests and motives as a source of human and social capital for Korea.

HETEROGENEITY AMONG KOREAN AMERICANS

Korean Americans range from individuals committed to their native Korean identities to those who disavow such identities altogether; they also range from freewheeling artists to business-minded individuals intent on climbing corporate ladders. To adequately address such diversity in our sample, we conducted a correspondence analysis of the 126 Korean American respondents to our survey, including all relevant characteristics of these students (i.e., variables). Figure 4.1, which shows the results of this analysis, reveals two main dimensions. The first dimension, shown on the X axis, corresponds to a respondent's familiarity with Korea. Individuals located to the right in Figure 4.1 tend to have spent more time in Korea and identify as a Korean, while those to the left tend to identify as an American (or Canadian). The second dimension, shown on the Y axis, corresponds to a respondent's business orientation.[5] Individuals located near the bottom tend to be pursuing careers in finance, management consulting, or corporations in general; they also aspire to earn an MBA. Individuals located near the top, however, tend to pursue nonbusiness careers in art, design, teaching, or academia. On both dimensions, the zero point indicates the sample mean.

TABLE 4.3
Comparison of four quadrants: Averages of social characteristics

Variable	All	I	II	III	IV
Family network characteristics					
Number of parents in the United States / Canada	1.33	1.53	0.85	0.76	1.86
Number of parents in Korea	0.61	0.43	1.08	1.16	0.09
Number of siblings in the United States / Canada	1.02	1.03	0.73	0.88	1.34
Number of siblings in Korea	0.12	0.03	0.15	0.32	0.06
Close extended family in the United States / Canada	0.75	0.65	0.88	0.84	0.71
Friend network characteristics					
Composition of friends in the United States / Canada	2.98	2.85	2.88	3.20	3.03
Has 21+ friends in Korea	0.19	0.05	0.12	0.56	0.14
Elementary/middle school friends in Korea	0.46	0.28	0.69	0.92	0.17
High school friends in Korea	0.33	0.18	0.38	0.52	0.31
Identity					
Self-described as Korean	0.32	0.08	0.65	0.56	0.17
Self-described as Korean American	0.71	0.85	0.50	0.60	0.80
Self-described as American	0.12	0.25	0.04	0.04	0.09
Cultural consumption					
Frequency of watching Korean movies	5.02	5.45	7.75	4.62	2.77
Frequency of listening to Korean music	7.12	7.80	7.90	6.60	6.13
Frequency of attending Korean church	2.88	2.20	2.02	3.30	4.00
Respondent intention to:					
Marry a Korean	3.86	3.48	4.35	4.40	3.54
Marry a Korean American	4.40	4.53	4.12	4.32	4.54
Marry a non-Korean Asian	2.86	3.35	2.65	2.16	2.94
Marry a Caucasian	2.45	3.00	2.12	2.04	2.37
Plans after graduation					
Work in finance	0.12	0.00	0.08	0.28	0.17
Work in consulting	0.11	0.03	0.04	0.28	0.14
Work for a large corporation	0.11	0.00	0.08	0.24	0.17
Work in entrepreneurship	0.06	0.03	0.04	0.12	0.09
Attend business school for an MBA	0.07	0.00	0.00	0.16	0.14
Work in medicine	0.30	0.30	0.35	0.28	0.29
Work in law	0.13	0.23	0.00	0.00	0.20
Work in computer science or engineering	0.08	0.10	0.12	0.04	0.06
Work in academia	0.09	0.18	0.12	0.04	0.00
Work as a teacher	0.11	0.18	0.00	0.08	0.14
Work in counseling or nonprofits	0.08	0.13	0.12	0.04	0.03
Work in art or design	0.07	0.13	0.08	0.00	0.06
Pursue a nonprofessional MA or PhD	0.22	0.33	0.23	0.12	0.11

NOTE: "Korean American" refers to both Korean Americans and Korean Canadians.

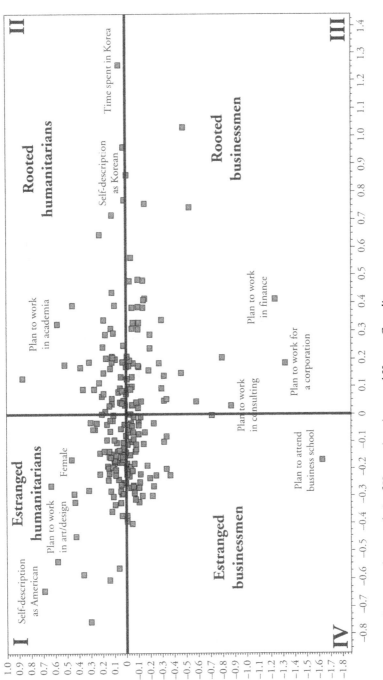

FIGURE 4.1 Correspondence analysis of Korean Americans and Korean Canadians

These dimensions divide Korean American students into four groups corresponding to the quadrants shown in Figure 4.1. According to Tables 4.2 and 4.3, respondents placed in quadrant I tend to be socially distant from their Korean origin, female (75 percent), interested in careers in teaching (18 percent), academia (18 percent), the arts (13 percent), or law (13 percent). As these individuals have become separated or "estranged" from their Korean roots and are largely following careers in education and the humanities, we call them estranged humanitarians. Respondents placed in quadrant II are similar to estranged humanitarians but tend to be more familiar with Korea and have closer contacts there. As these individuals remain connected with their Korean roots, we call them rooted humanitarians. Respondents placed in quadrant III tend to be male (80 percent), business oriented (28 percent interested in finance, 28 percent interested in consulting, 16 percent intending to attend business school), and socially proximate to Korea. Thus, we call them rooted businessmen. Respondents in quadrant IV share many similarities with their rooted businessman counterparts but are socially distant from Korea. Thus, we call them estranged businessmen.

Using both survey and interview data, we describe each category and relay main biographical characteristics and experiences that shape the key factors we investigate—their interest in living in Korea, their desire to work with Koreans or Korean firms should they choose to live overseas—and assess their chance to contribute to Korea's human capital and/or their potential to create bridging social capital.

ESTRANGED HUMANITARIANS

Estranged humanitarians have little familiarity with Korea and express little interest in business careers. These individuals, who constitute 32 percent of surveyed respondents, resemble Chang-rae Lee, an award-winning author and professor of creative writing at Princeton. Lee was born in Korea but moved to the United States at the age of 3 and grew up in suburban Westchester County near New York City. After attending a prestigious high school (Phillips Exeter Academy), he graduated from Columbia University with a degree in English and received a Master of Fine Arts degree from the University of Oregon. His award-winning first novel, *Native Speaker*, focuses on the nearly complete assimilation of a Korean American who nevertheless has difficulty fitting into U.S. society because he still desires to hold on to his Korean heritage. Although Lee did not write *Native Speaker* as an autobiography, it has nevertheless become iconic of the Korean American experience. Like Lee, other estranged humanitarians are characterized by a longing for a motherland that they never really knew.

Estranged humanitarians generally lack firsthand knowledge of Korea. Such respondents have spent the vast majority of their lives after age 7 in the United States and/or Canada (an average of 14.4 years) versus Korea (an average of only 1.0 years); only 15 percent have Korean citizenship and a further 8 percent Korean permanent residency (F-4). They also have relatively few friends and family in Korea. Not surprisingly, only 8 percent identified as Korean, compared to 85 percent identifying as Korean American or Korean Canadian and 25 percent simply as American or Canadian. Nevertheless, such individuals speak passable Korean on average (3.60/5.00) and frequently consume Korean culture. Indeed, four out of the six individuals we interviewed from this group mentioned that they had learned about Korea largely by watching Korean dramas. This phenomenon highlights a key aspect of this group—although estranged humanitarians retain a strong interest in Korea, they are so far removed from their Korean roots that they must learn about Korean culture and society from television programs.

Estranged humanitarians also aspire to work in female-majority fields such as art and design (13 percent), teaching (18 percent), and the nonprofit sector (13 percent). Unsurprisingly, 75 percent are female. Seven of 10 have majored in either the arts and humanities or the social sciences (excluding economics), noting that respondents were allowed to list multiple majors. Members of the group are also inclined toward academia: 33 percent plan on pursuing a nonprofessional MA or PhD. As a result, they show minimal inclination toward business-related fields such as finance, consulting, or employment by a large corporation.

Interest in Living in Korea Short Term

Estranged humanitarians show a below-average interest in living in Korea long term (2.05/5.00) or working for Korean firms (2.25/5.00). Yet they paradoxically express an average or above-average interest in living in Korea short term (3.87/5.00). Estranged humanitarians have spent very little time in Korea and have few connections there. Nevertheless, they are the most willing of all groups to return to Korea short term.

Why would this group be willing to live in Korea short but not long term? Our findings suggest that estranged humanitarians have a keen interest in exploring their Korean heritage. There are strong correlations between respondents' interest in living in Korea short term and the desire to return to Korea to study the Korean language (correlation of 0.37) or learn more about Korean culture (0.47). These correlations are particularly interesting as no other group was motivated by such a desire to learn about Korean culture and language. Our interviews with Korean American students belonging to this group suggest that they feel an affinity or kinship with Koreans whether or not they feel more comfortable living in the United States or Canada, and they would like to explore Korean culture and identity further by visiting their "homeland." Rebecca, a female graduate student in public health, expresses her desire to explore her Korean heritage even though she feels "really comfortable in American culture":

> I just feel like my identity is Korean American. . . . I want to know about the culture more, and with my future children I would want them to learn about my ancestry and everything. . . . I don't know why, but that's part of my identity. Just among Koreans there's a connection even when I go somewhere. I was traveling in Europe, and when I meet a Korean, I'm just so excited to meet someone who's of Korean decent. . . . There's a special bond, there's intimacy without knowing that person . . . but no concrete details.

John, a medical student, had not visited Korea since early childhood and shares Rebecca's desire to explore Korean identity:

> I just think [living in Korea short term] would be a good experience. One thing I really wish I had is a better sense of Korean-ness, I'd say. Just because I get kind of jealous of Korean Americans who can adapt very well to Korean culture. . . . I'm definitely not like that. . . . Just because I'm Korean I want to be part of that culture.

Other students are ambivalent regarding their Korean American identity and want to take a short-term visit to Korea as an opportunity to resolve their conflicting identities. Jasmine, another female undergraduate yet to declare a major, expressed anxieties when interacting with both Korean and American friends:

> Sometimes I feel like I wouldn't feel very comfortable talking with my Korean friends in trying to speak Korean with them, but sometimes when I'm with my American friends I just don't feel like I'm enjoying myself because we have

different values and different expressions. . . . When I'm at home I try to be really Korean to my parents, but when I leave the house I leave that identity for an American one. . . . It's hard to hide a part of me that I really value. . . . It's been with me my entire life.

Jasmine visited Korea partially to resolve such ambiguities about her identity but recognizes the difficulty of resolving such ambiguities even in Korea:

I try to seek out different places . . . somewhere I could feel a new flavor. I'd say Korea's a big attraction because it's definitely a different life as opposed to California. Maybe [the difference is] fitting in . . . we have to try to find a balance between our two heritages, cultures . . . the simple decision or solution would be to go to Korea and identify with the Korean heritage more, but I would say like just the difficulty of trying to fit in and accommodate both cultures is pretty difficult.

Our interviewees noted largely positive experiences with their short-term visit to Korea in terms of reaffirming their Korean heritage. Haley, a female student majoring in history, expressed comfort with Korea in contrast to her experiences back "home" in the United States:

I felt more comfortable in Korea in a way I didn't feel like at home. I think it's the same for every second-generation immigrant who goes back to their home country for the first time—when I went back, it was like the first time I felt like a part of the majority—it was like—the sense of privilege I had of being part of the norm. It is a very comfortable thing. I did like that a lot. [In the United States] just walking down the street . . . there isn't a moment where I'm not self-aware. . . . I could never feel fully American.

Other interviewees who had visited Korea expressed varying amounts of confidence and comfort with their American identities. Nevertheless, they unanimously showed feelings of kinship and warmth toward other Koreans, as well as a desire to learn more about their Korean heritage. Overall, estranged humanitarians appear to desire a short-term return to Korea to come to terms with their ethnic identity, even if they would like to pursue their careers in the United States.

Lack of Interest in Living in Korea Long Term or Working for Korean Firms

Despite their interest in a short-term sojourn, estranged humanitarians have little desire for a long-term return (2.05/5.00) or employment by Korean firms (2.25/5.00). Even as they feel an affinity with Korean heritage and culture, they still believe that they would face substantial barriers to building careers and lives in the country.

Estranged humanitarians reveal a strong distaste for Korea's rigid and hierarchical work culture. Our interviewees learned about the Korean work culture from several sources from their families, relatives, and personal friends. One respondent mentioned horror at her father's lifestyle while working for Samsung: "In Korea, you have to stay through the night and do that kind of work . . . and that's influenced by what I see my dad does. . . . I thought often about how hard such a lifestyle must be." Other estranged humanitarians also expressed concerns for the second- or third-hand accounts they had heard about Korea's excessively hard-working culture. In addition, nearly all interviewees' understandings of Korean work culture were negatively influenced by Korean television dramas. For instance, Daniel—a premed student—mentioned that "[Korean] dramas depict hierarchy. . . . It's so rigid there."

Students with firsthand experience of Korean companies expressed particularly strong distaste for their work culture. This insight is consistent with our quantitative findings. Those students who had recently spent at least one summer in Korea were less willing to work with Koreans (correlation of −0.28 between these variables) or work for Korean firms (−0.25). Haley—the history major—spent a year interning for a prominent nonprofit organization and described her experience as follows:

> No other country has as long hours as Korea . . . and it's very top-down. . . . There's hwoisik where all the decisions were made. . . . When I interned for [her employer], I was kind of exposed to the hwoisik, but I guess since it was in a nonprofit it was a little different from corporate companies. . . . They used to tell me that they do all the busy work at the office but make decisions during the hwoisik . . . and that it can be uncomfortable for women in that setting and that there's pressure to go to the hwoisik because that's when the company members bond and socialize.

Nearly all interviewees shared their concerns about the hierarchical nature, long hours, and compulsory after-work social events mentioned here: firsthand experience appears to have heightened interviewees' awareness of these problems.

Estranged humanitarians also reveal dissatisfaction with the conformity and sexism endemic to Korean society and culture. Haley told us about her personal experiences regarding conformity:

> I think everyone has to follow a trend and they have to fit into an ideal box, and if you're a little too creative, artistic, or somehow "out of the box," they'll sort of judge you and look at you strangely . . . and just the fact that I feel like Korea is very superficial and everyone, on the outside they're dressed very well, they just care so much about outward appearance with plastic surgery and even hiking, they wear heels to the mountains and all these girls were wearing heels [while hiking] . . . and even on the subway when I'm talking in English everyone stares at me.

Our respondents were even more concerned about the overt sexism found in Korea. All interviewees noted gender discrimination, whether or not they were female. Haley relayed the experience of her cousin:

> My cousin said it's hard for women to even get a job. . . . She applied for this administrative job at Hanyang University where she's an alum. . . . She was applying for this, and she made it to the final round of interviews, and ultimately she didn't get picked, and the people who got picked were nine guys and one girl, and the one girl was from Seoul National University. . . . She would tell me about the résumé, too, the very standard format with picture, height, and weight. . . . Your weight and height are kind of irrelevant. . . . It's like, they hire fewer women, and they are more selective with the women they choose based on appearance.

Rebecca—the female graduate student in public policy—disliked another phenomenon at the intersection of conformity and sexism, the expectation that women physically conform to widely expected social norms. She disliked being judged "because of my body weight. . . . People in Korea are really skinny." John—the medical student—recounted a similar story he had heard secondhand:

> My mom has a friend who has two daughters, and they weren't having too much success with jobs . . . and they were very smart . . . and afterwards they realized maybe it's their looks . . . and so they just got massive plastic surgery and became someone else . . . and they got hired the next month. It's just that shocking. Both of them are twins—it's just like fascinating to me—it's a huge investment, and I guess it worked out—I think in some ways it's superficial . . . and super competitive.

Finally, estranged humanitarians indicated that they would not live in Korea long term because of the language barrier. Their Korean language capabilities ranged between minimal and fluent. Even those who were fluent, however, reported difficulty with the technical jargon used in workplace environments and with the social detail attached to Korean vocabulary and manners.

These findings taken together suggest that estranged humanitarians have a strong desire to explore their ethnic heritage and culture with a short-term visit to Korea. Given their limited knowledge of Korea, however, they build an idealized image that is only shattered when they learn more about its society and culture, particularly after spending some time in Korea. Although they appreciate the chance to learn more about their heritage and identity, they are not likely to work with Koreans or for Korean firms, let alone return to Korea.

ROOTED HUMANITARIANS

Like estranged humanitarians, rooted humanitarians (21 percent of all respondents) express little interest in corporate careers. However, rooted humanitarians have much greater familiarity with Korea, having spent a good amount of time there. Such familiarity has opened doors in Korea's booming culture industry for Korean Americans who have maintained connections back home. For instance, Ok Taecyeon moved with his parents and older sister to the Boston area at the age of 11. Having retained his Korean language ability and interest in Korean culture, he was encouraged by his sister to apply to an audition held by K-Pop producer JYP Entertainment held in New York City. Returning to Korea at the age of 17, Ok has become the lead singer for the 2PM, a boy band popular across Asia. His story parallels those of other Korean American K-Pop stars. Contributing not only their command of English but also musical styles they enjoyed in the United States, the Korean American returnees in K-Pop groups have played an important role in the success of hallyu overseas.

Like Ok Taecyeon, rooted humanitarians understand Korea and its culture far better than their estranged humanitarian counterparts, as they have spent about the same amount of time after early childhood in Korea (9.4 years) and the United States or Canada (8.2 years) in addition to time spent elsewhere in the world. Consequently, 7 of 10 have retained Korean citizenship.[6] This group has a higher-than-average number of parents and siblings in Korea; furthermore, many stayed in touch with friends from their elementary and middle school years in Korea (69 percent). In total 65 percent describe themselves as Korean, while only 50 percent regard themselves as Korean American or Korean Canadian. Only 4 percent identify as American or Canadian. Furthermore, this group desires to marry a Korean (4.35/5.00) or a Korean American or Canadian (4.12/5.00) versus a non-Korean Asian (2.65/5.00) or Caucasian (2.12/5.00). In many respects, rooted humanitarians occupy a middle ground between estranged humanitarians and the Korean students overseas discussed in Chapter 3.

Jeannie, a 22-year-old premed student, spent 12 years in Korea and 10 years in the United States and says, "Even now I consider Korea as home and the United States more as a place where I can find my career. I think the fact that my parents live in Korea right now affects that." Karen, a 20-year-old student studying cognitive science, lived only 1.5 years in Korea but has nevertheless spent many summers there. Although she said she lost her Korean identity, she rediscovered it after visiting Korea before college and has maintained it ever since:

> Throughout high school, I was not open to having Korean friends. . . . Before, in middle school, I had gone to Korea every summer. But starting after middle school and throughout high school I didn't visit Korea. During that time I got disconnected. Also, my school had mostly white and non-Asian students. After I went to Korea, after graduating from high school, I got kind of interested in that. I found a lot of Korean friends through the Korean club that I'm involved in right now, mostly Koreans studying abroad. The funny thing is, I started to join the Korean American club here but didn't fit into it. I had another friend who lived here when she was nine. She introduced me to the club that I am in right now. Everyone there is like 1.5 generation.

Karen also credits a conservative upbringing for her close affinity with Korea:

> A big factor might be how my parents raised me. Korean Americans would always respond in English when parents talk in Korean. I grew up more conservatively. My parents always forced me to speak Korean to my sister and them. When we were alone, my sister and I wouldn't speak Korean. But now it's not much of a big deal anymore.

Both rooted humanitarians demonstrate a good understanding of Korean society and culture, unlike their estranged humanitarian counterparts.

Interest in Living in Korea Short Term

Rooted humanitarians have little interest in reclaiming Korean identities—largely because they had already done so or never lost their identity in the first place. They are willing to live in Korea short term (3.81/5.00), but for very different reasons than estranged humanitarians. Rooted humanitarians are not very interested in learning more about Korean heritage (correlation of –0.31 between the two factors): they are already quite familiar with Korean society and culture. Rather, they would like to see friends there (0.25) and "play" as we describe below. Many rooted humanitarians mentioned that they spent time seeing family members in Korea.

Interest in Living in Korea Long Term and Desire to Work for Korean Firms

Given their familiarity with Korea, rooted humanitarians show a greater interest in living in Korea long term (2.69/5.00) than members of estranged humanitarians (2.05/5.00), but less than Korean students studying abroad (3.30/5.00). They also were more willing to work for Korean firms (2.92/5.00) than estranged humanitarians (2.25/5.00). In these respects, rooted humanitarians once again represent a middle ground between estranged humanitarians and Korean students overseas.

The family and friends these individuals left behind in Korea continue to exert a powerful pull on them. We correlated a group member's interest in living in Korea long term and his or her motivations for a hypothetical return. Two of the three highest correlations were spending more time with friends (correlation of 0.52) and family (0.38). Both of our interviewees cited the desire to spend time with family members as a main motivation for returning long term. Karen mentioned that she was motivated to spend more time with her extended family: "Everyone on my mom's side is in Korea. I have two uncles from my dad's side living on the East Coast [of the United States], and the rest are in Korea. I'm quite close with my relatives in Korea." She also believes that her parents will someday move back to Korea after her father retires. She cites this as a good reason to get dual citizenship in Korea but also refers to work-related opportunities:

> This past summer, I went to get my dual citizenship there. There's no actual reason why I have to get that because I can still visit. The only gain is for working there, I guess. I got it for future opportunities.

Rooted humanitarians also have career-related motivations for returning to Korea. An interest in returning home long term is strongly correlated with a motivation to build a career in Korea (correlation of 0.41). Indeed, a desire to work in a chaebŏl (0.36) or to build a professional career outside the chaebŏl (0.27) also strongly correlates with an interest in living in Korea long term. Unlike estranged humanitarians who understand Korean work culture simply in negative terms, rooted humanitarians possess a more detailed and nuanced view. For instance, Jeannie characterizes Korea's work culture as "polarized" between two extremes:

> One end of the spectrum is very advanced or developed in terms of business and the way people interact, and they try to adapt, like, new business models and methods, and they try to adapt quickly. . . . The more up-to-date business environment . . . feels more free—they don't control your attire as much. I think those environments exist more in the capital, in Seoul. There are also still a lot of companies at the other end of the spectrum, where they value traditional values more. The way they work, the business is more based on their traditional way of doing things. The reason why I think that way is . . . based on what I hear from one or two friends that I have and their friends . . . right now in the middle of finding jobs [in Korea] and also my cousins who are working in Korea.

Karen, our other interviewee in this group, also shows an acceptance of Korean business culture, stating, "If I were to work in Korea, which I'm not opposed to . . . culturally I would be O.K., because I've been exposed to the drinking culture and the senior/junior relationship." These findings parallel our observation regarding Korean students overseas as examined in Chapter 3.

Although we might expect female members of this group to be concerned about gender discrimination in Korea, we find no correlation between this factor and their interest in living in Korea long term. Once again, we see a better and more balanced understanding among rooted humanitarians. Jeannie states that "there's much less gender bias in Korea than years before, years ago. That is still a major reason not to go back, but not so much as years ago."

Greater understanding, however, raised new concerns among rooted humanitarians. Notably, we find a negative correlation (−0.53) between concerns about Korea's educational system and interest in living in Korea long term. Karen indicated that she would be willing to stay in Korea for a long time, but: "Well, I really oppose raising my children in Korea. So up until there, I would be O.K." Rooted humanitarians also share concerns about the wage differential between the United States and Korea. Jeannie noted:

> I think money is one thing—some jobs . . . it really depends on jobs. For example, engineering makes a lot more money in the U.S. than in Korea, and people

value the work a lot more, and some other jobs make more money in Korea as opposed to the U.S., so money's one thing.

Overall, rooted humanitarians appear to include many Koreans who emigrated to the United States or Canada during high school, either with their parents or through the chogi yuhak process—representing the so-called 1.5-generation immigrants. Having gained permanent residency or citizenship in the United States or Canada, these individuals have indicated their intention to stay in North America. Nevertheless, they maintain close ties with Korea and would be open to pursuing attractive career opportunities there. Although such individuals might not be considered obvious contributors to Korea's economy, some—like Ok Taecyeon—may provide unexpected benefits by bringing new ideas into Korea and synthesizing them with those already prevalent there.

ROOTED BUSINESSMEN

Rooted businessmen, including 20 percent of the surveyed respondents, are the inverse of estranged humanitarians. Like their rooted humanitarian counterparts, rooted businessmen have a much stronger connection with Korea than estranged humanitarians. However, unlike both groups discussed so far, they are mostly male (80 percent) and oriented toward business (28 percent interested in finance, 28 percent interested in consulting, 24 percent interested in working for a large corporation, 12 percent interested in entrepreneurship, 16 percent interested in pursuing an MBA). Such respondents resemble Jeong H. Kim, founder of Yurie Systems and former head of Lucent's renowned Bell Labs. Born in Seoul, Kim emigrated to the United States at the age of 14, following his parents. While attending Johns Hopkins, Kim became involved in a startup, Digitus, before leaving and spending seven years in the U.S. Navy. After working in the military and, later, for defense contractor AlliedSignal, Kim studied for a PhD in reliability engineering at the University of Maryland. Soon afterward, Kim founded Yurie Systems, which was acquired by Lucent for $1 billion in 1998. After spending time at the University of Maryland as a professor, Kim returned to Lucent to head Bell Labs. Through it all, Kim remained connected to his Korean roots. Besides generous contributions to Korea-oriented charities, Kim visited Korea regularly and established a branch office of Bell Labs in Seoul. Recently, Kim was nominated as Korea's first

Minister of Science, ICT, and Future Planning by President Park Geun-hye, but withdrew his candidacy in part due to a strong nationalistic reaction against his U.S. citizenship.[7] Nevertheless, Kim exemplifies the potential for Korean immigrants to achieve success in mainstream U.S. society before bringing their expertise and connections back to Korea or its diaspora community.

Like their rooted humanitarian counterparts, rooted businessmen have a good understanding of Korea and its culture. Individuals in this group have spent about the same amount of time past age 7 in Korea (7.7 years) and the United States or Canada (7.3 years). Consequently, 65 percent maintain Korean citizenship. Like rooted humanitarians, rooted businessmen have a higher-than-average number of parents (1.16) and siblings (0.32) in Korea. Of these, 52 percent also have remained friends with their elementary and middle school classmates in Korea. Correspondingly, rooted businessmen more often identify with being Korean (56 percent) or Korean American or Korean Canadian (60 percent) than simply American or Canadian (4 percent). For instance, one of the three individuals we interviewed in this category—Jeongwon—even refers to the house he returns to in Korea every couple of years as home, considering how often he has moved across different cities in North America. Furthermore, this group is more willing to marry a Korean (4.40/5.00) or a Korean American (4.32/5.00) than a non-Korean Asian (2.16/5.00) or Caucasian (2.04/5.00). Peter—an economics undergraduate studying in entrepreneurial California—is even considering starting a dating website for Koreans and Korean Americans. Along with rooted humanitarians, rooted businessmen occupy a middle ground between more assimilated Korean Americans and the Korean students discussed in Chapter 3.

Unlike both types of humanitarians, rooted businessmen are strongly oriented toward business or business-related fields: its members show little or no interest in other career paths, with the exception of medicine (28 percent). Of the three interviewees, entrepreneurial Peter desires to enter management consulting, while Jeongwon is a 22-year-old premed student. The third interviewee, Paul, is a 23-year-old who moved to Korea and joined Samsung after graduating with a degree in economics. He answered our initial survey (spring 2011) as a student, graduated in June 2011, and was interviewed while working in Korea in the spring of 2012.

Interest in Living in Korea Long Term and Working for Korean Firms

Rooted businessmen are more willing to live in Korea long term (2.88/5.00) than respondents placed in other groups, even if they are no more willing than average to live in Korea short term (3.64/5.00), work with Koreans (3.08/5.00), or work for Korean firms (2.68/5.00). Interest in living in Korea long term is strongly correlated with the motivation to build a career in Korea (0.56), earn a substantial income (0.38), and spend time with friends (0.31). These findings indicate that rooted businessmen would be particularly likely to return to Korea should they find compelling career opportunities there. Peter indicates that he "wouldn't mind going to either [North America or Korea]. It'd be more dependent on what kind of opportunities I have rather than the locations I have or the culture."

Remarks made by two other business-oriented interviewees in this group suggest that the Korean chaebŏl are reaching rooted businessman individuals with an attractive recruiting pitch. For instance, Samsung, which has long recruited Korean students abroad and Korean Americans, sponsors an annual tennis tournament between Korean and Korean American students at Stanford and Berkeley. Our findings show that such efforts have sent an effective message that has resonated with rooted businessmen who emphasize that they are seeking the best possible opportunity to develop their careers. Peter, who is interested in finance, has been swayed by these messages, to the degree that he considers "getting into firms like Samsung Asset Management, Mirae Asset, or those types of companies. I would honestly consider them the same as top firms [in the United States]." In his view, Korean companies offer career opportunities that American firms may not be able to offer. He continues:

> Typically when you work at consulting firms like McKinsey, you are just one part of the ten thousands of employees. But in Korea, you will still be part of a very large company, but as someone coming in from the States you will be able to make more contributions to the company. And therefore you will be able to learn a lot. And also I think it's a really good environment to work in and to get exposed to since I haven't been in that culture since [the age of] ten. I see a lot of growth for finances in Korean companies. I could see a lot of regulations easing and therefore more investments coming in. So I see more growth opportunities in Korea.

Paul also responded favorably to this message, so much so that he relocated to Korea to join Samsung Electronics. He reflects on why he joined Samsung as follows:

I thought the place I would be the most valuable would be in a country that was looking for foreign hires and was willing and wanting to change, and I thought the rhetoric at Samsung suggested that. It was risky, but part of the hope was that if I go to Samsung, I would be able to do things there that I wouldn't have been able to do in the U.S. . . . I'm always looking, despite circumstance, if I feel like I can add value, and if that value outweighs the risk and the effort it takes to adapt, then I will make that move. It literally was that 'Is there a way that I can contribute in a way that, given my background, I couldn't in the U.S.?'. . . Would they trust me, if they were desperate for change? . . . Would they trust me to help them to bring the Silicon Valley culture or a hybrid model of it to help Korea to develop products?

Paul thought that he could make an impact earlier in his career by joining Samsung rather than working in Silicon Valley.

Both Peter and Paul initially had a positive image of opportunities in Korea despite being aware of the downsides of Korean business culture. As Paul recollects:

I had actually interned at [another Korean chaebŏl] so I had a little exposure [to Korean business culture]. But even before all that, some of the preconceived notions I had were [that Korean firms were] very hierarchical, very driven by a couple of people, risk-averse, not as much empowerment to the people lower down . . . paternal, as in the corporate management is paternal and takes care of its own, and requires loyalty in return.

Paul also knew that he would receive lower pay in Korea, but nevertheless rationalized the difference: "I knew I was going to take a hit financially. But at the end of the day, it was the savings left over. Given tax and everything, and California has a high tax rate, I thought it sort of helped that Korea's cost of living was low. I sort of rationalized it through, said that it could be worse."

After working there for several months, however, Paul has become less enthusiastic about Korea:

[I've] gotten more critical. . . . As an outsider, you're not as sure as to how much these preconceived notions [of Korean work culture] are correct, but I'd say it's pretty true. I guess now I have personal experience to back that up. . . . People straight out of college aren't necessarily expected to contribute in a highly significant way. The expectation isn't quite there. . . . *What you'll see for a lot of the Korean conglomerates is a disconnect between the rhetoric and what actually happens. What ends up happening is that "upper-upper" management knows*

> *something needs to get done, but the lower management or mid-management is kind of resistant—plus there's no clear roadmap as to how you would go about accomplishing this.* (emphasis added)

Indeed, Paul states that he will probably leave Samsung, lamenting that "there's no real incentive to stay—the only people that are willing to stay longer are the people that really feel that they have a vision here—people who are ridiculously motivated . . . and there are people who have been able to position themselves in a highly advantageous position so that they can make a career." Peter, who also worked at Samsung as a summer intern, likewise recognizes the problems with Korean work culture:

> [I am concerned about] things being more vertical in terms of rank. . . . That also contributes to the drinking culture. . . . I will be able to contribute but maybe not socialize well. Maybe I have the advantage of going to a better school than the other guys, but there's the psych factor of not going to the army and having less things to agree on. Maybe a little like *wangtta* [being shunned].

Nevertheless, Peter remains more enthusiastic than Paul about future employment in Korea, adding, "I'm pretty sure that, just in terms of contributions, I will be able to make a lot."

Overall, people like Peter and Paul—well connected in the United States and with in-depth knowledge of Silicon Valley's startup culture—can potentially help Korean firms compete with innovative corporate leaders such as Apple. However, Korean firms do not seem to be properly using the human and social capital such individuals possess. Thus, individuals fitting the rooted businessman profile appear to resist a long-term sojourn despite an initial desire to work in Korea, but they can be induced to play a bridging role between Korea and North America. Indeed, while expressing his desire to leave Samsung, Paul paints a nuanced portrait of work culture there, noting a heterogeneity not noticed by Korean Americans that have become estranged from their Korean roots:

> It's hard to make a blanket statement because it really differs from team to team . . . and fortunately enough the team I'm a part of is much more flexible. . . . Like dinner outings and alcohol, it's a lot better than I was expecting. The pressure is still there, but it's much better.

This suggests that Paul, like other rooted businessmen, believes that Korean business culture is not so broken as to be irredeemable. Such individuals might be willing to maintain the connections they forged with Samsung co-workers even after they leave and return to North America. With that, they can potentially bridge between the two countries.

ESTRANGED BUSINESSMEN

Estranged businessmen resemble rooted businessmen in their business orientation but are similar to estranged humanitarians in their social distance from Korea. Of the surveyed respondents 28 percent belong to this group. Eric Kim epitomizes this group, having left Korea at an early age, working in business, and possibly having little knowledge of the negatives associated with Korean business culture. Growing up in Southern California, Kim earned degrees from Harvey Mudd College, UCLA, and Harvard before learning marketing skills and experiences at places like Lotus and Dun & Bradstreet. When he returned to Korea to join Samsung, he was given an advertising budget of $3 billion per year to conduct a worldwide marketing campaign to propel Samsung into the ranks of top-tier electronics brands. Kim proved phenomenally successful. However, his first presentation to Samsung Electronics executives focused on American-style business concepts—and apparently drew an icy hostility from the executives gathered there. He was able to succeed only because the president of Samsung Electronics actively protected him and his endeavors, supposedly telling his subordinates that "if you touch him, you are dead." Eric Kim's experience highlights the challenges that estranged businessmen might face in Korean society—as well as their potential to contribute to Korean economic competitiveness.

Like estranged humanitarians, estranged businessmen have far stronger ties to the United States or Canada than Korea. Estranged businessmen have spent most of their lives in the United States or Canada and typically have both parents living there (average of 1.86). Few have elementary or middle school friends in Korea (17 percent). The majority (80 percent) describe themselves as Korean American or Korean Canadian; only 17 percent describe themselves as Korean. Accordingly, estranged businessmen are less willing to marry a Korean (3.54/5.00) than their counterparts in groups II or III. Finally, estranged businessmen also have the lowest Korean fluency (3.20/5.00) of the four groups. Our interviews with three members of estranged businessmen reflect the relatively high social distance separating them from Korea. One respondent—Richard, an MBA student—grew up in New Jersey, in a town without any other Korean families, and was later called a "twinkie" (yellow on the outside, white on the inside) by his Korean American friends. He lost touch with his Korean identity fairly early on in his life:

> When I was a little kid, I would spend summers in Korea—the last time I was in Korea was when I was twelve years old—after that point, since my parents shipped me off to boarding school and my summers were filled with doing extracurricular things for building my résumé, they didn't send me to Korea just to hang out with my cousins. . . . The sad part about that is my German's a lot better than my Korean.

Like their rooted businessman counterparts, estranged businessmen are interested in business-related careers. Besides medicine (29 percent), they are interested in finance (17 percent), consulting (14 percent), corporate positions (17 percent), and entrepreneurship (9 percent); 14 percent intended to pursue an MBA.

Interest in Living in Korea Short Term

Like all others, estranged businessmen are quite enthusiastic about returning to Korea short term (3.71/5.00). Like their estranged humanitarian counterparts, estranged businessmen indicated some degree of uncertainty regarding their identities. Brandon, a graduate student in computer science—expressed doubt and confusion about his identity:

> Ethnically, and just . . . well, I mean, culturally, I identify myself [with being a Korean]. . . . It's kind of weird—I don't agree with Korean values, but at the same time culturally speaking I feel like, I don't know—maybe—like little things—like some things, like—some values that I do identify with and . . . I don't know.

Given such uncertainty, estranged businessmen like to undertake a short-term return to Korea largely motivated by their desire to learn more about Korean culture (correlation of 0.55). Richard mentioned that "for me personally I would love to learn more about Korean culture . . . and my Korean friends telling me how to order some things—like eating some food in a certain way—like how to pour *soju* (Korean liquor) properly." Unlike estranged humanitarians, however, estranged businessmen are also motivated to return to seek career opportunities (0.27). All three interviewees emphasized that their primary interest was the pursuit of exceptional career opportunities and indicated that pay was more important than identity. When Brandon was asked whether he considered Korea or the United States home, he answered in very practical terms:

> I feel that neither is my home—it depends on what you're talking about—I mean I definitely like living in America because America is going to pay more than Korea—I mean, the salary in America is higher.

Given such practical attitudes, estranged businessmen would probably find it harder to justify a short-term sojourn in Korea unless it enhanced their career prospects.

Estranged humanitarians and estranged businessmen differ in another interesting and important respect. Unlike estranged humanitarian counterparts, estranged businessmen express little or no disappointment with Korea after actually spending time there. Having spent a summer in Korea has a positive correlation (0.23) with a respondent's desire to work for a Korean firm, not a negative correlation (–0.25) as found among estranged humanitarians. In other words, greater familiarity with Korean society and culture improved estranged businessmen's view of Korea-related opportunities, while greater familiarity worsened estranged humanitarians' view of such opportunities. Although we cannot conclusively explain this divergence based on our data, we suspect that the Korean mindset resonates with estranged businessmen while conflicting with basic values held by estranged humanitarians. Being oriented toward business and practical matters, estranged businessmen are likely to agree with modern Koreans' emphasis on achieving material, tangible results. In contrast, estranged humanitarians are oriented toward values of individual expression and nonconformity and may find the attitudes expressed by many Koreans toward such practical subjects such as cosmetic surgery somewhat off-putting. Estranged businessmen tend to be male, while estranged humanitarians tend to be female—making gender discrimination another possible explanation.

Interest in Living in Korea Long Term and Working for Korean Firms

Estranged businessmen have a below-average interest in living in Korea long term (2.11/5.00). Slower career progressions and lower pay appear to dissuade them from considering long-term careers in Korea. As Margaret, a female computer science major, says,

In Korea, just because I'm a girl and I grew up in America and I can't speak Korean as well as I should, I might get judged—there might be some injustice against people like me. . . . I've heard negative comments about those people, and there's very much a distinction between women and men. . . . My ability to advance is pretty limited if that is the case.

Brandon had little to say about gender discrimination but echoed Margaret's sentiment regarding lower pay:

They make you work super hard, and pay you so little—for their internships, you know how much they're making? Seven to eight dollars an hour—and they're working at pretty good companies. One of my friends was working at Naver as a coder—pretty smart guy. In America, do you know how much I'm getting paid? If I code for internship at Google, they will pay me forty an hour—*I don't care if my identity is Korean or what not—this is like game over.* For example, Samsung, they come with an info session, saying, "We're so good"—and I know they're good—but how much? . . . I mean, I'm not saying—I'm sure a lot of them are a lot smarter than me, but *they're getting paid like maybe 30k, 40k, whereas if I were to go to full time at Google, starting salary is 100k* or so . . . game over—that's my attitude. They make you work way more hard, pay you way less, make you do random stuff. (emphasis added)

Richard took a similar but longer-term perspective:

[Regarding opportunities:] Career growth and learning experience is number one, and number two is probably pay, and number three . . . sort of in the bigger scheme of things—geographically, is it the right fit? Culturally, is it the type of firm I want to work in? . . . [Regarding salary:] I wouldn't necessarily take less . . . I would take enough—a limited pay cut or same level as what I made before my MBA in order to position myself so that *if I come back to the States, I wouldn't be making any less than I would be making if I had stayed here in the U.S.* . . . They'll [firms] always ask you what you made previously, and they'll base your salary based off of that rather than what's competitive. (emphasis added)

However, Richard cited the existence of a glass ceiling as a reason not to go:

I could go over there with my degrees and do some good work, but at the same time because I'm not a Korean citizen, Korean-Korean, and especially as a Korean who didn't go to the army, there's no chance of me going high up in the Korean professional corporate structure—you have to be a citizen who served in the military in order to own your own business. I've dated Korean girls from Korea, and they have younger brothers who have to take over the father's business. They send them off to the military because they won't be respected if they don't go.

Estranged businessmen also expressed concerns about the work culture. Much like estranged humanitarians, estranged businessmen had little first-hand knowledge of Korean firms and relayed common stereotypes about the hierarchical, stressful work environment without detail. Margaret cited her father's experience as a senior manager at a large company, and how he was unceremoniously asked to resign when he reached a certain age. She also mentioned that Korea "seems so rushed and stressed. It's like a very high stress environment—there's kind of an environment where you're expected to really push yourself and excel—and it's . . . I don't think I can keep up." Margaret also expressed doubts regarding the work culture:

> What I know about it—what I hear about it—is that it's very tough working in corporations because a lot of it is you have to do hwoisik, and you have to go late at night—and you're kind of an outcast if you don't join in. . . . You start to care about what other people are thinking and compete—and you try to bring other people down.

Such impressions indicate that estranged businessmen remain unaware of the changes in work culture in certain Korean firms that some rooted businessmen noted. Also, they suggest that Korean corporations, especially chaebŏl, have not reached estranged businessmen as effectively as they have done with rooted businessmen, perhaps because they have targeted individuals with stronger connections to Korea (e.g., being associated with Korean student organizations). This is particularly important because estranged businessmen's interest in living in Korea long term is strongly correlated with a desire to work for a chaebŏl; other strong correlations include the motivation to earn a substantial income (0.52) and build a career (0.44) in Korea.

Estranged businessmen show a below-average interest in living in Korea long term (2.11/5.00) or working for Korean firms (2.57/5.00) but an above-average desire to work with Koreans (3.51/5.00), suggesting their potential as a social capital. In other words, they may not return to Korea to work for Korean firms but may be willing to work with Koreans, potentially bridging Korea with the country of their residency. In addition, desire to work with Koreans is very strongly correlated with consumption of Korean movies (0.50) and music (0.53). This has important implications as such motives are influenced by the consumption of Korean cultural products, despite their seemingly single-minded pursuit of career opportunities.

The Korean Diaspora as Global Talent

Korean Americans and Korean Canadians, especially those focused on business-related careers, have exceptional potential to contribute to Korea's development. Findings from our study reveal that these individuals are favorable toward Korean firms and culture and could potentially benefit the nation in two different ways. On one hand, Korean Americans and Korean Canadians could contribute mightily to Korea's pool of human capital, after returning home for the right career opportunities. Individuals like Eric Kim have made tremendous contributions. Rather than taking jobs away from Korean college graduates, they have created new ones for Koreans by enhancing Korea's economic competitiveness. Indeed, Korea is well poised to recruit the best and brightest of its overseas diaspora back home. As Korea's economy continues to develop, the salaries offered by Korean firms will become increasingly attractive. On the other hand, the same individuals could return to North America after a short sojourn in Korea, after having reestablished their Korean identities and developed social and business ties with Koreans. Such individuals would be particularly well positioned to function as transnational bridges, utilizing their embeddedness in their host societies and their reactivated embeddedness in Korea. Despite being geographically distant from the country, such individuals would nevertheless become transnationals making a contribution to Korea.

This study shows that both rooted businessmen and estranged businessmen have the best potential for helping Korea improve its economic competitiveness. Many of these individuals have the human capital (e.g., financial and business acumen) needed to help Korea expand into highly profitable service sectors like finance and consulting. Other individuals have both the human and social capital (e.g., creativity, foreign experience, ties with key individuals overseas) needed to help Korean corporations to understand foreign markets.

In many respects, rooted businessmen resemble the Korean students who generally return home after studying abroad with their strong interests in working in Korea or with Koreans. Thus, members of the rooted businessman group would be willing to take advantage of compelling economic opportunities in Korea, especially if they have friends and family there. However, their interest in returning home is attenuated by such unfavorable factors as Korea's rigid corporate culture. To recruit more such individuals back to Korea—or to secure the cooperation of those who remain overseas—Korean firms must continue their efforts to improve their work cultures. Specifically, reductions in hierarchical rigidity and forced socializing (e.g., hwoisik and drinking sessions) would have the greatest impact.

On the other hand, members of the estranged businessman group are motivated to construct their own identities by reconnecting with a homeland they know little about. Also, the Korean wave has exposed these individuals to largely favorable views of Korean culture and society as spread by television shows, movies, and music. However, these individuals remain somewhat hesitant about moving to Korea long term, mainly because they are unsure about the career opportunities that Korea offers and because they find more lucrative opportunities elsewhere.

Still, Korea has an opportunity to recruit members of the estranged businessman group as both human and social capital. Unlike estranged humanitarians who often discover that they do not fit into Korean society, estranged businessmen apparently have a positive experience with short-term sojourns. The challenge for Korea is to transform these positive short-term stays into longer-term commitments—or, perhaps even more usefully, to help estranged businessman members who return to North America maintain the ties they build with Koreans during short-term stays so that they can bridge the two countries across the Pacific. The Korean government may consider a new initiative along the lines of Birthright Israel, which not only awakens Jewish identities among members of its diaspora but also builds connections between those individuals and resident Israelis. Given its strong sense of ethnic identity and educational attainment, the Korean diaspora in North America can certainly be an important pool of global talent for Korea.

FIVE

Expatriate Indians and Korean Engineering

In the decade following the 1997 Asian financial crisis, LG and Samsung achieved a dominant position in the global market for high-end mobile phones. However, in 2008–2009, both companies lost that hard-earned position. As Korea's mobile phone exports dropped, LG Electronics' operating profit margins fell from 11.2 percent in 2008 to 1.7 percent in late 2009, while the average export price of Samsung phones dropped from USD 158 per unit in 2007 to USD 112 in 2009. What had happened? The electronics giants, filled with confidence from recent success, failed to anticipate the smartphone invasion. They underestimated how eagerly consumers would embrace the enhanced web-browsing experience and customization potential offered by a new generation of smartphones, epitomized by Apple's iPhone. Thus, when the iPhone swept North American and European markets starting in 2007, LG and Samsung had no answer. The iPhone even sold 2 million units in the Korean home market in little more than a year.

Industry observers in Silicon Valley had viewed the iPhone as a harbinger of revolutionary change and a clear threat to established mobile phone manufacturers. Nevertheless, executives at LG and Samsung either remained unaware of such warnings or dismissed them out of hand. For instance, Gee-sung Choi, CEO of Samsung Electronics, downplayed the iPhone's appeal to consumers, even as it was making serious inroads into the Korean home market. As late as January 2010, he claimed that the iPhone had achieved its impressive Korean sales partly because of the "excessive interest of (Korean) netizens" in the device. Furthermore, he contended that each country had different service environments—and that "Koreans' passion for the iPhone would soon disappear."[1] On the surface, Samsung's refusal to heed warning signs about the iPhone revolution appears to be a management failure, particularly as Samsung manufactured many of the iPhone's components. However, another possibility is that Samsung in specific—and Korean society in general—was so disconnected from Silicon Valley's hotbed of innovation that it simply lacked the capacity to comprehend why Silicon Valley's Technorati were so eagerly anticipating the iPhone. As we discussed in Chapter 1, raw information has little value in itself—it is only useful when combined with key background information (i.e., tacit knowledge) needed to understand what the information means and why it might be significant.[2]

Even if Samsung and LG had heeded warnings about the iPhone, it remains questionable whether they would have had the human capital in software engineering needed to devise effective countermeasures. Despite their strength in the hardware side, Samsung and LG had underdeveloped software capabilities—indeed, even today, they still mainly rely on the Android operating system developed by Google. Such poor software capabilities are becoming a serious challenge as LG's and Samsung's strongest competitor has combined world-class software and hardware engineering talent under the same roof. Apple has always had both hardware and software expertise in-house. Indeed, many have attributed Apple's success to its software prowess.

In this chapter, we investigate the recruitment of Indian engineers specifically as a way to enhance Korea's software engineering capacity, and more broadly as a case study to show how true foreigners could be leveraged. While many countries produce a surplus of engineers, India stands out for producing a large number of engineers focusing on software development. Furthermore, top Indian engineers have been among the most heavily recruited groups of skilled expatriates. Given the intensity of such competition, the recruitment of Indian engineers represents an ideal context for investigating expatriate recruitment under competitive conditions. We seek to show how countries like Korea can attract some of the most sought-after skilled foreigners despite being a nonsettler society—if they are willing to adopt creative approaches embodying strategic thinking. We also explore how Korea can unlock foreigners' social capital beyond their human capital.

Korea's recruitment of Indian engineers represents a conservative test of our proposition that nonimmigrant countries can recruit some of the most sought-after foreigners. The Institute for Management Development publishes a measure estimating a country's attractiveness to skilled foreigners, where 0 is very unattractive and 10 is very attractive. From 2002 through 2013, Korea ranged between 3.78 and 5.29, ranking between 23rd and 48th most attractive in the world. Although Korea was rated more attractive than Japan, it was rated far less attractive than countries like the United States and Singapore, which generally scored above 8 and ranked between first and fourth during the 2002–2013 time period.[3] Thus, by presenting how Korea can recruit Indian engineers, we also show that many other nonimmigrant countries considered similarly unattractive to foreigners may also do so.

Korea's Engineering Needs

HUMAN CAPITAL

Korea has historically been known for its deep, talented pool of human capital in engineering. However, it is now facing a massive shortage of software engineers. This shortage is threatening Korea's continued competitiveness in the electronics sector, particularly in telecommunications.

Korean Export Competitiveness

Korea's economic rise has been based on export-oriented industrialization, and the country continues to rely upon its high-technology exports. Compared with a 2011 gross domestic product of $1.116 trillion (USD), Korean exports totaled $427.3 billion (USD) according to the United Nations COMTRADE database, making the country a top-10 exporter in the world. As Table 5.1 shows, the vast majority of Korean exports consist of machinery and mechanical appliances (29.9 percent of the total); motor vehicles (15.7 percent); petrochemicals and plastics (15.0 percent); ships (12.7 percent); metals, including steel and steel products (8.6 percent); and liquid-crystal display (LCD) panels (6.5 percent). Mobile phones and associated technology constitute a quarter of all machinery, or 8.2 percent of total exports. Design and quality assurance based on strong hardware engineering capability have been cited as key factors for the rise of Korean firms such as Samsung, LG, and Hyundai in these segments, and such achievements would not have been possible without a pool of talented local engineers.

TABLE 5.1
Breakdown of Korean exports in 2011

Standard International Trade Classification (SITC) Rev. 4 commodity codes	Value (USD)	Percentage of total
Machinery and mechanical appliances	127,809,001,209	29.9
Wireless telephony	34,967,607,646	8.2
Petrochemicals and plastics	70,526,270,627	16.5
Vehicles other than railway or tramway rolling stock	67,096,998,404	15.7
Ships, boats, and floating structures	54,071,285,610	12.7
Base metals and articles of base metal (mostly steel)	36,534,733,162	8.6
Liquid crystal devices	27,656,217,630	6.5
Other	43,585,294,064	10.2
Total	427,279,800,706	100.0

SOURCE: Data from COMTRADE Database, United Nations Statistics Division.

The Engineering Talent Pool

During the 1960s, 1970s, and 1980s, Korean society produced a highly skilled pool of engineers. During these three decades, Korea dramatically expanded higher education; the total number of students at the tertiary level increased from only 100,000 in 1960 to 1.3 million in 1987. Many of the most talented students were funneled into engineering programs. Anecdotal evidence suggests that engineering was considered the most attractive field for college graduates in the 1960s and 1970s. For instance, electrical engineering used to be the most selective department at Seoul National University, as measured by entrance examination scores. As Figure 5.1 shows, engineers comprised a higher proportion of the Korean population than that of any other country—in early 2000s, Korea had almost twice as many engineers per capita as Japan and six times as many as the United States.

Nevertheless, Korea faces severe shortages of some types of engineers. As early as 2005, the Ministry of Science and Technology predicted shortfalls within some sectors of Korea's labor market for engineers and scientists. As presented in Table 5.2, *supply* indicates the number of individuals having the appropriate skills, produced via formal education and job training, and *demand* indicates the number of such individuals needed by the Korean economy. The supply of individuals with newly minted engineering BA or MA degrees (541,900) was predicted to be higher than the demand (461,800), but the supply of engineers with PhDs was projected to fall short. This estimate, however, failed to predict the increasing importance of engineers

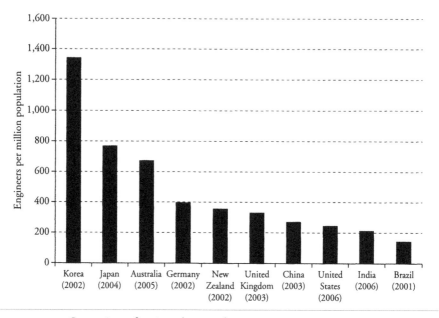

FIGURE 5.1 Comparison of engineer base as of 2004
SOURCE: Data from Ray, "Analysis of IITs," Working paper, Indian Institute of Technology, 2005.

TABLE 5.2
Supply versus demand of labor with tertiary educations by field of study and level of degree completed (in thousands of persons)

Field	PhD supply	PhD demand	MA supply	MA demand	BA supply	BA demand	AA supply	AA demand
Natural sciences	12.7	13.0	26.7	25.4	115.9	75.9	32.7	24.8
Engineering	22.0	31.0	116.3	109.4	425.6	352.4	217.5	112.6
Agriculture/forestry/fishery	1.8	2.8	2.6	2.1	7.3	13.7	0.9	1.6
Medicine and pharmacy	14.5	8.7	28.1	13.0	110.1	114.6	107.8	55.0
Total	50.9	55.4	173.7	149.8	658.9	556.6	358.9	194.0

SOURCE: Data from Ki Jong Lee, "Long-Term Forecast of Supply and Demand of Human Resources in S&T (2005–2014) and Preliminary Survey on the Status of Graduates in Science and Engineering," Republic of Korea Ministry of Science and Technology, 2005.

with skills in software and information technology (IT) and an increasingly severe shortfall in the number of such engineers. The Samsung Economic Research Institute recently estimated that Korea will face a shortfall of 500,000 qualified software engineers in the next five years. A Samsung executive recently lamented, "No matter how hard we try, we cannot find enough software engineers in Korea to meet our needs."[4]

Such a massive shortfall is unlikely to be alleviated by a recent uptrend in the number of Koreans majoring in engineering. It is encouraging that the number of undergraduate students choosing an engineering major in Korea has increased from 80,528 in 2007 to 92,522 in 2012 after many years of decline. This may reflect both government efforts to increase engineering majors and demographic changes, as the total number of incoming students increased from 342,250 in 2007 to 372,941 in 2012, an increase of 8.9 percent (see Table 5.3). Although a larger proportion of students are choosing engineering majors (increased from 23.5 percent in 2007 to 24.8 percent in 2012), the number of students majoring in software engineering—mainly computer science and information technology—has paradoxically declined through this time period. In 2009, nearly 20,000 students graduated with degrees in such majors. In 2012, only 17,188 students did.[5] Overall, an increase in the total number of engineering majors has not been accompanied by a growth in the number of software engineering majors, making it clear that Korean universities are not producing enough software engineers needed by Korean industry. This trend is troublesome, as Korea faces severe human capital shortfalls in software engineering, while being able to meet its human capital needs in hardware engineering.

Korea's software engineering weakness is already beginning to affect hardware exports. For instance, Korean consumer electronics have achieved global success by leveraging their strong engineering talent, creating products with innovative design and impressive reliability. However, the market for consumer electronics has shifted dramatically, converging with personal computers. Nowhere is this more evident than in mobile telephony. Hybrids between computers and telephones (i.e., smartphones) have

TABLE 5.3
Size of entering college cohorts by field of study, 2007–2012

Field	2007	2008	2009	2010	2011	2012
Natural sciences	44,067	43,736	46,372	47,030	46,975	47,828
Engineering	80,528	81,266	82,640	85,152	86,368	92,522
Medicine/pharmacy	13,497	14,371	14,688	17,953	20,750	23,337
Humanities/social sciences	147,042	146,869	145,695	148,484	148,059	148,775
Other	57,116	56,674	58,355	59,892	59,534	60,479
Total	342,250	342,916	347,750	358,511	361,686	372,941

SOURCE: Data from Annual Statistics, Korean Education Development Institute, http://cesi.kedi.re.kr.

displaced traditional mobile phones. In this emerging marketplace, consumers have begun choosing mobile phones based on the software they are running, rather than on design and technology—where Korean strengths traditionally lie. As discussed earlier, hardware manufacturers such as Samsung and LG lost ground to new entrants like Apple in the period following the iPhone's introduction.

Furthermore, the Korean weakness in software engineering has prevented LG from offering any effective responses. Instead of developing its own smartphone operating system and application ecosystem, LG adopted the Android platform made by U.S.-based Google. Samsung developed its own mobile platform (i.e., Bada), intending to give lower-tier phones some smartphone capabilities. Although Bada captured 3 percent of global smartphone sales as of the third (Q3) in 2012, its market share shrank rapidly to 0.7 percent in Q1 2013. Samsung was able to regain its dominance only after adopting the Android platform, combining that with its manufacturing power. Yet, this strategy is potentially dangerous, as Samsung lacks direct control over Android. While Samsung and Google have worked closely with one another, they remain potential competitors. Indeed, Google appeared to undercut its "partners" by purchasing Motorola, a rival smartphone manufacturer. Although Google eventually sold Motorola at least partly to reassure its partners, Samsung remains vulnerable to future changes in Google's strategic direction.

Software is becoming more important across all consumer electronics sectors, not just mobile telephony. Analysts note that many different consumer electronics goods, ranging from televisions to household appliances, will begin to run on operating systems connected to the Internet. Given this trend, software engineering capabilities will become more important across all of these categories. To save its hardware exports, Korea may have to rapidly improve its pool of human capital in software engineering.

SOCIAL CAPITAL

Korea also faces a shortage of transnational bridges in the software industry. Few expatriates currently work in the Korean software industry, in stark contrast to highly internationalized "industry clusters" for software development such as Silicon Valley. Lacking a substantial number of connections with leading centers for software development, the Korean software engineering industry is disconnected from trends developing in Silicon Valley,

Israel, or even Finland. For instance, in 2011, the Ministry of Knowledge Economy announced a government-led program to develop a computer operating system to counter the growing market power of software giants like Apple, Microsoft, and Google. This announcement, much to the government's chagrin, was criticized by a *Wall Street Journal* blog as having the "mentality of a developing nation." Considering that the government sought insufficient input from the private sector before making the announcement, this incident could charitably be attributed to policymakers' being out of touch with industry trends.[6] Nevertheless, the Korean government—acting in concert with major industry players—has repeatedly tried to develop and control software standards that no other country has adopted. Such tendencies to go against global trends indicate how peripheral Korea's software industry is and perhaps also indicate the industry's lack of transnational bridges.

Such peripherality has adversely affected Korean software firms in several important ways. Even more so than other Korean companies, software companies have had great difficulty in localizing their product to foreign markets, despite having commanding conceptual and technological leads over competitors in the United States and elsewhere. For instance, even with advanced technology and widespread adoption within the Korean home market as well as culturally similar Asian markets, software companies like the antivirus manufacturer AhnLabs and the video game manufacturer NCSoft have failed to gain traction in culturally dissimilar Europe or North America. Notably, the CyWorld case represents a tremendous missed opportunity not only for the company but also for Korea as a whole. CyWorld was one of the world's first online social networks, launched in 1999, long before Friendster's launch in 2002 and Facebook's debut in 2004. CyWorld became ubiquitous in the Korean market, gaining 19 million users by 2006. In its domestic market, CyWorld prospered by offering "mini-homepages" that users could decorate with flashy graphics and animations to express their unique personalities, as well as selling *dotori* (an online currency) that they could use to decorate their homepages or gift to their friends. CyWorld attempted to expand into the U.S. and European markets in 2006 but shuttered its European operations in 2008 and its U.S. operations in 2010.

Why did CyWorld fail in its international expansions despite its early success in Korea? Americans preferred Facebook's simpler layout over CyWorld's cluttered look. Furthermore, Facebook quickly incorporated

CyWorld-style virtual gifts into its platform, while CyWorld failed to incorporate Facebook's key innovation—the open architecture enabling embedded applications to run within Facebook. Had CyWorld been more integrated into broader developments in the online social network industry pioneered in Silicon Valley, it might have successfully entered the American market, prevented Facebook from growing into a global giant, and avoided being forced out of business even in its Korean home market.

All these missed opportunities point to Korea's lack of the transnational bridges needed to understand overseas consumer markets. How would Korean firms know about market conditions overseas if they lacked ties with "eyes on the ground" in that marketplace? Even if they did, how could they succeed if they disregarded the information they already had, as Samsung did with the iPhone?

Indian Engineers: Solutions and Challenges for Korea

This chapter investigates one potential solution to this problem—the recruitment of foreign software engineers. We illustrate it with a focus on software engineers from India, who are attractive to Korea for two reasons. First, India produces a surplus of skilled software engineers, a large proportion of which goes to overseas industry clusters such as Silicon Valley. While there are many reasons for India's success in software engineering, including knowledge of the English language, cheap bandwidth, and domestic entrepreneurship, its supply of well-trained engineers is undoubtedly another important factor. By recruiting some of these skilled individuals to Korea, firms located there would not only gain human capital but also transnational bridges to crucial software industry clusters like Silicon Valley and Bangalore. Second, Indian society privileges graduates of the Indian Institutes of Technology (IITs) over graduates of other leading universities—who are nearly as talented and skilled. For this reason, individuals from second-tier institutions appear particularly attracted to East Asian opportunities, rather than competing economically and socially against numerous IIT graduates in India and Silicon Valley. Korean firms can benefit from this pool of talent from India, if they are willing to strategically consider creative solutions. Here, we examine the challenges of identifying and recruiting such engineers and putting them in a position to succeed once they are in Korea.

BACKGROUND ON INDIAN ENGINEERS

India continues to produce a large surplus of well-trained software engineers, largely because its higher education system has dramatically increased the number of software engineers it trains—anticipating an increase in domestic demand that never materialized.

The Supply of Software Engineers

In India, most qualified software engineers receive their initial training across high-quality public and private universities. Over the past decade, the number of such trained engineers has grown tremendously. As of 2003 about 700,000 students were enrolled in undergraduate degree courses in engineering across all subfields. This number has risen rapidly in recent years and was estimated to be 3.26 million for the 2012–2013 academic year.[7] As Indian universities offer three-year programs, an estimated 1.07 million trained engineers entered the job market in 2013.[8]

India's public universities have long been recognized as leading centers of technical training, but nevertheless educate remarkably few students. Beyond setting and maintaining educational standards and accreditation procedures, the federal government also educates students directly by operating "centers of excellence." These national institutions are considered the best colleges and universities in India and include the highly prestigious IITs. During the 11th Plan Period (2007–2012), the number of federally run universities is scheduled to increase from 19 to 30, including an increase in the number of IITs from 7 to 15.[9] Yet, such schools will account for less than 20 percent of total student output.

India's private universities have expanded rapidly, given the scarcity of seats at public universities. Prior to 1991, the state took the view that higher education should be provided only by the state. However, the country experienced low rates of enrollment that have increasingly been attributed to exclusive state provision. Even as recently as 2010, India's gross enrollment ratio (the number of age-unadjusted enrollees as a share of the eligible population to go to university) remains at 12 percent, compared with 35 percent who complete secondary school. The state's failure to provide adequate higher education prompted a policy initiative in 1991 to encourage the growth of private institutions. Today, private institutions account for 80 percent of total student output—90 percent of the increase in student enrollment since 2001 has been in private institutions.

To be sure, the quality of engineers varies enormously. Without a doubt, the IITs produce engineers with excellent skills, but they represent less than 1 percent of the total at 9,647 in 2012. A much greater number of individuals have graduated from state and elite private universities in India. Although their quality may not be at the same level as that of ITT graduates, interviews with firms in Silicon Valley indicate that many such engineers have top-tier technical skills as well. Ten years ago, Intel had to vet the quality of engineers recruited from India. By 2009, this had ceased to be a concern.[10] Thus many—but certainly not all—Indian engineers can be qualified as the "global talent" we target in this chapter.

The Domestic Demand for Indian Engineers

The cost of hiring Indian engineers has remained remarkably stable over time despite rising skills and growing demand, as the supply of engineers has also increased. In fact, there has always been an oversupply of engineers in India. The domestic demand for engineers as a proportion of total supply peaked at 75.6 percent in 2007, before crashing to 18.2 percent in 2010 in the midst of the Great Recession. Since then, the proportion has fluctuated between 17 and 26 percent. With the demand being significantly lower than the supply, wages have stayed relatively low. In 2000, the wage of an engineer fresh out of college was $7,000 per year. Surprisingly, there has been virtually no change in the average wage for fresh graduates since that time. For this reason, Indian engineers have as strong an incentive to seek employment overseas as foreign companies are actively looking to hire them.

Identifying and Understanding Potential Recruits

In this chapter, we investigate which Indian engineers might be open to working in Korea and why. We primarily analyze data from an online survey of Indian engineers located in India and Silicon Valley, which we conducted in spring 2010. Working with Rafiq Dossani, an expert on India, we reached out to three well-established professional organizations known to have many Indian engineers as members. The first two organizations—the Silicon Valley Indian Professionals Association (SIPA) and the Indus Entrepreneurs (TiE)—mix socializing with professional connections. These organizations are notable for reinforcing ethnic identity while facilitating the information exchange, cooperation, and mentorship needed to succeed as profession-als in the information technology industry. TiE, headquartered in Silicon Valley, has 56 branches globally. Most are in India, followed by the United States. There are also branches in Kuala Lumpur and Tokyo (but not Seoul). The third organization—the National Association of Software and Services Companies (NASSCOM)—is a trade association of Indian information technology and business services organizations. NASSCOM plays a key role in advising the Indian government regarding technology policy. Like SIPA and TiE, NASSCOM maintains an email distribution list to individuals in-terested in NASSCOM events. We received assistance from SIPA, TiE, and NASSCOM in reaching their members through such distribution lists.

Our online survey collected information on the willingness of engineers to work overseas, including in Korea. The willingness was gauged in terms of opportunities for career development, job stability, earnings, innovation, and professional networks. Respondents were also asked about the attrac-tiveness of different locations based on various sociocultural attributes such as the hospitality of the local environment, adaptation in terms of language skills needed, and educational opportunities. The online questionnaire was distributed to SIPA and TiE members through the online SurveyMonkey platform.

Here, we closely analyze 27 respondents who completed the full survey.[11] While this group constitutes a relatively small proportion of all respondents, its members nevertheless have nearly identical biographical characteristics as the 79 respondents who provided biographical data but not geographic preference data, suggesting that the two groups are not significantly dif-ferent.[12] Nevertheless, we recognize the limitations of our sample, and our findings presented here should be taken only as suggestive. To add depth to our quantitative findings, we followed this survey with focus group discus-sions of both Silicon Valley and Indian respondents during summer 2010 and follow-up discussions during summer 2013, to ensure that the statistical findings found within our limited sample had external validity.

Table 5.4 presents key descriptive statistics for all respondents who com-pleted the survey. Survey respondents average 36.7 years of age, 81 percent have worked in India, and 63 percent have worked in the United States—56 percent are currently working there; 41 percent work in a nonmanage-rial technical role, while an additional 41 and 19 percent, respectively, work

TABLE 5.4
Comparison of four quadrants: Averages of biography and motivations

Variable	All	I	II	III	IV
Biographical characteristics					
Age	36.74	39.00	39.00	33.80	35.82
Has worked in India	0.81	0.50	0.80	0.80	1.00
Has worked in Japan	0.07	0.00	0.00	0.00	0.18
Has worked in Korea	0.04	0.00	0.00	0.00	0.09
Has worked in the United States	0.63	0.83	0.40	0.60	0.64
Currently working in the United States	0.56	0.67	0.40	0.40	0.64
Role at current employer[a]					
Nonmanagerial technical	0.41	0.50	0.20	0.20	0.55
Manager	0.41	0.50	0.60	0.60	0.18
Executive (director or above)	0.19	0.00	0.00	0.40	0.27
Entrepreneur (founder)	0.07	0.00	0.20	0.00	0.09
Investor (angel, vulture capital, or private equity)	0.04	0.17	0.00	0.00	0.00
Educational characteristics					
Degree from an IIT campus	0.26	0.50	0.00	0.00	0.36
Degree from a U.S. university	0.37	0.33	0.20	0.40	0.36
Determinants of geographic preferences[b]					
Current earnings	4.41	4.83	4.20	4.40	4.27
Career advancement	4.44	4.83	4.40	4.40	4.27
Job stability	4.15	4.17	4.80	4.40	3.73
Professional networks—local	3.70	3.33	4.20	3.80	3.64
Professional networks—global	4.04	4.17	4.20	4.00	3.91
Innovative environment	4.30	4.50	4.40	4.00	4.27
Startup opportunities	4.07	4.17	3.60	4.20	4.18
Investment opportunities	3.74	4.17	3.60	3.20	3.82
Educational opportunities: self/spouse	3.22	3.33	3.80	3.20	2.91
Educational opportunities: children	4.00	4.33	3.60	4.00	4.00
English speaking	3.59	3.50	3.80	4.20	3.27
Hospitable culture	4.15	3.83	4.20	4.00	4.36
Proximity to family	3.67	3.50	3.60	4.00	3.64

[a]Some respondents indicated multiple roles at their current employers.
[b]Measured on a 5-point scale with 1 indicating no importance and 5 indicating great importance.

as managers or executives. A small proportion worked either as entrepreneurs or startup-related investors. Regardless of their current roles, however, nearly all respondents had an engineering background (not shown). This finding is consistent with the perception that Indian engineers seek to climb the corporate ladder as quickly as possible, to move aggressively into management roles. At least 26 percent have one degree from one of several Indian Institute of Technology campuses, while 37 percent have at least one degree from a U.S. university, split evenly between elite institutions (e.g.,

U.C. Berkeley, MIT) and nonelite institutions (e.g., Santa Clara University, Portland State University).

Survey respondents referred to several different factors as important when choosing specific geographic locations. On average, survey respondents considered all of the factors listed in Table 5.4 to be important or very important when choosing a geographic location. The potential for career advancement (4.44/5.00), current earnings (4.41/5.00), and an innovative environment (4.30/5.00) were cited as particularly important, while educational opportunities for the respondent and his or her spouse (3.22/5.00), an English-speaking environment (3.59/5.00), local professional networks (3.70/5.00), and investment opportunities (3.74/5.00) were mentioned as comparatively less important.

Table 5.5 shows how respondents rated five selected geographic locations—China, India, Japan, Korea, and Silicon Valley in the United States—according to the work opportunities and the sociocultural environments they offered. Not surprisingly, Silicon Valley rated highest (4.96/7.00) on the *overall perception* aspect, followed by India (4.33/7.00), Korea (3.78/7.00), Japan (3.70/7.00), and China (3.07/7.00). This pattern is found in most other aspects as well with few exceptions, reflecting the significant attraction Silicon Valley holds for many Indian engineers. However, the preference for Silicon Valley and India over Asian locations is not uniformly held among respondents. For instance, India and Korea scored higher than Silicon Valley in the *proximity to family* aspect, given that many respondents had family members in India. This has important implications in formulating recruitment strategies.

DIVERSITY IN INDIAN ENGINEERS

As with other groups examined in the previous chapters, the Indian engineers responding to our survey reveal variation in several key dimensions—age and experience, geographic location, current role, and educational achievement. Consequently, to properly address heterogeneity rather than generalizing about Indian engineers as a whole, we conducted a correspondence analysis of our sample, including all characteristics of these 27 respondents that we described in Tables 5.4 and 5.5.

As Figure 5.2 shows, the empirical analysis finds two main dimensions here. The first dimension, shown on the *X* axis, corresponds with a respondent's geographic preferences. Individuals located further to the right on

TABLE 5.5
Comparison of four quadrants: Perceptions of selected geographic locations

Characteristic	Location	All	I	II	III	IV
Current earnings	China	3.15	1.33	2.60	5.20	3.45
	India	3.74	4.00	1.60	5.20	3.91
	Japan	4.22	3.83	1.60	5.00	5.27
	Korea (South)	3.85	2.33	2.20	5.80	4.55
	Silicon Valley	5.04	6.67	1.80	3.40	6.36
Career advancement	China	3.33	1.33	2.60	5.40	3.82
	India	4.26	5.00	1.60	3.80	5.27
	Japan	3.93	2.33	1.60	5.80	5.00
	Korea (South)	3.81	2.00	1.60	6.00	4.82
	Silicon Valley	4.74	6.67	2.00	3.40	5.55
Job stability	China	4.07	3.50	3.20	4.40	4.64
	India	4.93	6.50	1.80	4.40	5.73
	Japan	4.11	2.50	2.20	4.40	5.73
	Korea (South)	4.41	3.00	2.40	6.00	5.36
	Silicon Valley	4.85	5.17	3.60	5.60	4.91
Innovative environment	China	3.78	2.67	3.20	6.00	3.64
	India	4.33	4.33	2.60	5.00	4.82
	Japan	4.41	3.67	2.00	5.20	5.55
	Korea (South)	4.22	3.00	2.60	5.40	5.09
	Silicon Valley	5.15	6.50	2.00	3.20	6.73
Startup opportunities	China	4.00	3.33	2.80	6.00	4.00
	India	4.67	4.50	2.80	4.40	5.73
	Japan	3.81	1.83	4.20	5.60	3.91
	Korea (South)	4.07	3.00	3.00	6.20	4.18
	Silicon Valley	5.22	6.50	3.20	3.00	6.45
Investment opportunities	China	4.15	3.33	3.80	4.40	4.64
	India	4.41	3.83	1.60	4.00	6.18
	Japan	3.78	2.00	4.20	5.00	4.00
	Korea (South)	4.07	3.00	3.00	5.80	4.36
	Silicon Valley	5.26	6.17	3.80	3.00	6.45
Professional networks	China	3.26	1.33	2.80	5.80	3.36
	India	4.41	4.50	1.80	5.00	5.27
	Japan	3.70	2.00	2.00	5.80	4.45
	Korea (South)	3.81	2.17	2.60	6.00	4.27
	Silicon Valley	4.93	6.33	1.20	3.40	6.55
English proficiency	China	3.33	1.17	4.00	6.80	2.64
	India	4.93	5.33	1.80	3.80	6.64
	Japan	4.04	2.67	3.60	6.60	3.82
	Korea (South)	3.74	2.00	2.80	6.20	4.00
	Silicon Valley	5.04	6.50	1.40	3.40	6.64
Hospitable culture	China	3.11	1.50	3.40	3.80	3.55
	India	5.11	6.67	2.20	3.40	6.36
	Japan	4.11	3.17	2.40	4.00	5.45
	Korea (South)	4.00	2.50	2.80	4.20	5.27
	Silicon Valley	4.93	5.83	1.80	3.80	6.36

TABLE 5.5 (*continued*)

Characteristic	Location	All	I	II	III	IV
Education (self/spouse)	China	3.11	1.33	3.00	5.80	2.91
	India	4.81	5.33	3.20	4.40	5.45
	Japan	3.48	1.83	2.80	4.40	4.27
	Korea (South)	3.52	2.17	2.60	4.80	4.09
	Silicon Valley	4.70	6.33	2.40	1.60	6.27
Education (children)	China	3.07	1.50	2.40	5.20	3.27
	India	4.52	5.33	3.00	2.00	5.91
	Japan	3.63	1.83	3.00	4.00	4.73
	Korea (South)	3.74	2.17	2.00	4.80	4.91
	Silicon Valley	5.04	6.33	2.40	3.00	6.45
Proximity to family	China	3.63	3.17	3.80	4.60	3.36
	India	5.00	6.00	1.80	3.00	6.82
	Japan	3.78	3.17	3.20	5.00	3.82
	Korea (South)	4.07	4.00	2.80	5.20	4.18
	Silicon Valley	4.00	3.67	3.60	4.20	4.27
Overall perception	China	3.07	1.67	2.40	5.40	3.09
	India	4.33	4.67	1.80	3.60	5.64
	Japan	3.70	2.33	2.20	4.80	4.64
	Korea (South)	3.78	2.33	2.40	5.00	4.64
	Silicon Valley	4.96	6.33	2.20	2.80	6.45

NOTE: All variables are shown on a 7-point scale where 1 = weakest and 7 = strongest.

Figure 5.1 tend to rate Japan, Korea, and particularly China as superior environments to work and live, along all work-related and sociocultural aspects about which we queried respondents. In contrast, individuals located further to the left tend to rate India and particularly Silicon Valley more highly. Interestingly enough, individuals who had previously spent time in Korea or Japan were more likely to favor Silicon Valley and India, perhaps indicating dissatisfaction with their experiences. This dimension accounted for 12.3 percent of total variation among all variables in the analysis. The second dimension, shown on the Y axis, corresponds with a respondent's age and experience. Individuals located further to the top tend to be older and more experienced while individuals located further to the bottom tend to be younger and less experienced. Correspondingly, individuals higher on this dimension tend to place greater weight upon family-related quality-of-life issues such as educational opportunities for children, as well as investment opportunities. An interesting anomaly is that older, more experienced respondents tend to be managers—but that younger, less experienced respondents are more likely to be executives. The data suggest that this might

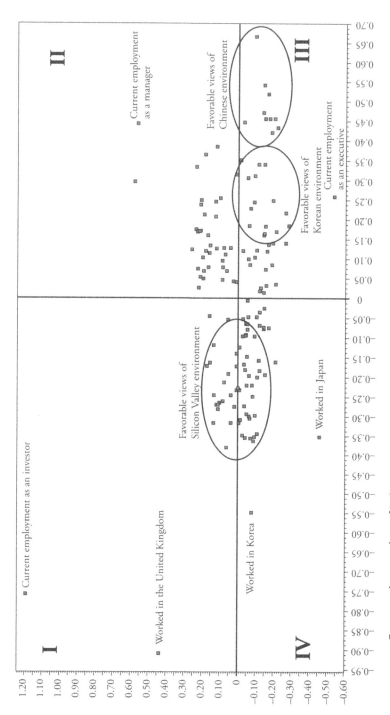

FIGURE 5.2 Correspondence analysis of Indian engineers

reflect the entrepreneurialism and aggressiveness of some young Indians with an engineering background, who ascend the corporate ladder quickly after receiving their MBAs. This dimension accounted for 7.9 percent of total variation among all variables in the analysis. On both dimensions, the zero point indicates the sample mean.

These dimensions divide sampled Indian engineers into four groups corresponding to the quadrants shown in Figure 5.1. Group I represents experienced engineers oriented toward the United States and India. While this group has an overwhelmingly positive overall impression of Silicon Valley (6.33/7.00) and a positive impression of India (4.33/7.00), it has very negative impressions of Korea (2.33/7.00), Japan (2.33/7.00), and China (1.67/7.00) (see Table 5.5). Group II represents experienced engineers that are more oriented toward East Asia—but only in relative terms. In stark contrast to group I, group II has negative impressions of all environments (1.80–2.40/7.00). Group III represents less experienced engineers oriented toward East Asia. In a reversal of group I's pattern, group III has much better impressions of China (5.40/7.00), Korea (5.00/7.00), and Japan (4.80/7.00) than India (3.60/7.00) or even Silicon Valley (2.80/7.00). Group IV represents less experienced engineers oriented toward Silicon Valley and India. Like group I, group IV has very positive impressions of Silicon Valley (6.45/7.00) and India (5.64/7.00). Group IV also has positive impressions of Japan and Korea (both 4.64/7.00), having a negative impression of only China (3.09/7.00).

Why is group III more receptive to Asian opportunities compared to the otherwise similar group IV? Table 5.4 offers some clues. While a substantial number of group IV respondents (36 percent) have received a degree from one of the IIT campuses, no group III respondent holds such a degree. Many Indians and non-Indians alike view the IITs as world-class institutions that provide an elite education far more cheaply than top U.S. or European institutions. IIT graduates gain substantial prestige, as well as job opportunities not available to graduates of other Indian or even U.S. universities—both in Silicon Valley and in India. Rather than competing with IIT graduates, those from quality Indian institutions other than the IITs may seek career opportunities elsewhere in which their lack of an IIT degree would not hinder their professional opportunities.

Our interviews with Indian engineers suggest that IIT graduates are treated very differently from graduates of other quality universities in India.

Ramesh—an experienced process engineer who worked in India and Japan and now is based out of Hong Kong doing significant amounts of work in mainland China—had much to say about this distinction. He acknowledged that the superiority of IIT graduates is a "fact" known to all engineers in India:

> The IITs are the only institutes that offer an engineering education with focus on practice, opportunities to explore, and freedom to investigate. The other colleges have a set curriculum that is fairly easy to master, but without much exposure to practical applications . . . it is also true that IIT graduates do have awesome aptitude and intellect and our country is proud of this.

Nevertheless, Ramesh—who had not graduated from an IIT—described the resentment that many other Indian engineers felt about the superior opportunities offered to IIT graduates, matter of factly expressing that "IIT engineers are the preferred choice of Indian and foreign tech companies due to IIT's reputation. They used to, and I believe still, receive higher salaries for same job profile." He suggested that non-IIT graduates found the social deference that IIT graduates received to be particularly galling:

> [The economic advantages that IIT graduates received] kept fuelling their attitude of superiority against non-IIT graduates. . . . It is not normal for IITians to mingle with non-IITians, perhaps both due to difference levels of intellect, completely separate curriculums, and maybe also attitude.

Such feelings might explain why graduates of quality Indian institutions other than the IITs would be interested in working in geographic locations where their lack of an IIT degree would not hinder their opportunities. Perceptions persist that the best Indian engineers end up working in Silicon Valley and India while those one tier down find their destination in various Asian countries. For instance, one Indian human resource manager at a large multinational firm, upon hearing that Ramesh was working in Japan at the time, asked him:

> Which institute have you graduated from? Not the IIT's, right? Because the cream of our engineers from IITs will go to US or UK, the not-so-skilled would go to Europe or Japan, followed by Hong Kong and Singapore. The remaining would go to Dubai.

After relating this quote to us, Ramesh vigorously countered its implications, saying, "While this would be based on [that individual's] experience in HR, I differ on this point. I've met several knowledgeable and highly skilled Indians in Japan and Hong Kong, much more skilled and talented than I am. [Such individuals] also seem to be well off in Asia, much more closely bonded to their families in India." Indeed, Ramesh mentioned that he had personally had an excellent experience working in Tokyo and had left only after the 2011 Tohoku earthquake and the following nuclear crisis.

Taken together, our quantitative findings, as well as our qualitative interviews with Ramesh and other Indian engineers, strongly suggest that the social divide between IIT and non-IIT graduates offers a real opportunity for countries like Korea that need high-quality software engineers but cannot attract IIT graduates.

KOREAN FIRMS FOR INDIAN ENGINEERS

Indeed, our findings indicate that individuals belonging to group III—predominantly not IIT graduates—would be especially receptive to opportunities in Korea if these were structured correctly. Our survey compared the attractiveness of five countries or regions, China, India, Japan, Korea, and Silicon Valley, across various dimensions (see Table 5.5). We presented above the results for several characteristics of these countries or regions that are deemed to be important by respondents. These are earnings potential, career development, job stability, the opportunity to build and benefit from professional networks, the innovativeness of the environment, and the opportunity to build startups in the environment. Note that the priority rankings—how important it is for the working environment to offer these characteristics—are high for all attributes. In other words, Indian engineers are most likely to think through all of these attributes before deciding to work in Korea.

Group III respondents have particularly favorable views of work opportunities in East Asian countries in general and Korea in specific. Why? Our focus group discussions with India-based respondents suggest that these perceptions are based on several factors.

First, Korea is viewed as a global leader in certain IT-related fields. Based on the strength of its consumer electronics products, Korean firms are respected as leaders in mobile applications, embedded software for operating systems and applications, digital entertainment, and displays. Working for a Korean company rather than a large Indian company would give engineers exposure to different kinds of products and technologies not available in

India, such as memory management and power consumption technologies. For such projects, Korean firms such as Samsung and LG would be very attractive to Indian engineers. Even if they return to India after working in Korea for a few years, the experience gained would, according to our respondents, yield them significant career advantages.

Simultaneously, Korean firms are viewed as innovators for low-cost economies. One interviewee noted that "unlike American firms such as Intel and SAP, Korean firms such as Samsung, LG, Hyundai, and the SK Group are able to produce innovative products suited to low-cost environments like India." This is taken as significant given the growing importance of low-income countries like India and China to the fortunes of the world's largest companies.

Some Indian engineers felt that they had better career prospects in Korea than in the United States or India. Such respondents, in their discussions about why this might be the case, note that it would take much longer to be able to do sophisticated work in Silicon Valley. They cite examples of their classmates working in the United States being assigned relatively low-end work, such as writing financial applications for mainframes. Thus, they believe that they would be given more responsibility more quickly in Korea. Along the same lines, many Indian engineers consider the working environment in the United States too competitive, leading to the likelihood of job instability without any significant earnings advantages. Korea was perceived to offer a stable job environment with adequate earnings potential. There is a sentiment that Korean and Japanese firms treat workers better like family, whereas in Silicon Valley younger engineers are not well treated.

Overall, our interviews with several Indian engineers suggest that they feel that Korean firms offer work-intensive but supportive environments. The work culture, especially compared to the one in Japanese and Chinese firms, was viewed as open and friendly. In the workplace, language was not a significant issue for doing technical work. Thanks to the success of large IT firms from India, such as TCS, Infosys, and Wipro, Indian engineers greatly respected process knowledge rather than just product development. The large Korean firms appear to be attractive in this respect.

EMBEDDING INDIAN ENGINEERS INTO KOREAN SOCIETY AND ECONOMY

These Indian engineers can offer much needed human capital for Korean firms, and leading Korean companies now actively recruit them. As of 2013, for instance, Indians constitute about one quarter of the 36,000 software engineers at Samsung, and this number is likely to increase as Korea continues to face a shortage of quality engineers in the software sector. To maximize the efficacy of Indian engineers, however, Korea must also pay close attention to their potential as social capital. At the very least, local bridges must be built between Indian engineers and their Korean counterparts. Otherwise, given that Indian engineers are likely to leave Korea after a few years, they risk becoming failed bridges.[13] Korea must assist them in becoming embedded into Korean society and economy to some degree. Those who are locally well embedded are more likely to play a transnational bridging role even after they leave the country.

It seems that the main concerns for Indian engineers working in Korean firms relate primarily to job tenure and the glass ceiling. Most Indian engineers, both in India and overseas, are not willing to build long-term careers in Korea, while those located in the United States see Silicon Valley as a more attractive destination for high-end work. Those in India are likely to want to work in Korea for three to five years early on in their careers as a career-building move. While in Korea, they would like to work in fields in which Korea excels. For a software engineer, this could include sophisticated fields such as embedded software for various purposes. After building these skills, the engineer would hope to move to higher value-added, more innovative environments such as Silicon Valley.

Another major concern has to do with the perception of a glass ceiling—the perception that a long-term career within Korea would mean that a foreign technician has little prospect of moving into the ranks of top management. Since Indian engineers are hierarchical and desire to move into management rather quickly, this is an important issue for them. Our interview with the director of the Korea Trade-Investment Promotion Agency (KOTRA) in India confirms this perception of a glass ceiling among Indians, consistent with the widespread belief that Korean firms remain reluctant to offer managerial positions to foreigners in general.[14] Yet, some of these concerns might arise from a lack of knowledge of the Korean language necessary to become a high-level manager.

Another challenge in embedding Indian engineers in Korea has much to do with sociocultural factors outside the workplace environment, such as barriers created by local language difficulties, poor acceptance of Indians by the local population, especially poor understanding of their religion and culture, reduced educational opportunities for children, and related factors (see Table 5.5). Of these, language, hospitality, and children's education were high-priority items for all respondents, even in group III. Our focus group discussions further indicate that working in Korea would become more difficult for a married engineer given the difficulty of managing dual careers in Korea. Respondents would also like to plan families in the United States, perhaps to obtain better education and/or citizenship for their children.

While the Korean government and firms can conceivably address some of the concerns that Indians have about the workplace environment, it will be more challenging and difficult to address non-work-related issues. On one hand, Indian engineers are concerned that they could not truly integrate into Korean society, be fully accepted, or ascend in economic or social status. This is particularly important because Indian engineers appear exceptionally status conscious. On the other hand, Koreans generally lack a good understanding of Indian culture, foods, and religion and have a strong jus sanguinis view of nationality and citizenship. Since Indians physically look different from Koreans and come from a very different cultural and religious background, Koreans are not likely to accept ethnic Indians as full members of Korean society, even if they regard them as valuable to the Korean economy.[15] For these reasons, Indian engineers and their Korean hosts may agree that the best strategy for Korea would be to continually recruit new Indian engineers to work in Korea for three to five years each until the country is better prepared to accept them socially and culturally, and that is indeed what has been happening in recent years.

Nevertheless, Korea can reduce many of these difficulties by building an ethnic enclave for Indians, most likely in Seoul or a nearby suburb. According to our interviews, Indian engineers were concerned about a language barrier in Korea, as well as their children's education. An ethnic enclave would provide a safe, secure haven for Indian engineers within Korean society, where they would have access to their home culture and perhaps socialize their children along Indian standards. To date, Korea lacks such an enclave. For instance, one of our focus group participants highlighted his difficulty finding decent Indian foods while working in Korea. This is consistent with Eun Mee Kim and Jean Kang's (2007) study of ethnic enclaves in Seoul, which finds Korean Chinese, Chinese Korean, Japanese, French, Italian, Mongolian, Filipino, and pan-Islamic enclaves, but not an Indian enclave. Indeed, the small Indian community there is centered on embassy staff and their families and excluded most other Indians. As Kim and Kang emphasize, the presence of an ethnic enclave provides ethnic minorities in Seoul with a home base from which to operate, where they might obtain key resources. Such an enclave would make Korea more attractive not only to Indian engineers but also to other foreigners wanting to experience Indian cuisine and culture.

Locally embedding Indian engineers into Korean society and culture is even more important from the social capital perspective. As mentioned above, Indian engineers and potential recruits want to work for three to five years in Korea early on in their career after completing an undergraduate degree. They would see this as a career-building move to acquire global skills in fields in which Korea excels on their way to other more attractive places such as Silicon Valley. In fact, some Korean executives who we interviewed lamented the high turnover rate among Indian engineers working for them. This is understandable as it is a loss for Korea from the human capital perspective. As argued throughout this book, however, this can be valuable insofar as they remain tied to Korea and play a crucial bridging role from the social capital perspective. Considering the well-established nature of global networks among Indian engineers, individuals well embedded into Korean culture and society may very well play a bridging role, and Korea should not overlook the importance of such social capital potential.[16]

SAMSUNG'S REVENGE

While LG has yet to mount an effective counter to the iPhone threat—and indeed, has faded as a manufacturer of high-end mobile phones—Samsung has countered Apple with an advanced smartphone of its own. Adopting Google's Android platform for some of its phones, Samsung has been extremely successful. In mid-2010, Samsung rolled out the Galaxy S line of smartphones across 110 different countries. The Galaxy S rapidly became the best-selling smartphone using the Android operating system, designed to compete with the iPhone. Despite being sold for only six or seven months in most major markets across the world, 10 million copies of the Galaxy S and its variants were sold in 2010 alone. Samsung followed up on this success by introducing substantial upgrades in the series every year. These phones were wildly successful across all global markets, and were sometimes called "iPhone Killers." Based on these successes, Samsung has sold more smartphones than Apple as of October 2013 and has reemerged as a strategic threat to Apple and its iPhone. By smartphone sales, Samsung is now "absolutely crushing Apple," selling 71 million smartphones into various sales channels in the second quarter of 2013 versus 27 million iPhones sold in the same period.[17]

Indian engineers have played a hidden but surprisingly important role in Samsung's resurgence. Samsung has nearly doubled its number of software engineers, from under 20,000 in 2009 up to 36,000 as of April 2013. Of these employees, 16,000 are foreigners—including 9,000 in India. Samsung has already opened large-scale software research and development centers in Noida, Bangalore, and Delhi.[18] Simultaneously, Samsung appears to be aggressively courting third-party Indian developers who had previously been committed to providing applications for the now-defunct Symbian platform, to develop applications for its in-house Tizen platform. Also, Samsung has started bringing Indian software engineers to its home research and development facilities in Seoul and Suwon in Korea.[19]

Samsung's resurgence nevertheless reflects Korea's weakness in software engineering. Instead of creating a direct competitor to the iPhone operating system, Samsung has either adopted a third-party alternative (i.e., Android) or competed in a lower-tier niche (i.e., Bada/Tizen). Media reports mention that Samsung and LG have been forced into this position because of their weakness in software engineering. More systematic recruiting of Indian software engineers may alleviate this position. However, they may not stay for long in Korea for the reasons mentioned above. Therefore, Korea should also seriously consider ways to utilize them as social capital (i.e., bridging Korea with the place of their future work) even after their departure. In a rapidly globalizing world, the value of such social capital will only increase.

SIX

Toward a Global Korea

In February 2013, Park Geun-hye—Korea's newly elected president—nominated Jeong H. Kim to lead the newly established Ministry of Science, ICT, & Future Planning. Kim, a Korean American scientist and entrepreneur who was then the president of Bell Labs, was eminently qualified for this cabinet-level position. Having emigrated from Korea as a teenager, he founded an information technology company that made him a billionaire before heading Bell Labs, legendary birthplace of innovations such as the laser, the transistor, and the C programming language. Kim would have been the ideal person to take charge of this new ministry and realize President Park's vision of the "creative economy." He would have brought to Korea not only his own professional knowledge and rich experience but also his social capital—the global network that he had assembled as a successful businessman and academic. President Park appeared to recognize the importance of global talent when she offered Kim a key ministerial position.

However, Korea was not ready to accept a "foreigner" as a top government official—even someone they had previously labeled a "proud Korean." Kim was well known to Koreans even before his nomination, as the story of how Kim achieved the so-called American Dream had been celebrated in Korea through documentaries and other media coverage. Yet, Kim's candidacy proved deeply divisive. Although some Koreans took his nomination as a positive sign of a globalizing Korea, others reacted less favorably. The news media, reporting on elements of Kim's American background, including his U.S. citizenship, service in the U.S. Navy, and former position on an external advisory board to the CIA, expressed unfavorable opinions like:

"No country in the world would appoint someone to a government post who had formerly served as an adviser to a foreign intelligence agency."[1] Some Koreans nicknamed Kim as "Mr. Import Jeong H." or even accused him of being a "CIA spy." To counter such concerns, Kim not only restored his Korean citizenship but also reportedly offered to forfeit his U.S. citizenship. Yet, such moves were not enough to appease his critics in the media and political opposition. Kim, who had stated, "I left behind what I have built in the United States and returned home so I could devote the rest of my life to the country where I was born," eventually withdrew his candidacy and returned to the United States with what he called "shattered dreams."[2]

This episode speaks to the central arguments of this book. Korea, as an advanced country, found itself needing to recognize the value of global talent to establish new engines of growth, or what the current Park administration is calling the creative economy. Many ethnic Koreans overseas, like Kim, remain closely attached to Korea and are willing to return to serve their motherland. These individuals, especially those whom we call "rooted businessmen," would return to Korea not only with their skills and knowledge—human capital—but also with tremendous social capital. Yet the potential for a strong nationalistic reaction, as seen in Kim's case, poses a significant challenge that Korea must overcome if it is to become a true leader in the global economy.[3]

A Global Korea?

Korea has undoubtedly established itself as an economic power, remaining among the largest 15 national economies for over two decades.[4] As a leading producer of ships, automobiles, and various electronic goods, the country currently stands as the world's seventh largest exporter.[5] Korea is the only member of the OECD to have become a provider of foreign aid after having been a recipient and has hosted a number of important global meetings in Seoul, including the G20 Summit and the Nuclear Summit. In fact, the Lee Myung Bak government (2008–2012) proudly proclaimed that the nation had become "Global Korea."

Korea's rapid rise from poverty to high-income OECD status has become an exemplary template for economic advancement to developing countries in and around the region. Unlike developed European and North American countries, Korea shares key cultural similarities with many neighboring countries in East and Southeast Asia. Furthermore, Korea's rise from poverty remains within living memory, unlike Japan's earlier ascent. For these reasons, Korea has been a particularly attractive model for many countries attempting to achieve economic development. As Chapter 2 shows, students from less developed parts of the world, especially in Asia, come to Korea specifically to study Korea's developmental model in hopes of realizing it in their own countries. The Korean government is also actively promoting its developmental model to developing countries through the Knowledge Sharing Program.

Ironically, respectful emulation has created new competitive challenges for the Korean economy. As many other industrializing countries such as China have become strong competitors in the same export industries that Korea recently dominated, it has experienced greater competitive pressures. In the 1990s, many Korea observers worried that the nation would succumb to a "medium-technology trap," sandwiched between lower-cost developing countries like China and high-tech Japan. Although Korea escaped this trap by mastering advanced technologies such as semiconductors and wireless communications, it nevertheless faces increasing competition in its niche of high-tech manufacturing. Korea's heavy reliance on this increasingly dangerous niche, rather than lucrative service-sector industries such as finance and business services, highlights how the country has reached the limits of its export-oriented industrialization.

Korean society is also beginning to show symptoms of social decline associated with many advanced economies, including declining fertility rates, an aging population, and a growing demand for unskilled laborers. In response to the lack of locals willing to take the so-called 3D (dirty, difficult, and dangerous) jobs, Korea has imported migrant laborers from other parts of Asia. According to the Korean Statistics Office, there were 791,000 foreign workers in the country as of June 2012, over 70 percent of whom were unskilled laborers.[6]

Acknowledging that unskilled migrant workers play an important role in the Korean economy, we propose that Korea should also recognize that a shortage of key individuals with technical or professional skills who can compete in the global market—global talent—may undermine its economic potential. Koreans should understand that globalization is not merely about building infrastructure or competing over sales in the global market. To attain sustainable growth in a globalized future, their nation must become more competitive in securing human talent. In other words, what will determine the country's economic vitality is no longer simply "hardware" such as capital investment; "software" such as human resources and social ties are becoming increasingly more critical for Korea as it moves into a more central position in the global economy. Accordingly, the political leaders and policymakers of Korea and other developed countries must devote greater attention to the value of global talent beyond unskilled labor. This opportunity is especially timely for Korea, as it is poised to shift its attention away from unskilled foreigners toward global talent, especially given its enhanced role in regional and global economies.

We emphasize that the most fruitful opportunities may involve social capital rather than human capital. In our first chapter, we called for a model of labor recruitment that acknowledges the human capital benefits valued by a so-called old model but that focuses instead on a new model highlighting social capital benefits—skilled foreigners' ability to bridge their home and host societies. Until recently, discussions of foreign labor have concentrated on human capital, overlooking the significant benefits that accrue from interpersonal social ties that spread market information, diffuse innovation, and facilitate trust between different cultures and societies. While human capital remains a key ingredient for national economic competitiveness, its contribution is limited as the technical skills and professional experiences possessed by individuals travel with them and cannot be separated from them. The new model, conversely, speaks to the potential of social capital and prizes bidirectional brain circulation rather than zero-sum brain drain. It points to the importance of recruiting global talent in transforming the country into the global Korea that the Korean government proclaimed it to be.

Attracting Global Talent

In this book, we have examined how advanced, nonimmigrant countries like Korea can recruit skilled foreign labor, not only as an embodiment of human capital but also for the social capital they potentially provide. We appreciate the old model's focus on recruiting skilled foreigners for their human capital. This model certainly remains relevant because many societies will soon be facing a serious decline in their working-age populations and will need to replenish their pools of skilled workers to support their growing number of retirees. However, we also draw upon the new model's focus on recruiting skilled foreigners for their social capital. The transnational bridges that they create should help nation-states and their associated ethnocentric corporations gain information on geographically distant markets, cooperate with foreign partners, and learn about disruptive innovations originating elsewhere. Overall, transnational bridges provide immediate competitive benefits in the international business arena.

Recruiting skilled foreigners and building transnational bridges, however, is not a trivial task—especially for nonimmigrant countries like Korea. To gain human and social capital, nation-states and their associated ethnocentric corporations are competing intensely against one another to recruit the most skilled, educated, and talented individuals worldwide. With intensifying globalization and demographic shifts, the competition for global talent among advanced countries will only increase in the coming years. Unlike the settler societies, a large group of developed, ethnically more homogeneous countries—including not only Korea but also others such as Germany, Poland, Italy, and Japan—face similar disadvantages attracting skilled foreigners because they have a national identity based upon shared ancestry and tend to exclude individuals lacking the same bloodline. Outsiders not only have difficulty assimilating to the culture but also tend to be socially ostracized. Here, we focus upon exploring creative strategies for such countries to overcome these disadvantages and recruit the skilled foreigners they need.

As our empirical chapters have demonstrated, global talent does not consist of a single homogeneous group, requiring a differentiated approach toward different target groups. That is to say, carefully differentiated strategies ought to be employed depending on which group of global talent a country is targeting. In this book, we empirically support our central arguments with analysis of four such groups for Korea.

The first group is foreign students in Korea. Our study shows that, whether they study technical or nontechnical subjects, they have great potential to contribute to Korea. To be sure, the specific skills (i.e., human capital) possessed by foreign students do matter, and those who study in technical fields (e.g., engineering) at top Korean universities can most likely provide immediate human capital for Korean firms. At the same time, foreign students' willingness and ability to bridge Korea with their home countries may matter no less. In fact, many of them—or those whom we call "Koreaphiles"—can provide reciprocal benefits to Korea and their home countries as they learn Korea's economic and technological developmental model to bring back home. It also should be stressed that a larger proportion of students willing to bridge Korea with their home countries may come from business-related fields rather than technical fields.

As such, foreign students in Korea may not only contribute human capital to Korea by working there short or long-term but also bridge Korea with their home countries by building relevant social ties in Korea before returning home. Given that most of these foreign students are likely to remain in Korea for some years of study and work, the primary task for the Korean government and universities alike is to foster their interest in bridging Korea and their home countries. As they link Korea with developing Asia and spread successful Korean practices, Korea would solidify its increasingly central position in that part of the region and become an economic hub beyond its current status as a cultural one in Asia. Once again, the current thinking among researchers and policymakers in Korea focuses disproportionately on students' human capital contributions and should be reconsidered to appreciate their potential as social capital.

Regarding Korean students abroad, a main task and challenge is to transform brain drain into brain circulation. While many of these Korean students return home and contribute their professional skills and experiences, there is also the opportunity for them to play another important role, becoming "private ambassadors" for Korea in their host countries. Even if they remain overseas, they may still contribute to Korea's social capital by remaining connected to Korea while becoming embedded in their host societies. Current debate on Korea's brain drain focuses on students who return home, while overlooking how students who remain in their host countries after graduation might function as social capital. In the old model, such students have little to contribute to Korean society and may be considered examples of brain drain. However, in the new model that we advocate here, they can potentially bridge Korea and their host countries. Accordingly, we should pay proper attention to Korean students who may not necessarily return home after education but who are nevertheless willing to work with Koreans and perhaps work for Korean firms. A key policy implication would be to provide rich identity-related social and cultural experiences for such individuals. If Korean students abroad can remain familiar with Korea and its culture, they may be considerably more likely to play a bridging role.

The diaspora community should also be thought of as a potential source of human and social capital for Korea. Until now, the majority of those returning to work in Korea have been ethnic Koreans from China. Being mostly unskilled workers, such returnees have provided Korea with low-end human capital in the manufacturing and service industries. Largely lacking professional ties in China, however, they remain limited in terms of the social capital that they could contribute. In contrast, other segments of the Korean diaspora could potentially contribute more human and social capital; those in North America represent one such group. These individuals are well educated, may have some experience as professionals, and remain attached to their ancestral homeland. The Korean government has recognized the strategic value of overseas Koreans—especially Korean Americans—and has implemented several government-led initiatives targeting this group. For example, the Kim Dae Jung government (1998–2002) instituted a special law to utilize overseas Koreans as a national resource for development in the global era.

While these individuals find Korea interesting and hospitable and their Korean heritage valuable, many are nevertheless likely to explore Korea for only a short time and then return to their "home" countries, where they are more comfortable. Accordingly, there is a need to search for creative ways to utilize their deep talent without necessarily bringing them to Korea. A few countries with strong ethnic identities have successfully instituted programs designed less to recruit their diaspora back home and more to strengthen their connections with their respective diasporas. For instance, the Birthright Israel program brings 51,000 religiously and ethnically Jewish young adults into Israel every year for sojourns to reawaken Jewish identities among members of the diaspora and to strengthen their ties to resident Israelis. Funded by the Israeli government in conjunction with private donors, Birthright Israel will eventually bring one of every two members of the Jewish diaspora into Israel. The program has been such a success that it was copied by Armenia and Greece, two other countries with large diasporas that maintain strong sense of ethnic identity. Although Korea lacks an official program like Birthright Israel, many members of the Korean diaspora, like Jeong H. Kim, nevertheless gravitate back to Korea.

The last group that merits Korea's close attention consists of "true foreigners" with no preexisting connection to Korea. To illustrate this group's potential as human and social capital, we examined Indian engineers who can address the shortage of software engineering in Korean firms. Indian engineers are among the most sought-after group of skilled foreigners in the world, mainly as they possess an increasingly important type of human capital—software engineering and programming skills. The influx of Indian engineers has proved spectacularly successful in the case of Silicon Valley, which also faced a severe shortfall of engineering talent. It is no surprise, then, that Korean firms like Samsung have been actively pursuing Indian engineers.

While most Indian engineers prefer to move to settler societies like the United States that appreciate cultural diversity—or simply stay home—some would be willing to relocate to a country like Korea in some situations. As we have shown in this study, social and work-related factors differentiate subgroups among Indian engineers, some of which may be more positively inclined toward specific countries than others. Working for a Korean company, for instance, would give engineers exposure to different kinds of products and technologies not available in India, such as memory management and power consumption technologies, which would represent an excellent opportunity for Indian engineers looking to build their skills. Even if they should choose to leave Korea after working there for a few years, the experience gained would, according to our respondents, yield significant career advantages. Such diverse motives and interests in turn offer an opportunity for a country like Korea, which is less favored by Indian engineers than the United States. While most of these engineers may not stay in Korea for long, they nonetheless can contribute badly needed software engineering skills while in Korea and may continue to provide social capital to Korea upon their return to India or move to Silicon Valley. Korea would benefit from assisting them in becoming embedded into its society and culture, as those who are locally well embedded are more likely to play a transnational bridging role even after they leave the country.

We emphasize that the recruitment of these four groups—foreign students studying in Korea, Korean citizens studying overseas, members of the diaspora, and Indian engineers—is only the first step. Recent studies have shown that social ties linking individuals across geographic space can only function as transnational bridges given two conditions. First, such individuals must maintain their rights and responsibilities in their home societies while becoming meaningfully embedded in their host societies.[7] In the Korean context, the challenge is to break down deeply ingrained tendencies to exclude outsiders arising from deep-seated ethnic nationalism. Second, individuals with bridging potential must join organizations willing to accept their contributions. Korean firms have long been believed to be hostile toward such contributions, being infamously rigid and hierarchical. The ethnographic interviews we have conducted with both corporate executives and potential employees suggest that such stereotypes do not necessarily reflect recent changes in Korean corporate culture. Nevertheless, Korean firms likely still have much room for improvement.

Comparison Cases

Although our research focuses on the Korean case, its findings can be relevant toward other developed, nonimmigrant societies. As we discussed in Chapter 1, a large number of European and Asian societies fall into this category, encompassing countries as diverse as Italy and Taiwan. We suggest that Germany and Japan are the most relevant comparative cases here, however. Like Korea and unlike the settler societies, both ground their national identities on shared ethnicity. Germany has experimented with multiculturalism in past decades but has retreated sharply in recent years. Indeed, Germany has had great difficulty assimilating second- and even third-generation Turkish immigrants despite its advanced economy and democratic politics. Japan has had even greater difficulty assimilating nearly a million ethnic Koreans who have been living there for many generations. Furthermore, Germany and especially Japan are facing the same economic and demographic pressures as Korea. Below, we illustrate how our findings in the Korean context might also apply to both countries.

GERMANY

Germany not only hosts more foreign students than any other non-English-speaking country but also has one of the largest diasporas of all European countries. Germany hosted 280,000 foreign students as of January 2014. However, Germany has had substantial difficulty retaining such students after graduation, much as Korea has. Germany has also historically drawn from 70 million ethnic Germans living abroad primarily in Eastern Europe, North America, and South America, excluding those in other German-speaking countries such as Switzerland and Austria. West Germany assimilated members of this diaspora fleeing from Eastern Europe after World

War II extremely well, so that they have become effectively indistinguishable from Germans born there. However, a unified Germany has not been nearly as successful at assimilating members of the diaspora who returned after the fall of the Berlin Wall.

Germany aims to increase its number of foreign students 25 percent to reach 350,000 by 2020 for two of the same reasons we discussed in the Korean context, seeking skilled workers to augment its shrinking workforce and recruiting top-end global talent especially in the sciences and engineering.[8] Germany seeks to capitalize upon two key advantages here. Its universities' low to nonexistent tuition fees are highly attractive to foreign students. Furthermore, Germany recently began allowing foreign graduates of its universities to spend up to six months looking for a job in the country. Nevertheless, Germany has had great difficulty retaining those students that it educates. According to a report by the Expert Council of German Foundations on Integration and Migration (2012), 80 percent of foreign students graduating from German universities desired to stay after graduation but only a quarter actually ended up staying. Indeed, only 12.5 percent intend to stay in Germany longer than five years, perhaps because they feel unwelcome in Germany. Indeed, among the foreign students surveyed by the Expert Council, 40 percent reported that they experienced xenophobia at some point during their sojourn. Given foreign students' desire to stay in the country short term but not long term, Germany can benefit from shifting away from the old model toward the new model, seeking to build transnational bridges by training and partially acculturating students who will eventually return home rather than trying to retain them long term for their human capital. Like Korea, Germany may benefit by adopting elements of the new model here.

Germany might benefit from taking a similar approach toward its diaspora. West Germany initially had tremendous success assimilating ethnic German returnees after World War II. West Germany's Basic Law, in Article 116(1), included refugees or expellees of German origin among the definition of a German. "Expellees" only had to originate from a Communist country to be labeled a "resettler." Many of these individuals had ancestors who had left "Germany" as long as eight centuries ago. From 1945 to 1987, 1.6 million "ethnic Germans" entered West Germany and quickly blended into the native population; ethnic German returnees from that era became socially invisible. However, an additional 1.6 million returnees arriving after the fall of the Berlin Wall have had a different and more challenging experience, experiencing much more unemployment than natives.[9] Besides attempting to assimilate members of its diaspora, Germany should pay close attention to their potential role as transnational bridges by encouraging them to reconnect with their German roots before they return to their host societies.

JAPAN

Japan was educating 137,756 foreign students in 2012, more than Korea. Japan also seems to recognize their potential to bridge Japan with their home countries. The Japanese government began to recruit foreign students into the Japanese education system because "Japanese industries, the research and development community, and society felt the necessity to attract talented human resources from Asia and all over the world, and foster them as to bridge Japanese labor and business customs with those of other countries" (Yonezawa 2014: 5). This motivation parallels our own findings in the Korean context. Nevertheless, Japan lags behind other countries (including Korea) in some important respects. For instance, Japan has only recently begun to allow foreign graduates to spend a year after graduation looking for a job, a policy that other countries like the United States, Canada, and even Korea implemented several years ago. Japan can still do much more to leverage the foreigners that it educates. Indeed, many students undoubtedly study in Japan for similar reasons why Koreaphiles come to Korea (see Chapter 2) based on their admiration of Japanese culture. Such students would have a strong motivation to bridge Japan with their home societies across Asia.

In contrast, Japan has successfully leveraged its large diaspora as unskilled labor. From 1885 to 1923, half a million Japanese left the country for reasons including poverty, unemployment, overpopulation, and heavy taxes. Japanese immigrants were not welcomed in most host countries except for Brazil, which had a shortage of labor after the curtailment of the Atlantic slave trade in 1850. By 1940, there were 205,000 Japanese and Japanese descendants in Brazil, constituting 0.5 percent of the Brazilian population.[10] In the 1970s, Japan began recruiting Japanese Brazilian labor in large numbers. The economic expansion of the era created shortages in unskilled labor. Foreign workers, particularly from Asia, were used to alleviate labor shortages, despite being prohibited by law. Recognizing this situation, the Japanese government amended the Immigration Control and Refugee Recognition

Law in 1989 so that Japanese descendants up to the third generation and their spouses were permitted entry for an indefinite period. Because these amendments favored returnees of Japanese descent (the *dekasegi*), the number of South Americans coming to Japan skyrocketed from 88,201 in 1991 to 274,442 in 1998, with 81 percent of them being Brazilian. Dekasegi are recruited through several channels: Japanese and Brazilian job-brokering agencies (the most popular option), directly by companies (about 35 percent of the whole), or by networks of friends and relatives working in Japan. Such dekasegi migrate to Japan for economic and identity-related reasons. The most common aspiration is to buy a house and start a business. Other motivations include experiencing life in a developed country, acquainting themselves with the land of their ancestors, meeting relatives, and learning about Japanese culture. The dekasegi emphasize the positives of their experience, encouraging others to follow in their footsteps. Most intend to return to Brazil after a few years, however.[11] Although the dekasegi lack the advanced skills of Korean Americans and Korean Canadians, Japan's experience with the dekasegi otherwise parallel our suggestions regarding skilled members of the Korean diaspora, that is, their potential for transnational bridging. Overall, a brief illustration of the German and Japanese cases attest to the applicability of the new model that we advocate in this study to other nonimmigrant countries in the world.

Theoretical Implications

Our investigation of four target groups in the Korean context not only addresses practical concerns with how nonimmigrant advanced countries such as Korea might recruit skilled foreigners but also fills crucial gaps in current research on this important group.

Our research builds on a relatively new theoretical approach that focuses on the growing role of brain circulation rather than brain drain in the global economy (i.e., the new model). This approach was foreshadowed by Castells (1996) but brought to fruition by studies in economic geography and economic sociology (e.g., Bathelt, Malmberg, and Maskell 2004; Saxenian 2006). Such scholarship strongly parallels studies in the sociology of immigration (e.g., Tilly 2007), differentiating transmigration from forms of immigration that socially and culturally uproot those who emigrate abroad. Our study connects these parallel but previously disconnected streams of research by calling for an attention to the importance of "transnational bridges."

Furthermore, our research goes beyond simply applying the new model toward a different empirical setting, addressing a key shortcoming of current works. Storper (2007), critiquing Saxenian's (2006) account of transnational bridging by the Argonauts, asks for more explanation why skilled foreigners abroad bridge their host societies with their home societies (see also Wang forthcoming). Our study helps answer this question. We find that different factors motivate different groups of skilled foreigners to actively bridge their home and host societies. Some individuals (e.g., Korean Americans) visit the host society seeking to answer longstanding questions about their identities. Developing and strengthening their ties with their ancestral homes, members of the diaspora gain opportunities to bridge as a further benefit. In contrast, other individuals (e.g., Indian engineers) have strictly economic motivations for sojourning in their host societies. The choice of bridging home and host societies represents an act that generates further economic opportunities for them. Still others (e.g., Koreaphile foreign students) are motivated by a desire to bring two countries they love closer together. Their ability to realize such desires, however, is strongly conditioned by the economic opportunities available to them. Finally, for students who never return after studying abroad, bridging is a way to remain connected to their roots, especially when economic benefits are involved. Overall, our findings show that bridging behavior is a consequence of sociocultural motivations as well as economic interests affecting different groups in different ways.

Additionally, our study adds to a relatively sparse body of research on the recruitment of skilled foreigners by nonimmigrant countries. The vast majority of research on skilled foreigners focuses on individuals sojourning in the settler societies—Canada, Australia, and particularly the United States. The body of research on skilled foreigners in nonimmigrant countries (e.g., Joppke 2005) is much smaller by comparison. Investigating this phenomenon is particularly important because nonimmigrant countries potentially benefit from skilled foreigners much more than the settler societies, experiencing pressures from demographic transition and changes in global economic structure largely bypassing settler societies. However, our study goes far beyond simply investigating skilled foreigners in a previously unstudied context (Korea). Acknowledging the difficulties that nonimmigrant countries face when recruiting skilled foreigners, we highlight an alternative way that such countries might benefit from skilled foreigners, by leveraging individuals who only stay in the country for a short sojourn before moving on to another country. Although we show that nonimmigrant countries can recruit skilled foreigners under some conditions, especially if they have an extensive overseas diaspora, we also argue that nonimmigrant countries do not necessarily have to fully assimilate skilled foreigners. What is needed is just enough socialization and social embedding to enable skilled foreigners to maintain their ties with the nonimmigrant country after they return home or move on to another foreign country.

Practical and Policy Implications

Besides their theoretical contributions, our findings have also important implications for many other areas within Korean economy and society. Below, we discuss the relevance of our key findings to industrial firms, entrepreneurial ventures, higher education, and public diplomacy.

EXPANDING OPPORTUNITIES FOR INDUSTRIAL FIRMS

Our findings suggest that transnational bridges might open new doors for Korean industrial firms abroad. Epitomizing ethnocentric corporations, Korean companies both large and small are staffed almost exclusively by Koreans at senior management positions, both at their Korean headquarters and at subsidiaries abroad. As prior international business research indicates, such an approach is conducive for generating global economies of scale for manufacturing companies but strongly hinders attempts to localize products and services for specific overseas markets. Indeed, Korean companies have been spectacularly successful at producing and selling manufactured goods such as electronics and automobiles, but equally unsuccessful at marketing highly localized consumer goods as well as services catering to businesses or individuals.

Transnational bridges can help Korean companies maintain their strong orientation to Korean society and culture—alignments they are unlikely to abandon anytime soon—while giving them a greater ability to localize their products and services. Some large Korean firms, such as LG Electronics and Lotte, have already recognized this possibility and initiated programs to hire, train, and employ foreign students in Korea as transnational bridges. Contingent upon the success of such programs, other Korean firms are likely to follow. Such transnational bridges can certainly help firms improve their manufacturing operations abroad, by reducing distrust between the Korean senior managers leading overseas subsidiaries and local staff who handle day-to-day operations. However, an even bigger payoff might be an ability to successfully enter foreign markets for goods and services that requires careful attention to local environments. This benefit is particularly important given that Korea must develop its service sector prowess to continue its economic advance.

While such initiatives would certainly improve performance, they might have an even greater effect on small and medium-sized enterprises (SMEs). Unlike chaebŏl that have established themselves on the global market, Korea's SMEs often have difficulty finding overseas partners and markets. Trapped within Korea's saturated market, SMEs have suffered from low growth rates and poor profit margins. Transnational bridges to key export markets or production bases have the potential to transform this unfortunate situation. Unlike some of the more forward-thinking chaebŏl, SMEs are unlikely to have the resources to aggressively hire foreign students, however. Such SMEs might benefit from government-sponsored initiatives matching the needs of specific SMEs to specific types of social capital possessed by specific foreign students, perhaps summer internships matching students with specific SMEs.

Overall, we emphasize how transnational bridges have the potential to create win-win-win situations among Korean industrial firms, foreign localities, and the individuals involved. As stated above, Korean firms not only gain key operational efficiencies but also the ability to enter previously impenetrable overseas markets. Foreign countries and localities also gain greater opportunities to partner with Korean firms as well as the chance to incorporate some of the elements that make Korean firms successful into home-grown companies. Perhaps most importantly, the individuals who bridge Korea with their home societies gain a potentially lucrative resource that enables them not only to earn higher salaries and eventually lead Korean firms' overseas subsidiaries but also to benefit from opportunities for innovation and entrepreneurship that combine resources drawn from both Korea and their home societies.

ENCOURAGING INNOVATION AND ENTREPRENEURSHIP

Our findings also suggest that transnational bridges might boost techno-logical innovation and entrepreneurship in Korea. Since its democratization in 1987, Korean entrepreneurs have scored numerous successes, including CyWorld (an online social network), Naver (a Korean-language search en-gine), NCSoft (a maker of massively multiplayer role-playing games), and AhnLabs (a computer antivirus platform). Yet none of these companies has had a global impact comparable to the likes of Facebook and Google.

Transnational bridges can solve part of the problem, which is that ad-vanced, locally successful services have had difficulty expanding overseas be-cause their managers do not understand foreign markets and cannot localize effectively to these markets. As discussed in Chapter 5, Korean entrepreneur-ial ventures repeatedly squandered technological leads by failing to establish themselves in overseas markets. For instance, CyWorld had the chance to preempt Facebook as the default online social network but was outcom-peted globally and now has shut down even in its Korean home market. Our findings suggest several solutions to this problem. By hiring foreign students, such ventures can better understand foreign markets and expand there. By hiring Indian engineers, such ventures can also synchronize with broader trends in a global network of technology entrepreneurship, pre-venting them from ignoring key innovations. By hiring U.S.-based Korean students and Korean Americans, such ventures can gain an opportunity to prove themselves in the world's most competitive technology market-place, placing them in an excellent position to spread globally. Transna-tional bridges of this kind have transformed other developed countries and regions in the past. Notably, the Argonauts of Silicon Valley, who returned to Taiwan, Israel, and India after being educated and trained in the United States, linked Silicon Valley with emerging technology clusters in Hsinchu, Israel, and Bangalore.[12] In doing so, the Argonauts transformed Silicon Val-ley from a localized hotbed of innovation into the central hub for a global network of innovation. U.S.-based Korean students and Korean Americans can better link Korea into this network, not only providing increased access to cutting-edge foreign innovations but also seeding local innovation.

Inflows of skilled foreigners, especially Korean Americans and Indian en-gineers, will also boost Korean innovation and entrepreneurship in a more subtle way. Although Koreans have produced several noteworthy entrepreneurial ventures, young Koreans nevertheless prefer to pursue stable jobs in the chaebŏl or even government service. This mindset stifles innovation and entrepreneurship by steering young Koreans toward traditional careers viewed as "stable." As prior studies (e.g., Saxenian 1994) have demonstrated, a risk-tolerant and entrepreneurial culture largely accounts for the continued success of entrepreneurial hotbeds across the world, while a risk-adverse corporate culture largely accounts for the failure and decline of previous entrepreneurial hotbeds. How can Korea transform its largely antientrepreneurial culture? Our study suggests that many Korean Americans and Indian engineers have a strong desire to be entrepreneurial and possess a substantial willingness to take risks (see Chapters 4 and 5). The hope is that they will not only continue their entrepreneurial activities by drawing from Korea's fertile technological resources but also inspire Koreans to join their ventures and undertake new ones of their own.

GLOBALIZING HIGHER EDUCATION

Korean universities seek to become centers of global talent, technological innovation, and creativity—the key drivers of today's economy and society. To achieve these goals, Korea has aggressively internationalized its higher education, with particular focus on three areas: increasing courses taught in English, promoting exchange programs with foreign (both Western and non-Western) universities, and attracting foreign students and faculty. Study Korea, a project begun in 2004, for instance, aimed to attract 100,000 foreign students by 2012. In 2006, the government launched the Strategy for the Internationalization of Higher Education, which eased regulations for running dual or joint degree programs and exchange programs between Korean and foreign universities. Brain Korea 21, aiming to develop 10 world-class, research-oriented universities by 2012, would place Korea among the world's top-10 countries in terms of the number of research articles published in reputable academic journals listed on the Science Citations Index. World Class Universities (WCU), a project launched in 2008, invited large numbers of prominent foreign scholars to conduct collaborative research with Korean faculty in key growth-generating STEM (science, technology, engineering, and mathematics) fields (e.g., nanotechnology, interdisciplinary studies), investing roughly US$740 million in the project over five years. Largely thanks to these efforts, the number of foreign students and faculty in Korean universities has increased: the former reached 86,878 in 2012, while the latter has increased steadily over the last decade from 985 in 2000 to 3,815 in 2010. Invited faculty, research, and graduate scholarships funded by Brain Korea 21 and WCU resulted in modest gains in research output in the sciences, and the global rankings of leading Korean universities have improved over the years.

Despite these achievements, the internationalization of higher education has not paid sufficient attention to producing global talent. While offering English-only degree programs and courses and increasing the number of foreign students and faculty brings more diversity to Korean university campuses, these measures in and of themselves do not automatically translate into a university community that is open to cultural diversity, nor do they produce global citizens with intercultural skills. In an increasingly globalizing world, corporations and societies seek talented college graduates who can work productively while interacting with different people, cultures, and perspectives. Yet the majority of Korean students leave college without experiencing diversity and with little or no interaction with non-Korean students or faculty. Also, Korean universities attract many talented foreign students but do not fully recognize their value as human and social capital as presented in Chapter 2. Korean universities have become more diverse without fully recognizing the benefits of diversity and enabling disparate people to engage one another in deeply productive ways (Moon and Shin 2014).

ENHANCING PUBLIC DIPLOMACY

Our findings suggest that familiarity with Korea, as well as a sense of attachment to Korea, its culture, its people, and its society, are key factors that motivate relevant individuals to play a transnational bridging role. Indeed, Korea has lately promoted various programs designed to increase foreigners' understanding of its history and culture and enhance its national image in the international community. For instance, the country is now actively exporting its culture through music, television shows, movies, food, and sports—all aspects of what has been termed hallyu (Korean wave). Private entertainment agencies and some governmental organizations produce programs specifically targeting international audiences. Hence, the export of Korean culture has become an important means of gaining recognition in the international community. As this study shows, music, dramas, and other cultural exports can have powerful effects on the way foreigners and overseas Koreans perceive Korea. For instance, *Gangnam Style* by K-Pop artist Psy has generated a surge of interest not only in the district (Gangnam District in Seoul) but also Korea in general.

The Korean government has also been promoting interest in Korea overseas. The Ministry of Foreign Affairs has recently appointed 16 foreign professors and researchers from Korean universities as honorary envoys for public diplomacy in early 2013. Putting together a group of academics as public diplomacy envoys is part of the ministry's efforts to enhance the country's soft power, mainly through creating interpersonal ties and promoting its culture. Overseas, the Korea Foundation under the Ministry of Foreign Affairs and the Academy of Korean Studies under the Ministry of Education have undertaken similar efforts. They have supported establishing Korean studies professorships at overseas universities, funding various seminars, workshops, and conferences on Korean affairs, and recruiting professors and scholars from other countries to Korean universities and research institutions to teach in and experience Korea. The Korean government has also sought to spread interest in Korean culture and language by creating and sponsoring language institutes named after King Sejong, the inventor of the Korean alphabet. Individuals studying Korean at these overseas institutes have risen steadily, from 740 in 2007 to 16,590 in 2012, according to the Ministry of Culture, Sports and Tourism. Such efforts have contributed to an increase in the number of nonnative speakers taking the Test of Proficiency in Korean (TOPIK) from 82,881 in 2007 to 151,166 in 2012.[13] Considering how strongly an interest in Korean language and culture may motivate an individual to bridge Korea with his or her homeland, these efforts certainly appear worthwhile.

More recently, Korea has begun stronger efforts through its Official Development Assistance (ODA) program. Beyond simple aid delivery, Korea has been trying to transmit its economic development model to less developed countries, encouraging such countries to adapt the model to fit their respective needs and situations. In particular, through the Knowledge Sharing Program, the Korean government aims to "share Korea's development know-how, assisting the partner countries and working towards lessening the knowledge divide."[14] If Korea combines its ODA measures with those public diplomacy efforts mentioned above, a tremendous synergic impact is likely to occur. After all, all of these efforts can have a significant role to play in the mobilization of global talent abroad.

Overall, the Korean government has increasingly emphasized the importance of public diplomacy. Effective public diplomacy can be a useful instrument for the recruitment and mobilization of global talent. At the same time, global talent can act as the most powerful and effective gateway to the promotion of Korea's soft power abroad because each individual is tied to at least one country other than Korea and thus may serve as a transnational bridge.

Nationalism, Racism, and Cultural Diversity

We conclude with the relevance of our findings to a key area of debate not only in Korea but other countries as well: the relationships between ethnic national identity, racism and xenophobia, and cultural diversity. As the Kim case shows, strong ethnic nationalism may be a double-edged sword in Korea's pursuit of global talent. On one hand, a strong sense of ethnic identity held among overseas Koreans may serve as a motivating factor for them to return home. Our findings suggest that ethnic nationalism does indeed have a positive side, by helping to maintain close connections between Korea and a diaspora community rich in human and social capital. On the other hand, even members of the Korean diaspora—not to mention "true" foreigners—face serious challenges in acclimating themselves to the nationalistic culture and society that they encounter in Korea. As we show in this study, Korean Americans and Korean Canadians must deal with greater reentry shock than Korean students returning from abroad. Migrant workers and foreign brides, who account for the majority of foreigners residing in Korea, still face discrimination in their pursuit of societal, political, and economic rights, and various laws and practices restrict immigration and limit immigrant rights. In contrast to most settler societies that rely on the jus soli principle to award citizenship, Korea defines citizenship and nationality according to the jus sanguinis principle. As a result, becoming a naturalized citizen in Korea is difficult, if not impossible, for individuals from other ethnic groups regardless of how long they have lived in the country and how well they have assimilated. Korea has therefore been depicted as an unwelcoming environment for foreigners and has had difficulty attracting highly skilled foreigners, despite widespread rhetoric about recruiting global talent among policymakers, academics, and the media. This puts Korea at a disadvantage relative to settler societies.

Indeed, the effectiveness of skilled foreigners in Korea is strongly hampered by racism, xenophobia, and a general unwillingness to accept foreigners into Korea's closed social networks. Recent studies (e.g., Saxenian 1994, 2006; Florida 2002) showing the human and social capital benefits that skilled foreigners can bring to a sociogeographic location have largely neglected a key factor that mediates the effectiveness of such capital—the social embeddedness of foreign individuals in the local context. It matters little if skilled foreigners settle in Korea, if they are not given the opportunity to productively use their skills. Similarly, it matters little whether foreigners are willing to bridge Korea with their home countries if Koreans refuse to accept them into local social networks (see Wang forthcoming).

For these reasons, Korea may squander the opportunity to leverage skilled foreigners for mutual benefit. As noted above, Korea has actively promoted globalization, but even these efforts have not uprooted or significantly weakened the power of ethnic nationalism in the country. Instead, as argued elsewhere (Shin 2006), Koreans have embraced and promoted globalization with a nationalist agenda by increasing their national competitiveness in a globalizing world. Accordingly, they have simultaneously sought to preserve and strengthen national heritage and culture. With the recent influx of migrant workers and foreign brides, however, the dark side of Korean ethnic nationalism has become salient. For some foreigners, subtle racial discrimination is a part of daily life in Korea.[15] In fact, the United Nations Committee on the Elimination of Racial Discrimination issued a report in 2007 stating that the concept of "pure-bloodedness" in Korea has produced various forms of discrimination against social "others."[16] According to the report,

> The emphasis placed on the ethnic homogeneity of Korea may represent an obstacle to the promotion of tolerance and friendship among the different ethnic and national groups living in its territory. Korea has to embrace the multi-ethnic character of contemporary Korean society. . . . The image of an ethnically homogeneous Korea is now a thing of the past.[17]

Other domestic and international organizations, such as Amnesty International, have since then expressed deep concerns about a Korean ethnic consciousness that encourages a false sense of uniformity and enforces conformity.

The Korean government has responded to such international criticism by promoting multiculturalism over the past decade. In 2005, the Roh Moo Hyun government designated "multiculturalism" as its primary policy initiative and established a wide range of multiculturalist institutes, policies, and practices, including the Committee for Foreigner Policy chaired by the prime minister.[18] Despite well-intended measures that have resulted in some progress, current multiculturalist policies are still limited, as their programs have been largely directed toward foreign brides, with the goal of assimilating them into Korean society. In contrast, migrant laborers (mostly unskilled) whose contribution is deemed only temporary have been largely excluded even from this multiculturalist agenda. It seems that Koreans do not fully appreciate the value that foreigners and cultural diversity can bring to their own society. Korea is becoming ethnically and culturally diverse but not yet tolerant or appreciative of such diversity (see Moon and Shin 2014; Shin 2012). The persistence of ethnocentric attitudes and a narrow application of multiculturalist policies will surely pose a challenge to Korea's efforts to attract foreign skilled labor. In order to compete with other advanced countries, especially the settler societies, for global talent, it is imperative for Korea to provide a more culturally diverse and ethnically tolerant environment for foreigners.

Reference Matter

Notes

Chapter 1

1. Organisation for Economic Co-operation and Development (2012b).
2. Prior studies on global talent management have highlighted two different aspects of the phenomenon. On the one hand, research on human resource management has emphasized that "better talent is worth fighting for" (Chambers et al. 1998), recommending that human resource professionals seek out the best and brightest individuals across the world. On the other hand, research on organizational behavior (e.g., Pfeffer and Sutton 2006) has found that an individual's natural talent has an overrated impact upon organizational performance, suggesting that the recruitment of "stars" fails to yield performance increases (for a review, see Beechler and Woodward 2009). Given this, we focus upon global talent as individuals with technical or professional skills conferring valuable advantages for firms competing in global markets.
3. *Foreign Policy* (2008).
4. We look more deeply into this problem in Chapter 5.
5. Becker (2008).
6. Judy and D'Amico (1997), Judy (1999), Burdette (1999), U.S. Department of Commerce Office of Technology Policy (1997), Information Technology Association of America (1997), and Kirkegaard (2007).
7. Morgan (2003).
8. For instance, Kim (2000) does not believe that large number of immigrants would be accepted into Korean society. See also Shin (2012).
9. Bae (2012).
10. Feere (2010).
11. Joppke (2005).

12. Becker (1964).

13. Bourdieu (1977), Coleman (1988), and Putnam (2000).

14. Becker (2008).

15. *Roll Call*, U.S. House of Representatives (2012).

16. Saxenian (2006) and Kirkegaard (2007).

17. Judy and D'Amico (1997), Judy (1999), Burdette (1999), U.S. Department of Commerce Office of Technology Policy (1997), Information Technology Association of America (1997), and Kirkegaard (2007).

18. Coleman (1988).

19. Bourdieu (1977), Powell (1990), and Putnam (1995).

20. Granovetter (1973) and Davis (1991).

21. Coleman (1988), Portes and Sensenbrenner (1993), and Putnam (1995, 2000).

22. Granovetter (1974) and Burt (1992, 2004).

23. See Cortright (2006) for a review.

24. Bathelt, Malmberg, and Maskell (2004), Maskell, Bathelt, and Malmberg (2005), and Bunker-Whittington, Owen-Smith, and Powell (2009).

25. Saxenian (1994), Dahl and Sorenson (2008), and Tharenou and Caulfield (2010).

26. Bunker-Whittington, Owen-Smith, and Powell (2009).

27. Shenkar (2001).

28. Bathelt, Malmberg, and Maskell (2004), and Maskell, Bathelt, and Malmberg (2005).

29. Choi (2003).

30. Prior research on immigration has focused mainly on bonding social capital, while somewhat neglecting both local and transnational bridges. For instance, bonding social capital has a strong effect within ethnic enclaves—localized concentrations of immigrants from a particular foreign country, such as Chinatown in San Francisco or Koreatown in Los Angeles. Within such enclaves, bonding social capital typically facilitates cooperation and productive exchanges, helping immigrant entrepreneurs flourish. Alejandro Portes argues that the strong bonding social capital present in ethnic enclaves helps them succeed in the United States by preventing undesirable contact with surrounding Americans. If the immigrants involved are situated in inner cities racked by drugs, violence, and gang activity, this argument is plausible. However, the strong bonding social capital present in these enclaves sometimes hinders upwardly mobile individuals from connecting with the mainstream. When particularly successful individuals attempt to join the host society's mainstream culture, they are sometimes shunned by the enclave they are leaving. For instance, Korean Americans who adopt mainstream habits and views are derisively called "twinkies" (i.e., yellow on the outside, white on the

inside) by fellow co-ethnics. This hinders immigrants from moving into lucrative occupations outside of the enclave (Portes and Sensenbrenner 1993; Portes 1995b; Portes and Rumbaut 2001; Tilly 2007; Chen 2010). This example shows both the benefits and drawbacks of bonding social capital—it creates internal solidarity but dissuades individuals from creating links with outsiders.

31. Granovetter (1985).

32. Dahl and Sorenson (2008).

33. Schiller, Basch, and Blanc (1995: 48).

34. Ong (1999); see also Roberts (1995), Bloemraad (2004), and Tilly (2007).

35. Greif (1989) and Meyer (1991).

36. Granovetter (1985) and Uzzi (1997).

37. Rauch (1999).

38. Porter (1990), Barnett (2008), and Powell et al. (2005).

39. See Porter (1990) for a review.

40. Maskell, Bathelt, and Malmberg (2005).

41. Perlmutter (1969), Prahalad and Doz (1987), and Bartlett and Ghoshal (1989).

42. See Granovetter (1974).

43. See Erickson (1982) and Uzzi (1997).

44. See Rauch (1999).

45. See Granovetter (1973), Burt (1992), and Watts and Strogatz (1998).

46. The distinction between skilled and unskilled foreigners is often unclear. Countries make a clear legal distinction between skilled foreigners, who receive visa exemptions, permanent residency, and even income tax exemptions, versus unskilled foreigners, whose entry is carefully restricted. Despite these common attitudes, the distinction between skilled and unskilled foreign labor is less clear than commonly believed. Sociological research suggests that immigrants are typically not a society's most destitute individuals; such individuals are unable to relocate elsewhere. Rather, many unskilled immigrants possess substantial social, cultural, and economic capital—including tertiary educations or college-level instruction. Migrants from the Philippines are an extreme case of this phenomenon. Of Filipino immigrants to the United States, 48.6 percent have some sort of tertiary education but, nevertheless, work predominantly in unskilled professions. For instance, Filipinas in Vancouver worked predominantly as domestic workers or nurse's aides but had previously worked in the Philippines as schoolteachers or accountants. Similarly, two-thirds of Filipina domestic workers in Hong Kong had some tertiary education. Conversely, highly skilled immigrants who lose their initial jobs can see their skills erode over time because they have difficulty finding suitably skilled jobs in the host country. For both reasons, immigrant overqualification appears to be universal. One OECD (2008) study found that immigrants

were more likely to be overqualified than native-born persons in all OECD countries except New Zealand and the Slovak Republic. Immigrant overqualification occurs largely because immigrants are willing to take jobs they are overqualified for, lack locally recognized professional credentials, and are restricted by work permits. Immigrant overqualification appears to dissipate over time, at least in the settler societies (Jasso and Rozenzweig 1995; Lowell 1996; Gallo and Bailey 1996; Portes 1998; Constable 2002; Pratt 2002). We acknowledge that the distinction between unskilled and skilled labor is somewhat artificial but nevertheless employ this analytical distinction to simplify our concepts.

47. Wallerstein (1974), Chase-Dunn (1975), and Sassen (1994, 2001, 2007).

48. Friedmann (1986), Meyer (1986), and Sassen (1994, 2001, 2007).

49. See Shin (2012).

50. Bae (2012).

51. Our focus is consistent with recent management research (e.g., Beechler and Woodward 2009), which emphasizes the importance of "creative and generative" approaches toward the global war for talent, noting that companies spend excessive energy chasing only the top individuals.

52. Although students studying abroad are not "foreigners" in the strict sense, we include them here as their values as human and social capital are similar to those of skilled foreigners due to their extensive experiences living in foreign countries.

53. See Tharenou and Caulfield (2010) for a review.

54. "Korean Residents Abroad" (Ministry of Foreign Affairs, annual year) retrieved from KOSIS (http://www.kosis.kr). Data as of 2005.

55. We use correspondence analysis rather than regression analysis for two reasons. First, we found a great deal of heterogeneity within all four groups, and each decomposed into several different subgroups with many shared characteristics. Regression analysis would have obscured—not illuminated—the existence of such subgroups. Second, our quantitative data fit the requirements for correspondence analysis but not regression analysis. Our sampling methods did not necessarily produce biased samples but, nevertheless, provided no assurance that the samples were representative of their respective populations. Also, our samples were insufficiently large for rigorous regression analyses. Given these limitations, we chose correspondence analysis as an alternative to regression analysis that had greater robustness when dealing with small, potentially biased samples.

Chapter 2

1. To protect interviewees' anonymity, we use pseudonyms and avoid providing personal characteristics that would allow specific individuals to be identified.

2. *Newstation* (2009).

3. Republic of Korea Ministry of Education, Science, and Technology (2001).

4. *CIA World Factbook* (2013).

5. International Monetary Fund (2010).

6. See Chapter 5, footnote 28 for details.

7. Kim (2011).

8. Also note that the Korean wave led to a backlash in certain parts of Asia like Japan and China, as frequently reported by the Korean media. For instance, see the *Joongang Ilbo* article at http://koreajoongangdaily.joins.com/news/article/article.aspx?aid=2932286.

9. Korea Export-Import Bank (2012).

10. The rapid increase in the number of foreign students has also created new challenges. On the one hand, the program has focused on increasing the number, rather than the quality, of incoming foreign students. Thus, not all incoming students have been sufficiently qualified. On the other hand, foreign students have complained about the support they received from institutions inadequately prepared to help them, as well as bureaucratic measures that are perceived as heavy-handed and demeaning (e.g., mandatory AIDS testing).

11. Republic of Korea Ministry of Education, Science, and Technology (2001).

12. For a review, see Jasso and Rosenzweig (1995), Gallo and Baily (1996), and Lowell (1996).

13. Mongolia is an extreme case. 1 out of every 100 Mongolians is currently in Korea, and half of all families have an extended family member there.

14. The resolution of these competing pressures represents perhaps the central question asked by research on multinational management. Foundational works in this tradition include Perlmutter (1969), Prahalad and Doz (1987), and Bartlett and Ghoshal (1989). Beyond these works, see also Ghoshal (1987), Ghoshal and Bartlett (1990), and Gupta and Govindarajan (2000) for reviews of this extensive literature.

15. Recruiting materials posted on LG Electronics website (http://www.lge.com), downloaded August 2012.

16. We interviewed these managers and executives with the explicit understanding that they will only be cited anonymously and that we will provide no information allowing readers to identify these individuals or their companies. We make no attempt at disguising company names when summarizing information already in the public domain (e.g., the recruiting programs conducted by Lotte and LG). The reader should note that other companies are conducting similar programs without posting publicly visible advertisements and that we may have interviewed personnel at these undisclosed companies.

17. We chose this particular focus since our study seeks to understand how foreign students can be a good source of global talent for Korea and believe that those majoring in engineering or business-related fields can be considered the best candidates.

18. Tongari are on-campus student groups centered around shared interests that typically generate substantial social interactions.

Chapter 3

1. Institute for Management Development (2005–2013).
2. Kirkegaard (2007).
3. Hong and Cho (2012).
4. Adler (1981) and Szkudlarek (2010).
5. We used the SurveyMonkey.com platform, a convenient and reliable way to send a customized online survey to email distribution lists.
6. Korea has only recently allowed dual citizenship, only for females and those males who have satisfactorily completed Korea's mandatory military service. Nevertheless, it has been common practice for Koreans overseas to acquire another nationality without informing the Korean government as required.
7. All interviews were conducted by a research assistant (RA) who had received methodological training at the graduate level. This RA matched the respondents in four important dimensions. First, the RA was a Korean student studying in the United States who faced many of the same concerns as her respondents. Second, the RA spoke fluent Korean and English and interviewed respondents in their preferred language (almost always Korean). Third, the RA matched the median age of our respondents. Finally, the RA had just finished an advanced degree from one of the three institutions where the interviews were conducted. For these reasons, our RA built rapport with the respondents much faster than the authors, who had more interviewing experience but diverged from the respondents in age and social status.
8. See Massey et al. (1993) for a review.
9. Indeed, some Korean students reported that they had no choice but to return to Korea, as they could not find jobs in North America.
10. http://www.urbanministry.org/wiki/being-korean-american-and-role-church-many-korean-peoples.
11. Kwon, Ebagh, and Hagen (1997).
12. See also Roberts (1995) and Tilly (2007).
13. See Saxenian (2006).

Chapter 4

1. Shin (2006).
2. Chen (2010).

3. Portes and Rumbaut (2001) and Noland (1993).

4. Republic of Korea Ministry of Justice (2008).

5. This dimension explained the third largest amount of variance, following *familiarity with Korea* and *inclination toward or away from the medical field*. Interest in medicine was not theoretically interesting for our purposes. Thus, we chose to focus on the next most important dimension—*inclination toward or away from business*—which explained nearly as much variance.

6. Korea does not grant dual citizenship until the age of 55, but many Koreans do not denounce their Korean citizenship even after obtaining American or Canadian citizenship.

7. Kim (2013).

Chapter 5

This chapter is adapted from a policy report by Gi-wook Shin, Rafiq Dossani, and Joon Nak Choi, "Building an IT Partnership: Indian IT Engineers in the Korean Marketplace," Shorenstein Asia-Pacific Research Center, Stanford University, 2010.

1. Press release by Gee-sung Choi at the 2010 Consumer Electronics Show.

2. Bathelt, Malmberg, and Maskell (2004).

3. Institute for Management Development (2002–2013).

4. *Chosun Ilbo* (2013).

5. *Chosun Ilbo* (2013).

6. *Joongang Daily* (2011).

7. University Grants Commission of India as cited by dreducation.com in August 2013, http://www.dreducation.com/2013/08/data-statistics-india-student-college.html.

8. *India Today* (2013).

9. http://www.aicte-india.org/#, May 8, 2010.

10. Intel (2009).

11. In total, 121 began the online survey, but we dropped 13 because they had been born outside India. We deleted an additional 29 responses from individuals who did not provide important biographical information about themselves. Of the remaining 79 respondents, 52 provided biographical information but not their opinions on various geographic locations.

12. As a robustness check, we estimated a logistic regression model predicting whether someone who started the survey would actually complete it. This model estimated the likelihood of survey completion based on respondent sociodemographic characteristics ($N = 79$), which we asked early in the survey, was far from being statistically significant ($p > 0.55$). Furthermore, none of the independent variables were significant at the $p < 0.05$ level. This robustness check confirms that

individuals who completed the survey were not significantly different from individuals who started the survey but did not complete it. Of course, we cannot rule out another source of selection bias—why a small proportion of the thousands of individuals who were made aware of the survey chose to begin it.

13. Wang (forthcoming).

14. Interview conducted by Rafiq Dossani on March 23, 2010. As shown in Chapter 4, even Korean Americans are concerned with the glass ceiling in Korean corporations.

15. Shin (2012).

16. Also note that a practical challenge has to do with the legal framework for recruiting Indian engineers. According to current regulations, Indian engineers would need one of three visas to enter Korea. Visas are needed even for short-term stays because Korea lacks a visa exemption or reciprocal visa waiver agreement with India. Korea has agreements with 99 countries, including Bangladesh and Pakistan, allowing citizens of these countries to enter Korea without a visa for 30 or 90 days. India is inexplicably not on this list. Thus, for short-term stays of 90 days or less, Indian engineers would need the C-4 Temporary Employment visa. Under this visa, information technology professionals must be recommended by the Ministry of Information and Communication. For longer-term stays, Indian engineers would need the E-7 Special Employment visa. This visa applies toward individuals who fit one of three conditions: (1) MA or higher in computer science, (2) BA in computer science + one or more years of work experience, or (3) five or more years of relevant work experience. The E-7 would allow individuals to work in Korea for three years for the specified sponsoring employer. Qualifying individuals must receive a recommendation letter from one of several quasi-government agencies, like the Korea Institute for Advancement of Technology (KIAT, loosely affiliated with the Ministry of Knowledge Economy) and the Small and Medium Business Administration, depending on their subspecialty and the size of their employer. The newly instituted Gold Card program, administered by KIAT, provides additional benefits. In 2009, the Korean government consolidated the old IT Card program into the Gold Card. This program targets specific industries, including information technology and e-commerce; all Indian software engineers would be eligible. The Gold Card expands on E-7 benefits. The Gold Card will have a five-year duration, during which they can change employment with the consent of the sponsoring firm. Holders of the Gold Card will also be eligible for permanent residency after three years, instead of the usual five years. Given these advantages, Indian software engineers would be expected to apply for the Gold Card program instead of the E-7.

There are several major shortcomings with the current framework. First, the lack of a visa waiver hinders Indians (e.g., from information technology consulting firms) from conducting short-term project work. In contrast, nationals of most other countries need no such visa to enter Korea. Government agency approval is appropriate for the longer-term E-7 visa. However, the process remains highly opaque. Different individuals even in the same subspecialty potentially require recommendations from different agencies. Furthermore, the criteria for recommendations remain unclear. Most of these shortcomings, however, have been alleviated through the Gold Card program, which is administered by a single entity through a more transparent process. Streamlining the visa process, especially with a visa waiver, should substantially increase Korean firms' ability to leverage Indian software engineers.

17. Epstein (2013).

18. *Chosun Ilbo* (2013).

19. *Economy Today* (2013).

Chapter 6

1. Interview with Park Jung-soo of Ewha Woman's University, according to the *Chosun Ilbo* (2013).

2. "As I watched the confusion over the government reorganization bill, my dreams were also shattered," Kim told a news conference at the National Assembly in Seoul.

3. His article in the *Washington Post* reflecting his experience provoked strong reactions in Korea too. See Kim (2013).

4. World Bank Indicator at http://data.worldbank.org/indicator/NY.GDP .MKTP.CD?page=4. For a summary of the data, see also "List of countries by largest historical GDP," *Wikipedia*, at http://en.wikipedia.org/wiki/List_of_countries _by_largest_historical_GDP.

5. World Trade Organization (2011).

6. Korean Statistics Office, http://kostat.go.kr/portal/korea/kor_nw/2/1/index .board?bmode=read& aSeq=268838.

7. Storper (2007).

8. Mechan-Schmidt (2014).

9. Joppke (2005) and Bommes (2006).

10. de Carvalho (2003).

11. de Carvalho (2003).

12. Saxenian (2006).

13. *Korea Herald* (2013).

14. Mission statement, Republic of Korea Knowledge Sharing Program website (http://www.ksp.go.kr/ksp/ksp.jsp).

15. The story of an Indian man, Bonojit Hussain, who was racially slurred on a bus made its way across the world to the pages of the *New York Times*. Hussain,

a 28-year-old professor at Sungkonghoe University, was called "smelly" and "dirty" by a Korean man. When he contacted the police, he was treated discourteously by police officers, who refused to believe that he was a university professor. "To me, it is obvious that racial discrimination is an everyday phenomenon in Korea, but nobody seems to talk about it in public," said Hussain in interviews after the incident Kim (2009).

16. United Nations (2007).
17. Moon (2010).
18. Moon (2010).

Bibliography

Adler, Nancy J. 1981. "Re-Entry: Managing Cross-Cultural Transitions." *Group and Organization Studies* 6 (3): 341.

Bae, Seoung-O. 2012. "Korea Needs to Groom More Top Scientists and Engineers." *Samsung Economic Research Institute Quarterly* 5 (3): 14–21.

Barnett, George A. 1993. "Correspondence Analysis: A Method for the Description of Communication Networks." In *Progress in Communication Sciences,* edited by William D. Richards and George A. Barnett, 12:136–163. Norwood, NJ: Ablex.

Barnett, William P. 2008. *The Red Queen among Organizations: How Competitiveness Evolves.* Princeton, NJ: Princeton University Press.

Bartlett, Christopher A., and Sumantra Ghoshal. 1989. *Managing across Borders: The Transnational Solution.* Boston: Harvard Business School Press.

Bathelt, Harald, Anders Malmberg, and Peter Maskell. 2004. "Clusters and Knowledge: Local Buzz, Global Pipelines and the Process of Knowledge Creation." *Progress in Human Geography* 28:31–56.

Becker, Gary S. 1964. *Human Capital: A Theoretical and Empirical Analysis.* Chicago: University of Chicago Press.

———. 2008. "Human Capital." In *The Concise Encyclopedia of Economics.* http://www.econlib.org/library/Enc/HumanCapital.html.

Beechler, Schon, and Ian C. Woodward. 2009. "The Global War for Talent." *Journal of International Management* 15 (3): 273–285.

Bloemraad, Irene. 2004. "Who Claims Dual Citizenship? The Limits of Postnationalism, the Possibilities of Transnationalism, and the Persistence of Traditional Citizenship." *International Migration Review* 38 (2): 389–426.

Bommes, Michael. 2006. "Migration and Migration Research in Germany." In *International Migration and the Social Sciences: Confronting National*

Experiences in Australia, France and Germany, edited by Ellie Vasta and Va-soodeven Vuddamalay, 143–221. New York: Palgrave Macmillan.

Bourdieu, Pierre. 1977. *Outline of a Theory of Practice*. New York: Cambridge University Press.

Bunker-Whittington, Kjersten, Jason Owen-Smith, and Walter W. Powell. 2009. "Networks Propinquity, and Innovation in Knowledge-Intensive Industries." *Administrative Science Quarterly* 54:90–122.

Burdette, Rebecca. 1999. "Testimony of Rebecca Burdette." Testimony to the U.S. House Judiciary Committee, Subcommittee on Immigration and Claims, Oversight Hearing on the Benefits to the American Economy of a More Educated Workforce, Washington, DC, March 25.

Burt, Ronald. 1992. *Structural Holes: The Social Structure of Competition*. Cambridge, MA: Harvard University Press.

———. 2004. "Structural Holes and Good Ideas." *American Journal of Sociology* 110 (2): 349–399.

Castells, Manuel. 1996. *The Information Age: Economy, Society and Culture*. Vol. 1: *The Rise of the Network Society*. Oxford: Blackwell.

Chambers, Elizabeth G., Mark Foulon, Helen Handfield-Jones, Steven M. Hankin, and Edward G. Michaels III. 1998. "The War for Talent." *McKinsey Quarterly* 3.

Chase-Dunn, Christopher. 1975. "The Effects of International Economic Dependence and Inequality: A Cross-National Study." *American Sociological Review* 40:720–738.

Chen, Ping. 2010. *Assimilation of Immigrants and Their Adult Children: College Education, Cohabitation, and Work*. El Paso, TX: LFB Scholarly Publishing.

Choi, Inbom. 2003. "Korean Diaspora in the Making: Its Current Status and Impact on the Korean Economy." In *The Korean Diaspora in the World Economy*, edited by C. Fred Bergstein and Inbom Choi, 9–29. Washington, DC: Institute for International Economics.

Chosun Ilbo. 2013. "Going All the Way to Bangladesh to Find Software Engineers." August 2.

CIA World Factbook. 2013. "Korea, South". https://www.cia.gov/library/publications/the-world-factbook/geos/ks.html.

Coleman, James. 1988. "Social Capital in the Creation of Human Capital." *American Journal of Sociology* 94:S95–S120.

Constable, Nicole. 2002. "Sexuality and Discipline among Filipina Domestic Workers in Hong Kong." In *Filipinos in Global Migrations: At Home in the World?* edited by Filomeno V. Aguilar Jr., 237–268. Quezon City, Philippines: Philippine Social Science Council and the Philippine Migration Research Network.

Cortright, Joseph. 2006. *Making Sense of Clusters: Regional Competitiveness and Economic Development*. Washington, DC: Brookings Institution.

Dahl, Michael S., and Olav Sorenson. 2008. "The Social Attachment to Place." Working paper.

Davis, Gerald F. 1991. "Agents without Principles? The Spread of the Poison Pill through the Intercorporate Network." *Administrative Science Quarterly* 36 (4): 583–613.

de Carvalho, Daniela. 2003. *Migrants and Identity in Japan and Brazil: The Nikkeijin*. New York: RoutledgeCurzon.

Economy Today. 2013. "Samsung Electronics, Hiring Another 3000 Indians with ICT Skills?" April 29.

Epstein, Zach. 2013. "Samsung Smartphone Sales Are Now Absolutely Crushing Apple." BGR.com.

Erickson, Bonnie H. 1982. "Networks, Ideologies, and Belief Systems." In *Social Structure and Network Analysis*, edited by Peter V. Marsden and Nan Lin, 159–172. Beverly Hills, CA: Sage.

Feere, Jon. 2010. "Birthright Citizenship in the United States: A Global Comparison." Center for Immigration Studies. http://www.cis.org/sites/cis.org/files/articles/2010/birthright.pdf.

Florida, Richard. 2002. *The Rise of the Creative Class: And How It's Transforming Work, Leisure, Community and Everyday Life*. New York: Perseus.

Foreign Policy. 2008. "The 2008 Global Cities Index." November–December.

Friedmann, John. 1986. "The World City Hypothesis." *Development and Change* 17 (1): 69–83.

Gallo, Carmenza, and Thomas R. Bailey. 1996. "Social Networks and Skills-Based Immigration Policy." In *Immigrants and Immigration Policy: Individual Skills, Family Ties, and Group Identities*, edited by Harriet Orcutt Duleep and Phanindra V. Wunnava, 203–218. Greenwich, CT: JAI Press.

Ghoshal, Sumantra. 1987. "Global Strategy: An Organizing Framework." *Strategic Management Journal* 8 (5): 425–440.

Ghoshal, Sumantra, and Christopher A. Bartlett. 1990. "The Multinational Corporation as an Interorganizational Network." *Academy of Management Review* 15 (4): 603–625.

Granovetter, Mark S. 1973. "The Strength of Weak Ties." *American Journal of Sociology* 78 (6): 1360–1380.

———. (1974) 1995. *Getting a Job: A Study of Contacts and Careers*. 2nd ed. Chicago: University of Chicago Press.

———. 1985. "Economic Action and Social Structure: The Problem of Embeddedness." *American Journal of Sociology* 91 (3): 481–510.

Greif, Avner. 1989. "Reputation and Coalitions in Medieval Trade: Evidence on the Maghribi Traders." *Journal of Economic History* 49 (4): 857–882.

Gupta, Anil K., and Vijay Govindarajan. 2000. "Knowledge Flows within Multinational Corporations." *Strategic Management Journal* 21:473–496.

Hayutin, Adele. 2010. "Population Age Shifts Will Reshape Global Work Force." Stanford Center on Longevity, Stanford University, Stanford, CA.

Hong, Sungmin, and Gawon Cho. 2012. "Entry and Exit Patterns of Sciences and Engineering Human Resources in 2012." Unpublished paper.

India Today. 2013. "Steep Fall in Demand for Engineers in the IT Industry." June 19.

Information Technology Association of America. 1997. *Help Wanted: The IT Workforce Gap at the Dawn of a New Century.* Arlington, VA: Information Technology Association of America.

Institute for Management Development. "World Competitiveness Yearbook," 2005–2013. http://www.imd.org/wcc/.

International Monetary Fund. 2010. *Direction of Trade Statistics.* Washington, DC: International Monetary Fund.

Jasso, Guillermina, and Mark R. Rosenzweig. 1995. "Do Immigrants Screened for Skills Do Better Than Family Reunification Immigrants?" *International Migration Review* 29 (1): 85–111.

Joongang Daily. 2011. "Engineers the Key to Software Woes." September 2.

Joppke, Christian. 2005. *Selecting by Origin: Ethnic Migration in the Liberal State.* Cambridge, MA: Harvard University Press.

Judy, Richard W. 1999. "Immigration Policy and America's Workforce Needs: Re-Establishing the Connection." Testimony to the U.S. House Judiciary Committee, Subcommittee on Immigration and Claims, Oversight Hearing on the Benefits to the American Economy of a More Educated Workforce, Washington, DC, March 25.

Judy, Richard W., and Carol D'Amico. 1997. *Workforce 2020: Work and Workers in the 21st Century.* Indianapolis: Hudson Institute.

Katzenstein, Peter J. 2005. *A World of Regions: Asia and Europe in the American Imperium.* Ithaca, NY: Cornell University Press.

Kim, Andrew Eungi. 2009. "Demography, Migration and Multiculturalism in South Korea." *Asia-Pacific Journal* 6 (2). http://www.japanfocus.org/-andrew_eungi-kim/3035.

Kim, Eun-jung. 2009. "Foreign Professor Launches Battle to Raise Local Awareness of Racism." *Yonhap News* (Seoul). Retrieved October 20, 2010 from http://english.yonhapnews.co.kr/national/2009/09/07/29/0302000000AEN20090907003300315F.HTML.

Kim, Eun Mee, and Jean S. Kang. 2007. "Seoul as a Global City with Ethnic Villages." *Korea Journal* 47 (4): 64–99.

Kim, Eun Mee, Ok-kyung Yang, and Hae-young Lee. 2009. *Multicultural Society of Korea*. Seoul: Nanam Sinseo.

Kim, Hye Jin. 2008. *Policy for Recruiting Chinese Students in Regional Universities*. Daegu, Korea: Daegu Gyeongbuk Development Institute.

Kim, Ik Ki. 2000. "Policy Responses to Low Fertility and Population Aging in Korea." Paper presented at the Expert Group Meeting on Policy Responses to Population Ageing and Population Decline, Population Division, Department of Economic and Social Affairs, United Nations Secretariat, New York, October 16–18.

Kim, Jeong H. 2013. "A Return to South Korea, Thwarted by Nationalism." *Washington Post*, March 29.

Kim, Pil-Soo. 2011. "Global Craze for K-Pop: A New Economic Engine." *Korea Focus*, August.

Kim, Wang-Bae. 2004. "Migration of Foreign Workers into South Korea." *Asian Survey* 44 (2): 327.

Kirkegaard, Jacob Funk. 2007. *The Accelerating Decline in America's High-Skilled Workforce: Implications for Immigration Policy*. Washington, DC: Peter G. Peterson Institute for International Economics.

Korea Export-Import Bank. 2012. "Analysis of Korean Cultural Exports Impacts and Financial Support Measures." Overseas Economic Research Institute, Korea Export-Import Bank, Seoul.

Korea Herald. 2013. "Hallyu Fuels Korean Language Boom Abroad." http://www.koreaherald.com/view.php?ud=20130429000600.

Korean Educational Development Institute. 2012. *Research on Strengthening Universities' Foreign Student Management and Support Practices* (in Korean). Research Report RR 2012-15, Seoul, Korea.

Korea Research Institute for Vocational Education and Training (KRIVET). 2008. *A Policy Study on Utilizing Overseas High Skilled Human Resources in Science and Engineering Fields in Korea*. Seoul: KRIVET.

Kwon, Victoria Hyonchu, Helen Rose Ebaugh, and Jacqueline Hagen. 1997. "The Structure and Functions of Cell Group Ministry in a Korean Christian Church." *Journal for the Scientific Study of Religion* 36 (2): 247–256.

Lee, Ki Jong. 2005. "Long-Term Forecast of Supply and Demand of Human Resources in S&T (2005–2014) and Preliminary Survey on the Status of Graduates in Science and Engineering." Republic of Korea Ministry of Science and Technology, Seoul.

Lowell, B. Lindsay. 1996. "Review and Policy Commentary—Skilled and Family-Based Immigration: Principles and Labor Markets." In *Immigrants* and *Immigration Policy: Individual Skills, Family Ties, and Group Identities*, edited by Harriet Orcutt Duleep and Phanindra V. Wunnava, 353–372. Greenwich, CT: JAI Press.

Marshall, Alfred. 1920. *Principles of Economics*. London: Macmillan.

Maskell, Peter, Harald Bathelt, and Anders Malmberg. 2005. "Building Global Knowledge Pipelines: The Role of Temporary Clusters." DRUID Working Paper 05-20, Danish Research Unit for Industrial Dynamics, Copenhagen.

Massey, Douglas, Joaquin Arango, Graeme Hugo, Ali Kouaouci, Adela Pellegrino, and J. Edward Taylor. 1993. "Theories of International Migration: A Review and Appraisal." *Population and Development Review* 19 (3): 431–466.

Mechan-Schmidt, Frances. 2014. "Germany Pledges to Increase Foreign Students by 25 Per Cent." *Times Higher Education*, January 16.

Meyer, David R. 1986. "The World System of Cities: Relations between International Financial Metropolises and South American Cities." *Social Forces* 64 (3): 553–581.

———. 1991. "Change in the World System of Metropolises: The Role of Business Intermediaries." *Urban Geography* 12 (5): 393–416.

Moon, Kyoung-Hee. 2010. "The Challenge of Becoming a 'Multiethnic Korea' in the 21st Century." *East Asia Forum*, March 18. http://www.eastasiaforum .org/2010/03/18/the-challenge-of-becoming-a-multiethnic-korea-in-the-21st -century/.

Moon, Rennie J., and Gi-Wook Shin. 2014. "Globalization without Cultural Diversity? Internationalization of Higher Education in Korea." Unpublished paper.

Morgan, S. Philip. 2003. "Is Low Fertility a Twenty-First-Century Demographic Crisis?" *Demography* 40 (4): 589–603.

Newstation. 2009. "Pursuing Degree in Korea? Foreign Scientists Attracted Attention by Their Performance." July 7.

Noland, Marcus. 1993. "The Impact of Korean Immigration on the US Economy." In *The Korean Diaspora in the World Economy*, edited by C. Fred Bergstein and Inbom Choi, 61–76. Special Report 15. Washington, DC: Institute for International Economics.

Ong, Aihwa. 1999. *Flexible Citizenship: The Cultural Logics of Transnationality*. Durham, NC: Duke University Press.

Organisation for Economic Co-Operation and Development. 2006. *PISA 2006 Technical Report*. Paris: OECD.

———. 2008. *A Profile of Immigrant Populations in the 21st Century: Data from OECD Countries*. Paris: OECD.

———. 2011. *Education at a Glance 2011: OECD Indicators*. Paris: OECD.

———. 2012a. *Connecting with Immigrants: A Global Profile of Diasporas*. Paris: OECD.

———. 2012b. *Education at a Glance 2012: OECD Indicators*. Paris: OECD.

———. 2012c. "Glossary of Statistical Terms." http://stats.oecd.org/glossary/.

Perlmutter, Howard V. 1969. "The Tortuous Evolution of the Multinational Corporation: A Drama in Three Acts." *Columbia Journal of World Business* 4:9–18.

Pfeffer, Jeffrey, and Robert Sutton. 2006. *Hard Facts, Dangerous Half-Truths, and Total Nonsense: Profiting from Evidence-Based Management*. Cambridge, MA: Harvard University Press.

Porter, Michael E. 1990. *The Competitive Advantage of Nations*. New York: Free Press.

Portes, Alejandro. 1995a. "Economic Sociology and the Sociology of Immigration: A Conceptual Overview." In *The Economic Sociology of Immigration*, edited by Alejandro Portes, 1–41. New York: Russell Sage Foundation.

———. 1995b. "Children of Immigrants: Segmented Assimilation and Its Determinants." In *The Economic Sociology of Immigration*, edited by Alejandro Portes, 248–279. New York: Russell Sage Foundation.

———, ed. 1998. *The Economic Sociology of Immigration: Essays on Networks, Ethnicity and Entrepreneurship*. New York: Russell Sage Foundation.

Portes, Alejandro, and Ruben G. Rumbaut. 2001. *Legacies: The Story of the Immigrant Second Generation*. New York: Russell Sage Foundation.

Portes, Alejandro, and Julia Sensenbrenner. 1993. "Embeddedness and Immigration: Notes on the Social Determinants of Economic Action." *American Journal of Sociology* 98:1320–1350.

Powell, Walter W. 1990. "Neither Market nor Hierarchy: Network Forms of Organization." In *Research in Organizational Behavior*, edited by Barry M. Staw and Larry L. Cummings, 12:295–336. Greenwich, CT: Jai Press.

Powell, Walter W., Douglas R. White, Kenneth W. Koput, and Jason Owen-Smith. 2005. "Network Dynamics and Field Evolution: The Growth of Inter-Organizational Collaboration in the Life Sciences." *American Journal of Sociology* 110 (4): 1132–1205.

Prahalad, C. K., and Yves Doz. 1987. *The Multinational Mission: Balancing Local Demands and Global Vision*. New York: Free Press.

Pratt, Geraldine. 2002. "From Registered Nurse to Registered Nanny: Discursive Geographies of Filipina Domestic Workers in Vancouver, B.C." *Filipinos in Global Migrations: At Home in the World?* edited by Filomeno V. Aguilar Jr., 111–143. Quezon City, Philippines: Philippine Social Science Council and the Philippine Migration Research Network.

Putnam, Robert. 1995. "Bowling Alone: America's Declining Social Capital." *Journal of Democracy* 6 (1): 65–78.

———. 2000. *Bowling Alone: The Collapse and Revival of American Community.* New York: Simon and Schuster.

Rauch, James E. 1999. "Networks versus Markets in International Trade." *Journal of International Economics* 48:7–35.

Republic of Korea Ministry of Education, Science, and Technology. 2001. "Master Plan for Recruiting Foreign Students: Study Korea Project."

Republic of Korea Ministry of Justice. 2008. "More Advantages for Overseas Koreans who Reported Domestic Residency." Press release, 11 June 2008.

Roberts, Brian R. 1995. "Socially Expected Durations and the Economic Adjustment of Immigrants." In *The Economic Sociology of Immigration*, edited by Alejandro Portes, 42–86. New York: Russell Sage Foundation.

Sassen, Saskia. 1994. *Cities in a World Economy.* Thousand Oaks, CA: Pine Forge Press.

———. 2001. *The Global City.* 2nd ed. Princeton, NJ: Princeton University Press.

———. 2007. *A Sociology of Globalization.* New York: Norton.

Saxenian, AnnaLee. 1994. *Regional Advantage: Culture and Competition in Silicon Valley and Route 128.* Cambridge, MA: Harvard University Press.

———. 2006. *The New Argonauts: Regional Advantage in a Global Economy.* Cambridge, MA: Harvard University Press.

Schiller, Nina Glick, Linda Basch, and Cristina Szanton Blanc. 1995. "From Immigrant to Transmigrant: Theorizing Transnational Migration." *Anthropological Quarterly* 68 (1): 48–63.

Shenkar, Oded. 2001. "Cultural Distance Revisited: Towards a More Rigorous Conceptualization and Measurement of Cultural Difference." *Journal of International Business Studies* 32 (3): 519–535.

Shin, Gi-Wook. 2006. *Ethnic Nationalism in Korea: Genealogy, Politics, and Legacy.* Stanford, CA: Stanford University Press.

———. 2012. "Racist Korea? Diverse but Not Tolerant of Diversity." In *Race and Racism in Modern East Asia: Western and Eastern Constructions*, edited by Walter Demel and Rotem Kowner, 369–390. New York: Brill.

Shin, Gi-Wook, Rafiq Dossani, and Joon Nak Choi. 2010. "Building an IT Partnership: Indian IT Engineers in the Korean Marketplace." Shorenstein Asia-Pacific Research Center, Stanford University, Stanford, CA.

Spradley, James P. 1979. *The Ethnographic Interview.* New York: Holt, Rinehart and Winston.

STEPI (Korea Science and Technology Policy Institute). 2010. "Constructing Global Knowledge Networks in the Bio and Pharmaceutical Industry: Focus on Skilled Expatriate Labor" (in Korean).

Storper, Michael. 2007. "The New Argonauts: Regional Advantage in a Global Economy" (book review). *Journal of Economic Geography* 7:113–117.

Szkudlarek, Betina. 2010. "Reentry—A Review of the Literature." *International Journal of Intercultural Relations* 34 (1): 1–21.

Tharenou, Phyllis, and Natasha Caulfield. 2010. "Will I Stay or Will I Go? Explaining Repatriation by Self-Initiated Expatriates." *Academy of Management Journal* 53 (5): 1009–1028.

Tilly, Charles. 1990. "Transplanted Networks." In *Immigration Reconsidered. History, Sociology, and Politics*, edited by Virginia Yans-McLaughlin, 79–95. New York: Oxford University Press.

———. 2007. "Trust Networks in Transnational Migration." *Sociological Forum* 22 (1): 3–24.

United Nations. 2007. *Report of the Committee on the Elimination of Racial Discrimination*. General Assembly Official Records A/62/18.

U.S. Department of Commerce, Office of Technology Policy. 1997. *America's New Deficit: The Shortage of Information Technology Workers*. Washington, DC: U.S. Department of Commerce.

Uzzi, Brian. 1997. "Social Structure and Competition in Interfirm Networks: The Paradox of Embeddedness." *Administrative Science Quarterly* 42:35–67.

Wallerstein, Immanuel. 1974. *The Modern World-System*. Vol. 1: *Capitalist Agriculture and the Origins of the European World-Economy in the Sixteenth Century*. New York: Academic Press.

Wang, Dan. Forthcoming. "Activating Brokerage: Inter-Organizational Knowledge Transfer through Skilled Return Migration." *Administrative Science Quarterly*.

Watts, Duncan J., and Steven H. Strogatz. 1998. "Collective Dynamics of 'Small-World' Networks." *Nature* 393 (6684): 409–410.

World Trade Organization. 2011. *International Trade Statistics*. http://www.wto.org/english/res_e/statis_e/its2011_e/its11_toc_e.htm.

World Values Survey. 2005–2008. http://www.worldvaluessurvey.org/.

Yonezawa, Akiyoshi. 2014. "Japan's Challenge of Fostering 'Global Human Resources': Policy Debates and Practices." *Japan Labor Review* 11 (2): 1–16.

Index

"knowledge-based economy" strategy, 2
Knowledge Sharing Program, 169
Kojong (emperor), 98
Korea, 157; Asian students in colleges in, 21; distrust/dislike of foreigners, 4, 20–21; engineering needs, 128–134; foreign students and faculty in, 167–168; history of foreign labor in, 17–18; immigration policy, historically, 96–99, *97*; during Japanese colonial rule, 96–97; jus sanguinis citizenship, 4; key shortages of skilled individuals, 153; lower pay in, 117; as model for other nations, 153; as "nonimmigrant society," 4; overall perceptions of, 139, *140–141*; as perennial "second option," 82; students not experiencing diversity in, 168; transition from foreign aid recipient to donor, 34, 152; universities, 32, 167–168; work culture of, 61, 108, 123
Korea Foundation, 169
Korean diaspora, generally: size of, 25; as source of human and social capital, 95
Korean diaspora in North America: defined, 72; estranged businessmen, *103*, 104, 119–124; estranged humanitarians, *103*, 104, 110, 120–121; as global talent, 124–125; heterogeneity among, 101–104; interest in long-term return, 112–114, 116–119; interest in short-term return, 105–112, 120–121; "Korean effect," 98; Korean enclaves, 87; military service not required of, 99; as potential returnees, 99–101; retaining Korean citizenship, 110; rooted businessmen, *103*, 104, 114–119; rooted humanitarians, *103*, 104, 110–114; three waves of migration, 96–97; working in Korea during recession, 98. *See also* Korean versus Korean American identity
Koreans studying abroad, 24–25, *66*; biography and time spent in Korea, 76–77; culture shock on visits home, 86–87; effect of chogi yuhak, 65–66, 83–87, *84*, 89–92; effect of church attendance, 83–85, *84*, 87–90; high proportion return home, 25; historically, 68; identity, 73;

78–79; increasing brain drain, 65–66; interest in returning home, 75–76; interest in working with/for Koreans, 82; job opportunities, 79–82; networks and embeddedness in Korean society, 77–78; in North America, 73–75, *74–75*
Korean versus Korean American identity: ambiguity in, 106–107, 121; basing on legal residency, 73; basing on self-description, *74*; chogi yuhak status and, 86, 89, 93; as global talent, 124; key factor in residency decision, 78–79; kirŏgi kajok and, 91; Korean church attendance and, 87–90; social characteristics, 101
Korean wave. *See* hallyu
Koreaphile foreign students, 57–63
KOTRA (Korea Trade-Investment Promotion Agency), 147
K-Pop, 34, 110, 123, 169

labor, types of, 16–17, *17*
labor shortage, projected, 3
language fluency as motivation, 44, *48*, 52, 57, 106, 109–110
language skills: foreigners studying Korean, *32*, 32; and foreign student residency choice, 56–57, 62, 76; and long-term residency choice, 109–110
Lee, Chang-rae, 104–105
Lee, Hae-young, 21
Lee Myung-bak, 2, 152
LG Electronics: attractive to Indian engineers, 146; losing market to iPhone, 126–127, 132, 149–150; recruiting foreign students, 39, 164–165
Lotte Group, 68, 164–165
lower pay in Korea, 117

Malaysia, 43, *48*, *50*, 58, 62
Marshall, Alfred, 14–15
"medium-technology trap," 153
migration: career, 80, 93; migrant workers, 4, 18, 153, 170–172; units of, 78; "voluntary," 92
military service and citizenship, 99, 122–123, 180n6

salaries, U.S. versus Korean, 80

Samsung: attractive to Indian engineers, 146; Economic Research Institute, 4; Eric Kim at, 119; Galaxy S smartphones, 149; importance of Indian engineers to, 150; losing market to iPhone, 126–127, 132; student choices regarding, 116–117

Saxenian, AnnaLee, 6, 15, 67, 163

Scandinavia, tolerance for foreigners in, 4

Schiff, Adam, 8

Sejong (king), 169

selective acculturation, Korean churches and, 89

self-identity and living preference, 73, 74, 78. *See also* Korean versus Korean American identity

Seoul: ethnic enclaves in, 148–149; international rankings of, 2; more up-to-date work environment in, 113; overseas Koreans living in, 99; as world/global city, 19

service sector, 2, 124, 153, 165

settler societies: attractiveness to foreigners, 3–4, 21, 163; cultural diversity of, 56–57; defined, 3; Indian engineers' preference for, 158; and jus soli citizenship, 3, 170; Korea as steppingstone to, 42; rising birthrates in, 10; trusting of foreigners, 4

sexism in Korea, 108–109, 113, 121–122

Shin Kyŏkho, 68

short-term study abroad, 70

Silicon Valley, 3; as industry cluster, 11, 132; Korean disconnected from, 127; opinions of Indian engineers on, 139, 146; overall perceptions of, 139, *140–141*; transnational bridging from, 67

SIPA (Silicon Valley Indian Professionals Association), 136–137

SITC (Standard International Trade Classification), *129*

SK Group, 146

skilled foreigners, defined, 177–178n46

skilled foreigners in global economy: brokering cross-national deals, 14; combined model, 16–17, *17*; local responsiveness from corporations, 15; new model, 6, 10–16, *12*; old model, 6–10; as positive-sum game, 6–10; spreading key innovations, 14–15

skilled foreigners in Korea, 22, *22–23*; citizens educated overseas, 24–25; data sources and research methods, *26*, 26–28; foreign students educated in Korea, 23–24; overseas diaspora, 25–26; true foreigners, 23. *See also* foreign students in Korea; Korean diaspora in North America; Koreans studying abroad; "true" foreigners in Korea

small and medium-sized enterprises (SMEs), 165

smartphones, 126–128, 131–132

social capital: brain circulation potential, 71; defined, 6; in engineering, 132–134; of estranged businessmen, 123; foreign students as, 35–36, 58, 70–72; immigrants from diaspora as, 95; Indian engineers as, 147, 149–150; as key resource, 10–11; Korean Americans, 98; lack of hurting software industry, 132–134; types of, *12*; ways to leverage, 40

social identity, 42, 60–61, 78–79

social motivations, *41*, 60–61

software engineering, Korean: effect on export competitiveness, 128; not competitive in recruiting Indians, 128; talent pool, 129–132, *130*, *131*; weakness in, 127

sŏnbae-hubae (senior-junior) relationship, 46. *See also* hierarchical social structure

South Asia, 43, *48*, *50*, 54–56

"stars," recruitment of, 175n2

STEM (science, technology, engineering, and mathematics), 8, 167

Storper, Michael, 163

Strategy for the Internationalization of Higher Education, 167

study abroad. *See* Koreans studying abroad

"Study Korea" program, 33

Test of Proficiency in Korean (TOPIK), 169

Printed and bound by CPI Group (UK) Ltd, Croydon, CR0 4YY

23/04/2025

14660937-0002